Stealing Sisi's Star

Stealing Sisi's Star

*How a Master Thief
Nearly Got Away with
Austria's Most Famous Jewel*

JENNIFER BOWERS BAHNEY

McFarland & Company, Inc., Publishers
Jefferson, North Carolina

LIBRARY OF CONGRESS CATALOGUING-IN-PUBLICATION DATA

Bahney, Jennifer Bowers, 1967–
    Stealing Sisi's Star : how a master thief nearly got away with
Austria's most famous jewel / Jennifer Bowers Bahney.
        p.   cm.
    Includes bibliographical references and index.

    ISBN 978-0-7864-9722-5 (softcover : acid free paper) ∞
    ISBN 978-1-4766-1939-2 (ebook)

    1. Jewelry theft—Austria—Case studies.   2. Elisabeth,
Empress, consort of Franz Joseph I, Emperor of Austria,
1837–1898.   I. Title.

    HV6665.A8B34 2015
    364.16'28739278—dc23   2015018914

BRITISH LIBRARY CATALOGUING DATA ARE AVAILABLE

On the cover: Nineteenth century postcard depicting Sisi in
her coronation regalia as Queen of Hungary, a title she
cherished above all others (author's collection)

Printed in the United States of America

McFarland & Company, Inc., Publishers
    Box 611, Jefferson, North Carolina 28640
    www.mcfarlandpub.com

For Mearan and Harrison, with love

Acknowledgments

I owe a debt of gratitude to the following people for helping this book come to fruition: journalist Joshuah Bearman; Gerald Blanchard and attorney Judith Karfiol; Sergeant Larry Levasseur (retired); Winnipeg Police Superintendent Gordon Schumacher (retired); Terry Kolbuck of the Winnipeg Police Department; attorney Danny Gunn; Jeffrey Oliphant, senior associate chief justice of the Court of Queen's Bench of Manitoba (retired); executive assistant to the chief justices and chief judge of the Manitoba courts, Aimee Fortier; manager of provincial court administration for the Winnipeg courts, Elizabeth Dahl; Schönbrunn and Hofburg Palace officials Franz Sattlecker, Josepha Haselböck, Brigitte Wachtl, and Olivia Lichtscheidl; Theatrical Stylist Hannelore Uhrmacher; Nancy Koreen, director of sport promotion for the United States Parachute Association; Martin Kriegel of *Kronen Zeitung*; Frank Luba of *The Province*; Patricia Dean of the Medill School of Journalism and Annenberg School for Communication; my mother Bette Bowers and my husband Robert H. Bahney, III; my Bahney, Bowers, Ferrante, and Paselsky family members; and all of the wonderful friends who kept me on my toes by continuously asking "How's the book coming?" Thank you all.

Table of Contents

Table of Contents

Preface

The story of Empress Elisabeth of Austria and the theft of the Köchert Diamond Pearl was a match made in heaven for a journalist with a penchant for nineteenth-century European history. I am a firm believer that journalism is "the first rough draft of history," a sentiment made popular by publisher Phil Graham, because we journalists usually don't have the time or resources to delve as deeply into a story as we would like before going to print or live on the air. Thus, our work often remains the roughest of rough drafts until a historian comes along and gives a subject the attention it deserves. To thoroughly research a subject for years and spend months writing about it is a luxury I have not had up until now.

I have been fascinated by Empress Elisabeth of Austria since I was a history major at Smith College, when I first learned of her eccentricities and how she manipulated her image to create the legend of a forever youthful and glamorous icon. I read all of the best biographies of Sisi, those by Count Egon Corti, Brigitte Hamann, and Andrew Sinclair, and even the not-so-great biographies by sensationalist or grudge-holding authors who may or may not have known the empress in her lifetime. But I never could bring myself to watch the sugar-coated "Sissi" [sic] movies from the 1950s, directed by Ernst Marischka and starring Romy Schneider as the perpetually cheerful "fairytale empress" when I knew how far those romantic comedies veered from the truth.

I found myself wanting to learn the details behind certain facets of Sisi's life, like the Franz Xaver Winterhalter painting of the empress with the glittering stars in her hair. What was the full story behind the one image that remains the most famous depiction of this much-painted and photographed woman and that which so completely represented

1

the height of Europe's imperial majesty? How did her trademark hair stars come into being, and what happened to them down through the ages? And how could a woman who seemingly had everything—beauty, riches, a loving family—be so utterly miserable with the fate she had been handed?

One winter morning I was doing a rather routine computer search on Sisi to see if any new research had surfaced, when I stumbled across an April 2010 article for *Wired* magazine: "Art of the Steal: On the Trail of the World's Most Ingenious Thief," by journalist Joshuah Bearman, whose exceptional piece on the CIA's foray into the Iran Hostage Crisis was turned into the multiple Oscar-winning film, *Argo*.

"Art of the Steal" told the unbelievable story of a Canadian man in his early twenties who used spy tactics to break into Sisi's summer residence, Vienna's Schönbrunn Palace, and pilfer the last remaining diamond-and-pearl "Sisi Star," formally called the Köchert Diamond Pearl, from under the unblinking eye of the museum's electronic surveillance system. Searches of Canadian newspaper archives showed that although there were plenty of reports on the crime itself, no one seemed to really understand what the Sisi Star was or who had once owned it; the Star was referred to in more than one piece as a brooch, and Sisi herself was referred to several times by her pre-marriage title of princess. And despite some perfunctory facts, no report ever delved deeper into the rich and tragic history of the Star's original owner.

At that moment, I knew I wanted to tackle the complete story, combining the modern-day crime story with the thoroughly-researched history. I would be weaving together a tale of two narcissists from two very different centuries: the master thief who stole the Köchert Diamond Pearl and Empress Sisi herself. In the case of Sisi, I would have to uncover as much information as I could on this enigmatic woman through her artifacts, poems, and contemporary news clippings. And I had to figure out a way to get in touch with the man who plucked the Sisi Star from the red velvet pillow under the bulletproof glass: Gerald Daniel Blanchard.

I immediately cold-emailed Josh Bearman in the hopes that he might be willing to share a little information on how I could communicate directly with Blanchard. But much to my surprise and delight,

Bearman was incredibly generous and supportive. He readily gave me Blanchard's contact information, a few words of advice, and an encouraging, "Let me know how it goes!"

I fired off an email to Blanchard explaining who I was and what my project was about, then waited. And waited. And heard nothing back. After a little digging, I found out that at least one Schönbrunn Palace insider was skeptical of Blanchard's story of how he broke into the imperial apartments and how long it took before the theft was discovered. Fingers crossed, I felt this might be the ammunition I needed to get Blanchard to respond to my interview request.

I emailed him again, this time telling him that some in the palace didn't believe he was quite the James Bond character he said he was and that he was the only person on earth who could clear this up for me. Within a day, I had a response, and the next thing I knew I was on the phone with the man who stole the Köchert Diamond Pearl.

In addition to extracting new information from Gerald Blanchard, I also gave him an opportunity to rectify any erroneously reported information on his crime. He corrected the details of one news report in particular but concurred with other accounts, including the Bearman article, one hundred percent. "Everything in the article," he told me, "I agree. And not only do I agree with it, the Winnipeg Police Service also backed up the credibility of the article."[1] Winnipeg authorities may have confirmed the story of how they investigated and put an end to Blanchard's crime spree, but no one but Blanchard himself truly knew how the Sisi Star ended up in his possession.

Jeffrey Oliphant, who was the senior associate chief justice for the Queen's Bench Court of Manitoba and the sentencing judge for Gerald Blanchard, provided me a thorough background on the Canadian court system. He also shared as much as was legally permitted on the Blanchard case and made himself available to answer my numerous email questions. So, too, did Gordon Schumacher, the Winnipeg Police superintendent who oversaw the Blanchard investigation and arrest. Both men had the opportunity to examine the Sisi Star up close and, with their unique insights, were able to add important dimensions to the book that I hadn't anticipated when I first began writing.

The last influential biography on Sisi came out in 1999, by historian

Preface

Andrew Sinclair, and many more facts and artifacts pertaining to the Empress have come to light since then. The Hofburg's Sisi Museum, opened in 2004, has been instrumental in helping me glean some of this previously obscure material, including more information on the Sisi Stars, the empress's poetry, her beauty regimen, and the story behind her ruby jewelry that disappeared along with twenty-seven additional Sisi Stars during the collapse of the Habsburg Empire in 1918. Contemporary newspaper articles from Austrian and British publications helped me further round out Sisi's narrative with first-hand accounts of the empress's actions and the public's reactions.

I had the pleasure of interviewing Hannelore Uhrmacher, a theatrical makeup artist and hair stylist who recreated three of Sisi's most famous hairstyles for the Sisi Museum. Ms. Uhrmacher gave invaluable insight into what Sisi's hairdresser, Fanny Feifalik, must have gone through while dressing the empress's extraordinary hair each day. Without Fanny's uncommon skills, the Sisi Stars might never have reached their fabled status.

There remains a question as to whether the imperial jeweler Köchert created hair stars for Sisi both with and without center pearls. Through my research, I have come to believe that either the jeweler did, in fact, create both versions, or that Sisi actually wore the Köchert Diamond Pearl stars while sitting for the famous Winterhalter painting and the artist decided, for creative reasons of his own, to remove the center pearls in his finished work.

Sisi's last remaining hair jewel disappeared from Schönbrunn Palace in 1998 and wasn't seen again until nine years later. Already a legend, the Köchert Diamond Pearl has continued to grow in mythic stature as Austria's most famous jewel because of one remarkably talented and inscrutable thief. Sometimes truth is more fascinating than fiction—I believe it's certainly the case with this story.

A Note on Currency

In nineteenth-century Austro-Hungary, monetary values were listed as *gulden* or *florin*. Although the currency names are interchangeable, I have used florin throughout the book for consistency. According to the *Congressional Serial Set*, published in 1896, two gold crowns equaled one Austro-Hungarian florin, and one florin equaled 40 U.S. cents.

For monetary values, I gave the rough 2015 equivalents of nineteenth-century Austro-Hungarian currency in parentheses so the reader could more easily relate to prices or salaries. To calculate these values, I turned to measuringworth.com, a web site produced by Lawrence H. Officer, professor of economics at the University of Illinois; and Samuel H. Williams, professor of Economics, emeritus, of Miami University. I learned about this site from one of my favorite historians, Alison Weir, famous for her biographies of the English monarchy.

According to measuringworth.com, "real price commodity" value of 40 U.S. cents in 1896 was $11.40 in 2013 U.S. dollars. Thus, 1,000 florins in 1896 would be about $12,000 today in U.S. currency.

Prologue

"We couldn't figure out how they could have done it. It was definitely very clever. And very uncomfortable for us."
—Franz Sattlecker, Director, Schönbrunn Palace[1]

In early June 1998, at the height of Vienna's tourist season, an international crowd packed the east wing of Schönbrunn Palace to catch a rare glimpse of the "Sisi Star" that had once adorned the magnificent tresses of Empress Elisabeth of Austria, known affectionately as Sisi. Now a museum, Schönbrunn was previously the preferred summer residence of Austria's ruling Habsburg dynasty. Up to 9,000 visitors flock to the palace daily to tour the grand apartments where Sisi, her husband, Emperor Franz Joseph, and their surviving children carried out their imperial lives. It had been seventy-five years, however, since anyone but a handpicked few had laid eyes on this one particular relic—the fabled ten-pointed star of sparkling diamonds surrounding an impressive pearl set in a bed of white gold. The private owner agreed to loan the star, officially called the Köchert Diamond Pearl, to the palace in honor of a very special and solemn occasion: the centennial anniversary of the empress's assassination.

The single diamond-and-pearl jewel is the last vestige of original hair ornaments created for the empress by the firm of master goldsmith Jakob Heinrich Köchert following Sisi's marriage to Emperor Franz Joseph in 1854. Köchert designed two sets for the empress, each comprised of twenty-seven individual stars—with and without center pearls—that created a halo effect when pinned into the empress's braids. According to legend, Sisi got the idea for the hair stars after attending a production of Shakespeare's *A Midsummer Night's Dream* at

7

Prologue

Vienna's Burgtheater. A strikingly beautiful, eccentric royal with obsessive-compulsive tendencies and a decidedly independent streak, Sisi had always identified a kindred spirit in the Bard's strong-willed and daring protagonist, Titania the Fairy Queen. In fact, Sisi's bedroom ceiling and walls at Vienna's Hermes Villa, the home she called "Titania's enchanted castle," was painted at great expense with scenes from the play by a young Gustav Klimt. The actress portraying Titania for that particular performance wore a sprinkling of glittering stars in her hair that captivated the Empress. Inspired, Sisi then requested her own fairy stars from the imperial jeweler. (Emperor Franz Joseph wasn't quite as enamored with the play that so enraptured his wife, calling it "rather boring and very stupid."[2])

Peering intently through his jeweler's loupe, Köchert's son had mounted some thirty diamonds of graduated sizes and one large center pearl onto each star for this particular set. The empress's hairdresser then carefully pinned all twenty-seven stars into Sisi's braided chestnut locks via an attached *agrafe* or hook-and-loop clasp that was also studded with diamonds. The stars were designed to be worn in two styles: pinned individually throughout the empress's coiled braids or connected together to form a diadem, or crown-like headband. Sisi was very particular about what accessories adorned her imperial mane; it inched toward her ankles when loose—no small accomplishment on a nearly five-foot eight-inch frame. Indeed, her unusually long, thick hair was one of her greatest obsessions, and she would spare no expense for its care and dressing.

Although not officially part of the Austrian Crown Jewels, the Köchert Stars were some of the most recognizable gems in Europe, largely due to the depiction of the all-diamond version in the famous 1865 Franz Xaver Winterhalter portrait of Sisi in court gala dress. Today, the romantic image is considered the most valuable exhibit in the Hofburg's museum dedicated to Sisi.

One hundred years after the empress's violent death at the hands of an anarchist, the single remaining star, measuring just under one-and-a-half inches, was on public display at Schönbrunn Palace lit from above with special jeweler's lights for maximum sparkle and presented to the public on a pedestal—a weight-sensitive pedestal surrounded by a bulletproof glass case wired with alarms. The room was further monitored by security guards, cameras and motion sensors. No precaution was too great for the last remaining Sisi Star, which was a priceless national treasure. As the crowds peered into the case, marveling at this material link to the ethereal Sisi, they could not have known the terrible secret that palace security wouldn't discover for another two weeks: the star was an impostor—a replica from Schönbrunn's own gift shop. A lone thief had surreptitiously stuffed the original inside a scuba respirator that he had brought along on vacation and was quietly making plans to spirit it out of the country.

I

"I am on show like a freak in a circus."

—Empress Elisabeth of Austria

Before the thief had fled Schönbrunn Palace for good, he couldn't help but admire the audacious undertaking he had carried out the night before. Paying his admission fee of about $7.80 and standing in the seemingly endless line leading up to the fake Köchert Diamond Pearl nestled on its red velvet cushion, he carefully monitored the imperial room now filled with daylight, scrutinizing the security guards and each visitor who marveled at the jeweled star that had once graced Sisi's tresses—or so they thought. His secret was still safe—no one had yet noticed that the piece in the case was made from cheap metal alloy and synthetic crystals that had been purchased for a few schillings just around the corner. As reckless and arrogant as it was to return to the scene of the crime and observe his handiwork, the thief just couldn't stay away. His narcissism was matched only by Sisi's.

—⚬⚬⚬—

The image that Empress Elisabeth of Austria cultivated over her forty-four years on the Austrian throne was of a woman—generally accepted as the most beautiful in Europe, if not the world—who spent all of her time and the empire's money on traveling with her entourage, riding expensive thoroughbreds, and doing whatever she felt necessary to beautify herself and prevent the manifestations of age. She became

The Köchert Diamond Pearl was stolen from Schönbrunn Palace in 1998. Court jeweler Köchert designed two sets of twenty-seven diamond stars for Sisi, one with and one without center pearls. She wore them in her hair and was immortalized on canvas wearing the all-diamond version. This is the last remaining "Sisi Star" of either set (© Schloss Schönbrunn Kultur- und Betriebsges.m.b.H., Sisi Museum/Hofburg, Vienna, photograph by Mr. Hannes Wagner).

obsessed with herself and her needs first, while her family and the empire had to learn to get along without her.

She was born Her Royal Highness Duchess Elisabeth Amalie Eugénie, Princess of Bavaria, on Christmas Eve, 1837, in Munich's Herzog Max Palais and spent her summers in the country at Possenhoffen Castle on Lake Starnberg. The family relished free time at their beloved "Possi" and whiled away their summer days hiking, riding, and fishing in the pastoral countryside. To Sisi, nature and the freedom it afforded her amounted to heaven.

Sisi was the fourth child of Duke Maximilian and Princess Ludovika, who was daughter of the first King of Bavaria. Ludovika and Max's fathers were first cousins, making the marriage one of first cousins once removed, and both had initially fallen in love with individuals their families found unsuitable due to political incompatibility or insufficient rank. After much conferring, the family threw the cousins together into an arranged marriage in order to prevent any further lapses in romantic judgment. Maximilian told Ludovika straight away that he did not love her and was marrying her solely because he was being forced to; thus, the union got off to an inauspicious start that would never fully recover in all of its sixty years. Ludovika gradually came to tolerate her husband's coarseness and restless spirit, but she would forever remain unfulfilled, saying, "When one is married, one feels so abandoned."[1] In time, Sisi herself would come to understand this statement all too well.

Sisi's father, Duke Max, as he was called, was from a junior branch of the House of Wittelsbach. The Wittelsbach dynasty had ruled in southern Germany for more than seven hundred years as dukes, electors, and kings of Bavaria. But since Duke Max did not belong to the royal branch as his wife did, he had no official functions at the Bavarian court and was free to devote himself to his rakish private life—a life he took very seriously.

Duke Max was a free spirit and political liberal, often cash poor, who enjoyed nothing more than wine, women and song. He fancied himself a poet, a talent that Sisi would inherit and use throughout her life to record her deepest sentiments, and her cruelest taunts for those she despised. In addition to the ten children Duke Max fathered within his marriage (eight of whom survived to adulthood), he had dozens of other offspring with Munich actresses and peasant girls near Possenhoffen. He ran a loose household, free from burdensome courtly restrictions, and taught his legitimate heirs to think freely and act on emotion in keeping with the philosophy of the Romantic movement that swept Germany during his lifetime.

As a child, Sisi adored her father, who was often off wandering the countryside or traveling to foreign lands. She showed signs of being highly intelligent, sensitive, and imaginative, a head-in-the-clouds idealist who was said to "spend hours dreaming in front of her mirror combing and arranging her hair," but she "would become nervous and impatient as soon as she had to try on a frock."[2] In fact, she was so fidgety and unfocused when doing her schoolwork that her tutors often tied

13

her to a chair to prevent the energetic child from dashing out the door to play with her numerous dogs and horses.

Under Duke Max's tutelage, Sisi learned to become a trick horse-back rider, acrobat, and street performer. She also learned to play the harp, piano, zither, and mandolin. Her father once told her, "If you and I had not been princely born, we could have performed in a circus."[3] Indeed, when looking back on her childhood, Sisi said that the only honest money she ever earned were the coins showered on her and her father by a cheering audience when they performed a song and dance act outside the Munich beer gardens.

Engraving of Sisi around the time of her 1854 wedding to Emperor Franz Joseph, based on a portrait by Swedish artist Amanda Bergstedt. Sisi was just sixteen when she married her first cousin and was catapulted to fame as the new Empress of Austria. Having grown up mostly in the Bavarian countryside, she never fully adjusted to her new life in Vienna nor her imperial position (photograph by Rischgitz/Getty Images/iStockphoto).

Sisi's chief personality trait as a child, the one that would adversely affect the rest of her life, was her melancholia, the tendency to become sad and withdrawn, retreating within herself and keeping everyone else at bay. Mental instability was a trait shared by both her hereditary lines, the Wittelsbachs, and her future husband's, the Habsburgs; their ancestors were extensively endogamous and had a long history of depression, hallucinations, and delusions. Sisi would fear for her own sanity all her life due to the "Wittelsbach curse," which she would come to call the "black clouds" that hung over her family.[4]

Although it was assumed she would marry well due to her princely blood, Sisi was never expected to become Empress of Austria; that honor was reserved for her elder sister, Helene, who was educated and groomed specifically for the title. It was fifteen-year-old Sisi's natural beauty and charming timidity, however, that infatuated her first cousin, Emperor Franz Joseph. After meeting Sisi at the imperial vacation villa of Bad Ischl for his twenty-third birthday celebrations, where he was also expected to become engaged to Helene, the emperor gushed only about Sisi to his mother, Archduchess Sophie, who recorded her son's thoughts in her journal: "She is as fresh as a newly peeled almond, and what a splendid crown of hair frames such a vision! How can anyone help loving such tender eyes and lips like strawberries!"[5] At the time, Sisi's hair was still dark blond—it had yet to turn the chestnut brown of maturity.

Fortunately, the emperor realized that Sisi was, in fact, still a child and handled her mercurial moods as gently as he could. She had been raised under such insular conditions that she became completely overwhelmed by her new position and grew frantic at the thought of leaving her close-knit family behind when she would be required to move to Vienna. Crying fits were commonplace, so Franz Joseph had a child's swing installed in the Hofburg gardens in order to mollify and brighten his frazzled bride.

One of the thousands of people on hand for Sisi's much celebrated arrival in Vienna at the end of her nine-month engagement was the Countess of Westmorland, who recorded her account of the young Sisi amidst the fanfare.

> She is a thousand times better than her portraits; none of them give an idea of her freshness, her air of candour and gentleness and intelligence, and of the perfect grace of all her movements. If her features are not perfect, they are delicate; her complexion white and clear, her lips like coral, her brown eyes not large, rather deep set, but bright, pretty hair.... Her figure is charming, medium size, slender and lissom, pretty shoulders and round arms, a most distinguished air and a young soft voice.[6]

The countess reported that once Sisi's ship arrived at Nussdorf, the emperor ecstatically ran onto the dockside bridge to openly embrace his young fiancée. Thousands of onlookers burst into cheers at the completely natural display of affection, and the countess wrote that she and many others dabbed away tears of joy.

Sisi and Franz Joseph would carry on the tradition of intermarriage between the Habsburgs and the Wittelsbachs, as they were related through both their mothers' and fathers' bloodlines. This extreme consanguinity required the couple to obtain an official papal dispensation, which they readily received in time for a spectacular royal wedding on April 24, 1854. Following days of parades and receptions, more than 1,000 invited guests packed the Vienna parish church of St. Augustine, which was lit with 15,000 candles, to witness the glamorous, young couple exchange their wedding vows and usher in a new age for the Austrian Empire. Sisi was somber and reticent at the ceremony, but she dazzled the attendees in her white gown of silk moiré with silver embroidery and a simple gold filigree crown of blossoms with matching decorative combs for her hair.

The people of Vienna flocked to wherever Sisi was making a public appearance, trying to catch a glimpse of their lovely new empress. But Sisi was a sensitive, painfully shy sixteen-year-old who was completely dismayed by her newfound fame. As she waved her lace handkerchief to acknowledge the crowds whose incessant cheering unnerved her, she remarked to her mother, "I am on show like a freak in a circus."[7]

Life behind the closed doors of the Hofburg Palace, home to the Habsburgs for more than 600 years, was no easier for the new empress. Her domineering mother-in-law, Archduchess Sophie, ran the most formal court in Europe and did not allow Sisi the comfort of any familiar faces from Bavaria. Instead, she introduced Sisi to a new entourage of middle-aged servants, all handpicked by Sophie herself. The girl who grew up running wild in the Bavarian countryside presently belonged to the empire and was no longer permitted to do anything for herself. From now on, all her needs would be met by her secretary, chatelaine, chamberlain, ladies-in-waiting, maids, footmen, grooms, and porters.

Archduchess Sophie was a stickler for properly observed court hierarchy and etiquette, and made it her mission to mold Sisi into a proper Viennese royal. To help achieve this goal, Sophie chose a fifty-six-year-old mistress of the household, the dour countess Esterházy-Liechtenstein, to act as a sort of governess to the still developing teenager. Sisi considered the countess nothing more than a spy who reported her most minor flaws back to the Archduchess. Both the countess and the archduchess continually reminded Sisi that people from southern Germany

A photomechanical print of Vienna's Hofburg Palace from 1890. Home to the Habsburgs since 1279, the Hofburg's 2,600 rooms served as the preferred winter residence of Emperor Franz Joseph's imperial family. Today, it houses the Sisi Museum that features 300 exhibits, including the Köchert Diamond Pearl (photograph by Library of Congress Prints and Photographs Division).

did not know how to behave as properly as the Viennese, and therefore she must learn her lessons well if she were to become a fitting Empress. The variety of courtiers from exalted Viennese families who came in contact with the new Empress each day agreed fully with Archduchess Sophie; they regarded Sisi as an unrefined country bumpkin to whom they would grudgingly be required to bow and curtsy. In order to prevent any missteps, Countess Esterházy-Liechtenstein presented Sisi with a thick manuscript titled "Most Humble Reminders," with all of the rules of etiquette and court hierarchy carefully spelled out for her.

Thirty years earlier, it was Sophie who had been considered the unpopular provincial outsider when she first came to Vienna to marry Archduke Franz Karl. Sophie had ambitions to become Empress of Austria herself when she suspected that Franz Karl's epileptic and childless older brother, Ferdinand I, would eventually be forced to abdicate due to his diminished health and his advisers' lack of confidence in his leadership. This would open the door for Sophie's husband, the heir presumptive as long as Ferdinand had no children, to become emperor sooner rather than later. However, grasping that her own husband was dull and unambitious, the politically shrewd Archduchess gave up her dream to become empress in favor of advancement for her more promising eldest son, eighteen-year-old Franz Joseph. In 1848, upon Ferdinand's abdication, Sophie persuaded her ineffectual husband to renounce his claim to the throne, paving the way for Franz Joseph to become emperor.

Revolution was upending the empire at the time of Franz Joseph's accession, and he took the motto *viribus unitis* (united peoples) to express his desire to reconcile his dominion of some twenty-nine million subjects with eleven distinct nationalities through unification and centralization. The citizens comprising Franz Joseph's vast empire included Czechs, Poles, and Ukrainians in the north, Serbs and Croats in the south, Romanians and Hungarians in the east, and Italians and Austrians in the west. Franz Joseph believed in a patriarchal autocracy and vehemently opposed the liberal democratic ideas that would in time be espoused by his wife and son. He regarded himself as taking full responsibility for his peoples' needs, and throughout his reign permitted general audiences twice a week to hear the requests and grievances of more than one hundred subjects at a time. For her efforts to orchestrate Franz Joseph's accession, Sophie became known throughout Europe as the power behind the empire's throne and pejoratively as "the only man at court." As such, the empress-mother was absolutely used to controlling every aspect of court life, and Franz Joseph's new bride was no exception.

Although Sisi and Franz Joseph had a tender relationship at the beginning of their marriage, politics and paperwork occupied Franz Joseph's entire days, leaving little time for his new—and very needy—young wife. In many ways, Sisi and Franz Joseph were completely incompatible; his heart lay with the military, court protocol, and official duty (he wore a military uniform throughout his life, even to complete his daily paperwork), while Sisi treasured the freedom to think, dream, and live without structure. The couple's differences may have been readily apparent to Sisi's mother, who may also have been concerned with her daughter's extreme youth. But when asked if Sisi ever thought of turning down Franz Joseph's proposal, Ludovika famously answered, "One does not send the Emperor of Austria packing."[8]

The morning after their wedding, Sisi and Franz Joseph were confronted at breakfast by their respective mothers, who learned that the marriage had not been consummated on the wedding night. Before the day was out, the entire court knew the truth, much to the teenaged Sisi's mortal embarrassment. Sisi would never fully forgive her husband or her mother-in-law for putting her through this humiliation. On the third night following the wedding the marriage finally became official, clearing Sisi to receive her *Morgengabe*—or "morning gift"—of approximately $240,000 to compensate her for the loss of her virginity.[9]

Franz Joseph was consumed with countless political crises including the Crimean War during the early days of their marriage, and his hectic schedule meant a proper honeymoon was out of the question. This important period right after the wedding when the young couple should have spent time getting to know one another was squandered, and Sisi was consumed with despair. She was often left alone in the royal household with her controlling mother-in-law and countless courtiers she didn't know. She remembered later to one of her ladies-in-waiting,

> I was alone all day long and was afraid of the moment when Archduchess Sophie came. For she came every day, to spy on what I was doing at any hour. I was completely *à la merci* of this completely malicious woman. Everything I did was bad. She passed disparaging judgments on anyone I loved. She found out everything because she never stopped prying. The whole house feared her so much that everyone trembled.[10]

Only later in life did Sisi admit that Sophie meant well for the good of the empire even if her methods were questionable. Sophie's own journal entries often expressed compassion and good will toward her daughter-in-law, but the archduchess was never able to understand Sisi's extreme moods or why she wouldn't fall in line with the imperial family.

Just two weeks after the wedding, Sisi literally became ill with homesickness for her carefree Bavarian home and family. She fell into a deep depression and turned to poetry to express her feelings of extreme loneliness and despair.

> I waken in a prison cell
> And fetters heavy on me weigh.
> I long far more than I can tell
> For freedom—it has turned away![11]

Inspired by her idol, Heinrich Heine, Sisi kept a poetic diary throughout her life in which she set to verse her myriad disappointments and few joys. Heine was a prolific writer and an outcast, banned in Germany for his Jewish heritage and radical political views, even though he had himself baptized a Christian at the age of twenty-eight in order to further his professional appeal. It was a move he would later regret, lamenting that instead of being accepted, he had become hated by both Christians and Jews.

Heine credited himself with moving beyond the emotional poetic techniques of the Romantic era; "with me, the old German lyrical school was closed, while at the same time the new school, the modern German lyric was inaugurated by me."[12]

Instead of writing sentimental poetry as had been popular in his day, Heine preferred to smatter his verse with sarcasm and irony.

> My songs, they say, are poisoned.
> How else, love, could it be?
> Thou hast, with deadly magic,
> Poured poison into me.
> My songs, they say, are poisoned.
> How else, then, could it be?
> I carry a thousand serpents
> And, love, among them—thee![13]

Heine's criticism of German nationalism and its censorship of his work led him to spend the last twenty-five years of his life as an exile in Paris where he supported France's decidedly more liberal political climate. Sisi felt an affinity with Heine's ostracism from his homeland, just as she came to believe that she had been forced out of Bavaria. And in the same way that Heine's words could be biting, Sisi's poetry could be cruel to those she blamed for her unhappiness, or those she simply found

I. "I am on show like a freak in a circus."

unattractive and unworthy of her attentions. When she wasn't composing verses, Sisi also kept a sketchbook in the early years of her marriage as a lighter form of expression where she drew self-portraits and images of Franz Joseph hard at work at his desk.

Sisi bolstered herself enough in the early years of her marriage to fulfill her chief duty as empress: she gave birth to two princesses, Sophie, named after the archduchess, and Gisela, named for a medieval Habsburg ancestor, although a son would have gone much further toward securing her position at court. Without consulting her daughter-in-law, Archduchess Sophie took immediate charge of the imperial children's rooms and situated them in her own Hofburg apartments as far from Sisi's rooms as possible. The archduchess also installed all of the children's nurses and attendants. Sisi was precluded from nursing or taking any active role in childrearing because Sophie felt the young empress could not be trusted with the monumental task of raising Habsburgs, the dynastic family that had ruled Austria since 1279. The House of Habsburg was so prolific, it could be traced to rulers in Spain, the Netherlands, Italy, and some twenty German emperors. Sisi's husband was the fifty-fourth successor to Charlemagne himself, and it was expected that a son would one day follow suit.

Sisi was not as impressed by the auspicious lineage as she was by what she believed was her young children's need for their mother. Of being separated from them by the archduchess, Sisi recalled,

> She took my children from me straight away. I was only allowed to see them when Sophie gave her consent. She was always present when I went to visit the children. Eventually I could only concede to her and only seldom went up to see them.[14]

Following Sisi's prodding and many tantrums, Franz Joseph finally interceded against his mother's objections, and Sisi won the battle to have the children's rooms moved closer to her own.

Since he owed his imperial position to his mother, Franz Joseph treated Archduchess Sophie with great reverence and continually looked to her for validation. He regularly had his daily schedule sent to her apartments for approval and deferred to her good judgment on such subjects as the best times and locations for their meals. Although bright, dedicated, and ambitious, Franz Joseph was emotionally immature and so entirely dependent on his mother's assent that he readily took her side over his wife's during the women's many petty arguments.

Sisi continued to bristle at her mother-in-law and, as she slowly gained confidence, began to push back; Sisi won a battle about wearing a pair of shoes more than once—the Empress of Austria was expected to exchange her shoes for a brand new pair each day, a custom Sisi found wasteful and ridiculous. Sisi also began restricting her food, which was something she could absolutely control herself. Meals with the empress frequently lasted just twenty minutes, which meant her disgruntled staff had to leave the table hungry. And when she did eat, Sisi refused to wear her white gloves, which was a time-honored dining tradition of the imperial family.

Sisi also defied her mother-in-law by insisting on taking two-year-old Princess Sophie and the baby, Gisela, on a trip to Budapest, Hungary, in 1857. Sophie protested greatly, believing the children too young to travel. The Archduchess finally acquiesced but sent along her approved medical adviser, Dr. Johann Seeburger, just to be cautious. Perhaps because he was firmly in Archduchess Sophie's camp, Dr. Seeburger harbored a poor impression of the empress. He remarked that "she was unfit for her position both as Empress and as wife, although she has really nothing to do. Her relations with the children are most perfunctory, and though she grieves and weeps over the noble Emperor's absence, she goes out riding for hours on end, ruining her health."[15]

During the trip to Hungary, both of Sisi's daughters became ill with measles. Sisi desperately wished to remain with the children in Budapest instead of traveling on for an official visit to the countryside. Franz Joseph insisted that they fulfill their obligations, and Sisi reluctantly left the girls in Dr. Seeburger's care. Toward the end of their journey, the couple received news that while baby Gisela was rallying, Sophie had taken a turn and was fighting for her life. Once back in Budapest, Sisi stayed by the toddler's bedside for eleven hours until Sophie died in her arms. Sisi's act of defying her mother-in-law had backfired in the worst possible way, and this major emotional blow to the already fragile twenty-year-old empress was the impetus for her first major psychological break. Sisi completely withdrew from court, cried constantly, and spoke of suicide for the first time. She also utterly gave up trying to be an attentive mother and left the future child rearing completely in Arch-duchess Sophie's hands.

Sisi's mother, Ludovika, hurried from Bavaria to attend to her despairing daughter during the crisis. But the official period of court mourning came to an obligatory end after three months when Franz Joseph's brother, Maximilian, and his new wife (and second cousin), Belgian Princess Charlotte, stopped in Vienna following their Brussels wedding. The occasion was certainly not a pleasant one for Sisi and may have been made worse by her mother-in-law's fawning over the new bride. Archduchess Sophie wrote in her diary that Charlotte was "charming, beautiful, attractive, loving, and gentle to me. I feel as if I had always loved her."[16] In the event that Sisi never gave birth to a male heir, Sophie felt satisfied that Charlotte would, and the succession would pass to Max.

Once Sisi finally began to recover from her grief, she commissioned a memorial bracelet featuring a portrait of the deceased child surrounded by diamonds. The jewelry can be seen on Sisi's left wrist in an official portrait of her in full court regalia by artist Franz Russ. Sisi's physical and mental health continued to improve until joy filled the Hofburg once again on August 21, 1858, just over a year after her daughter's death, when Sisi gave birth to a healthy boy named Rudolf, after the medieval Habsburg King of Germany. Sisi biographer Brigitte Hamann contends that the baby's name was politically motivated: Franz Joseph hoped to reestablish Habsburg rule over Germany, which had ended with the dissolution of the Holy Roman Empire in 1806 prompted by the military defeat of Austrian Emperor Franz I by Napoleon at Austerlitz.

Rudolf's was a difficult birth and Sisi recovered slowly, but she had to take satisfaction in knowing there would be no more talk of the succession passing to Max and Charlotte's branch of the family. Tears were said to have streamed down Franz Joseph's face as he met his son for the first time and described the baby as "not beautiful, but magnificently built and very strong."[17]

Around the summer of 1860, another crisis rocked the royal marriage, but this one would have the most seriously lasting implications. Franz Joseph was rumored to be having extra-marital affairs—not particularly unusual for a high-born gentleman of the time. Instead of ignoring the affairs as dozens of Habsburg wives before her had, however, Sisi refused to acquiesce to the infidelity. The twenty-two-year-old empress left her husband and small children and fled back home to Possenhofen, nearly three hundred miles away.

Attempts at reconciliation failed, and in the fall, Sisi packed up a small circle of courtiers and sailed to the subtropical island of Madeira, Portugal, under the guise of being gravely ill. Since none of the empire's ships was available for the journey, Sisi chartered Queen Victoria's private yacht. According to *The Irish Times*, "The *Victoria and Albert* ... has been placed at the disposal of her Majesty by the Queen, who is said to have expressed and shown very great sympathy for the youthful invalid."[18]

The official reason for Sisi's flight, and the reason for which Queen Victoria lent her the yacht, was the need to recover from tuberculosis or "galloping consumption," as it was known in the day. It was believed that the Empress was so acutely ill that she might never recover. During a layover in Dublin, *The Irish Times* reported, "During the time [the empress] remained here she was so unwell that her physician had given directions that no one should speak to her."[19] A flurry of letters ensued between Sisi's mother, Ludovika, and Archduchess Sophie about the state of Sisi's health. Both feared the young empress was in fact dying, and Ludovika believed Sisi had fled the court to spare the emperor from seeing her in such a distressing condition.

As it turns out, Sisi was not as concerned with the emperor's feelings as with her own. Although she suffered from a well-documented cough, in actuality, Sisi wanted to be as far away from her husband as possible. Dr. Seeburger had diagnosed her with a sexually transmitted disease, probably syphilis, in his attempt to explain the cause of the unusual swelling at her wrists, ankles, and knees. However, even into old age, Sisi never manifested any other symptoms of syphilis, at least none that was recorded by any doctors, courtiers, or other court watchers. Syphilitic symptoms include small open chancre sores; a spotty, reddish-brown rash on the palms of the hands; large, raised mouth lesions; and eventually blindness and dementia. Although Sisi was certainly eccentric and depressive, she was never suspected of having dementia. And if she had suffered from patchy hair loss, another syphilitic symptom, someone—even the empress herself, who prized her beautiful hair above all else—certainly would have recorded it.

The joint swelling was most likely a symptom of malnutrition due to Sisi's refusal to eat, as her protein-starved body retained fluids that could not be flushed by her increasingly stressed kidneys. Another doctor named Fischer diagnosed the empress as having acute anemia and edema, and was unable to state for certain whether she had a venereal infection as Dr. Seeburger had been quick to do. Sisi's mother, Ludovika, would ultimately place her faith in Dr. Fischer, stating, "Fischer was the only one who diagnosed her correctly always."[20] We may never know for sure if Franz Joseph infected his wife, but she believed he was the cause of her suffering and this belief changed the dynamic of the imperial marriage forever.

Feeling a grave amount of guilt, Franz Joseph denied Sisi nothing on her flight away from him. He supplied the vast financial backing needed to pay for the voyage that took Sisi from Madeira, Portugal, to Venice, Italy, and on to Corfu, Greece. During her absence, the emperor periodically sent a courier to report back on Sisi's health. The news was always perplexingly positive, and the empress did not seem to be on her deathbed after all. In fact, while Franz Joseph struggled to keep his empire together, Sisi spent her time romping with her animals, strumming her mandolin, and playing card games like Old Maid with her ladies. Clearly the warmer climate and less rigid atmosphere had been good for her, and Sisi felt well enough to return to Vienna in 1861. But from the moment she reentered the Hofburg doors, Sisi's cough returned with a vengeance, and her continued refusal to eat started to garner attention outside of the family. According to Austria's Foreign Minister Count Louis Rechberg, "The Empress has the deepest aversion to any kind of nourishment. She no longer eats anything at all, and her energies are exhausted all the more as … severe pain robs her of the sleep that might still be able to keep up her energies."[21] Malnourishment aside, esteemed lung specialist Dr. Josef Skoda ordered Sisi out of the capital once again for more restoratively temperate climes.

Intense whispers circulated around Vienna as courtiers began to suspect Sisi's persistent cough was brought on by emotional instability rather than physical infirmity. Once Sisi settled again in Corfu, Ludovika, and the emperor "ardently begged" Sisi's sister Helene, now married to the Hereditary Prince of Thurn and Taxis and with young children of her own, to travel to the Greek island to get to the bottom of Sisi's illness. At first, Helene was said to be frightened by Sisi's "puffiness and pallor."[22] She observed how her younger sister exercised to extremes while barely eating, and Helene made her own diagnosis that Sisi was suffering from malnutrition. From then on, Sisi was put on a regimen of goat meat three times a day, and her constitution started to improve.

Although she was feeling better, Sisi did not look forward to her eventual return to court. She wrote to a confidante, "It will take me a little while to get used to taking up the domestic cross again."[23] But the time finally came in 1862; After a full two-year absence from court, the

Schönbrunn Palace, the 1,441-room Rococo summer residence of the imperial family and the scene of Gerald Blanchard's daring theft of the Sisi Star. Blanchard said he parachuted onto the roof at night and slipped through a window he had managed to unlock the day before while on a palace tour (photograph by Dan Breckwoldt for iStockphoto).

emperor himself traveled to Corfu, along with the Austrian Navy, to fetch his wife and put an end to her flight. Sisi was welcomed home with trepidation. One of her nieces wrote, "Now we have her back in this country just as we had two years ago; yet how many things lie between— Madeira, Corfu and a world of troubles."[24]

And yet, through all of her travels supposedly in search of health, Sisi seemed to have finally gained some much-needed confidence. Gone was the timid girl who burst into tears when she became overwhelmed or couldn't get her way. Sisi was now a self-assured woman of twenty-five who had been completely in charge of her traveling household and had thrived under her own autonomy. She had also learned that in her blossoming beauty lay tremendous power. During her trip, a Russian naval ship had docked at Madeira, and Sisi had invited the officers to a dinner dance. A Russian admiral later reported that every officer present had fallen in love with the young empress. A handsome Austrian officer who was part of her retinue was also reported to have been smitten with her charms. Sisi rebuffed them all, always remaining the cold, untouchable beauty floating above reproach. But she undoubtedly loved the attention and would soon decipher precisely how to use this new power to her benefit back at court.

The Austrian *Reichsrath*, or parliament, welcomed Sisi home with a congratulatory address in September 1862. Sisi granted the representatives an audience at mid-day in Schönbrunn Palace's Hall of Ceremonies as an imposing portrait of Empress Maria Theresa as the "First Lady of Europe" gazed down from her perch. Sisi graciously accepted the government officials' kind words, replying, "I am most grateful to Providence for having restored me to health, and for having allowed me to return to the Emperor, to my children, to Austria." News reports described the empress as looking "remarkably well" but said "she was nervous, and read her speech in such a low voice that the deputies in the background could not distinctly hear what she said." The newspapers then turned their attentions to her appearance, describing Sisi as being "very simply dressed, and she wore no jewelry, but nature has done so much for her that she needs no artificial ornaments. Her beautiful hair was dressed in such a way that it fell in a loose bow round the nape of the neck."[25]

Now home in Vienna, Sisi tried to retain some of the control she had experienced on her travels and began to wield her new power to freely make demands of her husband. One of her most significant stipulations was regarding the education of Crown Prince Rudolf. Rudolf's chief educator, Count Leopold Gondrecourt, applied sadistic military tactics to toughen up the sensitive seven-year-old boy, whom Franz Joseph referred to as "the wretch."[26] Gondrecourt's methods included cold water therapy, hours of exercise in the rain, and waking the boy each night by shooting a pistol. Rudolf was turning into a nervous, miserable child, and Sisi insisted that he be given a more liberal, academic education. In addition to Gondrecourt's dismissal, Sisi also requested the removal of the austere Countess Eszterhazy-Liechtenstein as mistress of the household. Perhaps concerned that Sisi would leave again if he defied her, Franz Joseph capitulated to all of his wife's demands.

Sisi also made a bold move by deciding to learn Hungarian, much to her mother-in-law's dismay. Archduchess Sophie hated all things Hungarian and believed that the ethnic Magyars were continuously conspiring to split the empire. The Revolution of 1848, when mass demonstrations led to the dethronement of the Habsburgs in Hungary, was still fresh in her mind, and she cared nothing for the country's desire for autonomy and a constitution. After all, it had been a Hungarian nationalist named János Libényi who had attempted to assassinate Franz Joseph when the emperor was just twenty-two and at the beginning of his reign. As the young emperor and one of his officers took a stroll in Vienna on February 18, 1853, Libényi lunged at Franz Joseph and struck him in the neck with a knife. Fortunately, the emperor had been wearing his military uniform, and its stiff collar prevented any life-threatening injuries. The assassination attempt had rattled Archduchess Sophie so much that she immediately pushed Franz Joseph to find a wife and continue the Habsburg succession. Franz Joseph and Sisi were engaged six months later.

Recent history aside, Sisi regarded the Hungarian freedom-fighters as heroes battling for independence just as she was battling for independence from the archduchess. In a bid to irritate her mother-in-law and the Viennese courtiers, Sisi sent to Hungary for a reader to teach her the language. According to the *Ost-Deutsch Post*, "Her majesty is so

I. "I am on show like a freak in a circus."

fond of this language that she has recently taken into her service a *femme de chambre*, a native of the district of Raab, who speaks nothing but Hungarian."[27]

Sisi chose Ida Ferenczy from a list of potential tutors in part because she liked the simplicity of the Hungarian's name. But because Ida was a member of the Hungarian gentry and not of sufficiently high birth, she could not be given the title of "court lady," so Ida was called "Reader to Her Majesty" instead. Over the years, Ida became one of Sisi's closest confidantes and best friends, and in time even referred to her beloved empress informally as "the dewy flower." Ida was the last person Sisi saw each evening as she loosened the empress's hair and helped her prepare for bed. Sisi readily admitted that she could hardly sleep without Ida as her "soporific."[28] The two women confided in each other regularly, and it was Ida who first encouraged Sisi to become involved in Hungarian politics. This advocacy ultimately led to the establishment of the dual Austro-Hungarian Monarchy with Sisi crowned as its queen.

Now back at court following her two-year hiatus, Sisi turned completely inward in order to regain some sovereignty over her own life. Since she had very little say over her children or her household, Sisi became obsessed with what she could control: her physique. She came to believe that beauty was her only path to power—after all, it was the only thing the newspapers and her subjects seemed to talk about—and she started making a cult of it, turning each act of grooming into a sacred ritual that could last all day. Sisi wanted to be known as the most beautiful woman in the world, and her attention to detail developed into an obsession that would last until her violent death just shy of her sixty-first birthday.

Sisi was particularly preoccupied with two aspects of her appearance: her extraordinarily long hair and her weight. She was terrified of gaining an ounce and weighed herself several times each day. One of her doctors once remarked in exasperation, "If it were not for those damned scales! Devil take the man who advised her Majesty to weigh herself all the time!"[29]

Although it is difficult to diagnose an historical figure with a psychological disorder, it's relatively safe to say that Sisi displayed signs of anorexia nervosa. She purposely maintained just one hundred to one hundred-ten pounds on her nearly five-foot eight-inch frame all her adult life, despite giving birth to four children. In fact, her weight only significantly increased when she retained fluids as a result of malnourishment. Her mother became so alarmed at seeing Sisi's slight frame that she remarked that her once-healthy daughter resembled "a bean-pole."[30]

Sisi often ate just one meal a day, consisting of warm bouillon or egg whites with salt, or she simply ate nothing at all and drank only milk. She also tried the fad diets of the day that included eating only oranges or grapes, and even ocean sand to fill her up and control her appetite. Yet, despite her doctor's admonitions that she nourish herself, Sisi would only agree to increase her calories with a few pieces of fruit or glasses of milk each day.

Sisi once told her eldest daughter she was deathly afraid of growing "as fat as a tub."

"When I am not feeling well," she wrote, "my weight goes up, and of all my ills this upsets me the most."[31]

To keep in shape, Sisi had exercise equipment installed in her apartments so she could hoist herself onto the gymnastics rings or wall bars whenever she felt she had overindulged and needed to burn off extra weight. Sisi's "wasp waist" was particularly important to her; in addition to slimming cures and other extreme activities like riding to hounds sidesaddle, fencing, lifting dumbbells, and taking strenuous hikes that could last up to ten hours, Sisi budgeted an hour each day to having herself tightly laced into silk corsets that rendered her waist no larger than twenty inches. As a result, she often experienced lightheadedness and shortness of breath. To keep her hips slim, Sisi wrapped her body in tight compresses doused in vinegar and slept in them overnight.

A recipe for her favorite vinegar, infused with violets, listed specific instructions for the court pharmacist:

Place the violet blossom in layers in a bellied bottle and pour the apple vinegar over it. Close tightly and let stand for two days. Then filter with a hair sieve and squeeze out the blossom with a wooden spoon. Remove some of the distilled water and mix the violet root powder in it. Pour into the distilled water and shake the mixture well.[32]

The empress was also known to binge on large quantities of food in one sitting before fasting again. In 1878 her niece, Countess

I. "I am on show like a freak in a circus."

Marie Larisch, recorded a situation in which the empress visited a restaurant under an assumed name and proceeded to eat an entire chicken, vegetable salad, and pastry for dessert while her ladies looked on in astonishment. Sweets turned out to be one of the empress's favorite overindulgences; she was known to splurge on violet-flavored ices, confections and pastries. Once she finished bingeing, Sisi managed to regain her composure and continue with her starvation diets for weeks on end.

Sisi's poor eating habits terribly worried her husband, who wrote of his feelings of helplessness: "I am only depressed by the thought of the gnawing hunger which you punish by fasting, instead of appeasing it as other sensible people do, but the case is beyond all remedy, so we will pass it over in silence."[33]

In the 1800s, the medical community was slowly starting to recognize self-starvation as an illness, but doctors were still unsure of how to treat the problem. Victorian newspapers recounted the tales of "fasting girls" who starved themselves mainly for religious transcendence of the flesh. But by the 1870s, some doctors began diagnosing self-starvation as a disease completely separate from religious delusions or insanity, noting that the symptoms often began in adolescence and therefore must be a manifestation of hysteria, or extreme emotional turmoil brought on by female puberty. In 1873, Queen Victoria's physician Sir William Gull coined the term *anorexia nervosa*, or "nervous absence of appetite," and believed the disease occurred in men as well as women. He treated his patients with a mixture of medicines, a change in diet, and sometimes a change in environment. That same year, however, French physician Ernest-Charles Lasègue postulated that the lack of appetite originated from emotional and psychological beginnings: dysfunctional family dynamics and a desire to avoid pain. It was not until a full one hundred years later, however, that obsession with body image would be considered a symptom of anorexia. Sadly, the best Sisi's doctors could do at the time was to simply encourage her to eat without yet having the knowledge to get to the psychological root of her problem.

Although never formally recognized as having the still nascent disease anorexia nervosa, Sisi was repeatedly diagnosed with "greensickness" or anemia, exhaustion, and painful joints throughout her life. Finally, in 1898, the doctor who performed her autopsy reported that

Sisi had signs of "edema of hunger," or severe swelling around the joints due to malnutrition. This was probably the same swelling that was earlier diagnosed by Dr. Seeburger as a sexually transmitted disease. Yet, miraculously, the lack of adequate nutrients throughout her life never caused Sisi to be bedridden, have organ failure, or even break a bone. Neither did it significantly affect the length or thickness of the empress's other obsession—her abundant chestnut locks. The intricately braided styles she wore would become as famous as her slender figure, and when she dressed for court occasions, some of the most spectacular jewels on display were the ones she wore in her hair.

II

"It's just a natural thing."

—Gerald Blanchard

The stolen Köchert Diamond Pearl wouldn't be seen again until 2007, when investigators liberated it from its dank hiding place in a basement crawlspace in Winnipeg. How it got there, no one but the thief knew for sure. After carefully extricating it from behind an insulated panel, natural light reignited the star's dormant fire. The detectives turned the exquisite piece over in their hands, holding it up closer to take in every detail, while the thief stood by nervously in handcuffs. Soon, the Sisi Star would be heading back home to Austria, while its abductor would gain international recognition as a master criminal.

—ʍ—

In 1998, this master criminal was a slight, bespectacled kid in his 20s, with a super-human ability to detect security flaws in banks, and as it turns out, museums. Conversing with Gerald Daniel Blanchard, one recognizes the characteristics of both James Bond and Rain Man rolled into one polite, soft spoken package with a steel trap mind. As Blanchard explained it, "It's like the Italian Mafia boss. He's a little, fragile-type person. But he controls a big empire. It's not the size, it's the mind that gives the power to control people and have people do things for you."[1]

Blanchard had been having people do things for him and his budding criminal empire ever since he was a twelve-year-old in Omaha, Nebraska. That's when he first realized he could make money—a lot of

33

money—by "rehashing," a scam whereby the perpetrator uses fabricated receipts to return stolen merchandise. The idea first occurred to Blanchard when he bought a remote controlled car with his frugally saved-up allowance. When he opened the bag after making his purchase, he realized that the receipt sitting inside was actually more valuable than the merchandise itself. After stashing his new toy, Blanchard went back inside the store, picked up an identical car, then used the original receipt to "return" that car and get his money back.

"I realized, I have a $99 car basically for free and money back in my pocket," Blanchard said.[2]

That serendipitous discovery led Blanchard to develop his own rehashing scheme with the assistance of some close accomplices who would help net him hundreds of thousands of dollars.

"I would know people who worked at department stores and they would sell me merchandise for twenty-five percent on the dollar," Blanchard explained. "And I would have other people print receipts and return them back to the store for the full price plus the fourteen-percent sales tax." None of these people ever turned him in, Blanchard said, because, "I could just tell who would work with me. It's a gift, I guess."[3]

And just as his crew members remained loyal to him, Blanchard was a thorough believer in "honor among thieves" himself. Throughout his criminal career, Blanchard would pride himself on taking good care of his people. He would be the one to take the heat from an even bigger crime boss down the line when money went missing. And he would eventually be the one to confess to possessing the Sisi Star and serve extra prison time just to keep his crew members out of prison. Blanchard would also remain something of a gentleman criminal, never using violence or deliberately going after the possessions of ordinary people. Instead, Blanchard targeted institutions—the big guys with big money—like major banks and even a Viennese museum. This way, he rationalized, he wouldn't feel guilty about hurting little guys like himself.

Blanchard figured that by 1998, the rehashing scheme had netted him some $230,000, and he finally felt financially stable enough to marry his sweetheart, a German citizen he had met in Edmonton, Canada. The two posed for photos in their matching white wedding ensembles and red roses, the picture of hopeful young love. Another major life event would happen the same year when Blanchard would break into Schön-brunn Palace and steal the Sisi Star thousands of miles away in Austria. How did he go from simple retail scams to single-handedly pulling off one of the most sophisticated international jewel heists of all time? Chalk it up to another gift: Blanchard was born with an almost sixth sense that allowed him to recognize security flaws and dismantle complex surveillance systems like the one at Schönbrunn Palace, so he could slip in and out completely unnoticed.

As incredible as such a heist was, Blanchard remained relatively nonchalant about his abilities. "It's just a natural thing," Blanchard said. "I have the ability to look around and realize where the flaws are."[4]

Blanchard was born at Victoria Hospital in Winnipeg, Canada, where he was immediately handed over for adoption by his birth mother. He grew up poor with his sister and adoptive mother, who would soon divorce and struggle daily to provide for her small brood. At the age of six, he decided to help out by stealing some just-delivered bottles of milk from a neighbor's porch. As a child, Blanchard knew that stealing was wrong, but he was the man of the house now and couldn't let his little sister go hungry. He ran home with the bottles as fast as his six-year-old legs could carry him, then laid low for a while until he was sure he hadn't been caught. It was then that he realized the experience hadn't been so bad; in fact, there was a kind of rush to getting away with taking something that wasn't his. "After that, I was hooked," he said.[5]

Blanchard had something more than the average petty thief: intellectual curiosity and plenty of natural talent. "His mother indicated that … from a young age, he was always very good at taking apart toys, and dismantling them effectively," his lawyer said. "And I think probably that curiosity in life has obviously served him to develop his skills."[6]

According to Blanchard, his mother would eventually learn to look the other way and even accepted a house he bought her with the help of a lawyer and more than $100,000 in cash. Blanchard was just sixteen at the time and told her that the house belonged to a friend. But, just as he was protective of his crew, Blanchard was equally protective of his mother's blind spot and firmly put the onus on himself. "I tried to keep it all from her," he said.[7]

At the age of seven, Blanchard's family immigrated to the United States and as a school kid in Nebraska, he started going by his middle name, Danny. Blanchard struggled with dyslexia and had a hard time fitting in. That's when he started stealing again, perhaps for the attention or maybe for the ego boost he got when he was able to outsmart an unsuspecting victim. Eventually, his troublemaking landed Blanchard in reform school, where he met a home-mechanics teacher while trying to steal a school VCR. It was a heck of an introduction, but the two developed a mentorship that would foster Blanchard's skills for construction, woodworking, model building, and automotive mechanics. The teenager finally had an advocate and some direction.

"He could see that I had talent," Blanchard said of his mentor, "and he wanted me to put it to good use."[8] But instead of applying his natural skills in the workforce, Blanchard was more interested in circumventing the system. His life's ambition became to find a direct route to big money and be his own boss. So, the teenager decided to stop wasting time stocking groceries after school, which netted him only peanuts, and set to work recruiting department store employees to move tens of thousands of dollars' worth of stolen goods.

Blanchard was proud of his newfound status as a nascent crime boss. A photo taken at the time shows a skinny, shirtless teen with huge glasses that threaten to swallow him whole. He's counting stacks of dollar bills while accomplices loiter nearby. On the table next to the loot is a bulky and expensive Motorola portable phone, the pound-and-a-half brick type with a long rubber antenna. A status symbol at the time, it clearly represented Blanchard's growing clout.

But Blanchard's luck ran out one night in 1992 when he was caught by a store security officer at an Omaha mall after heaving a bag containing stolen clothes into the trunk of his car. The officer remembered grabbing Blanchard by the neck through the open driver's side window. When Blanchard stepped on the gas to make his getaway, the officer held on tight and managed to climb over the suspect and into the passenger seat. He punched Blanchard several times until the thief finally stopped the car and the police arrived.

Even the mall security guard realized he was dealing with an uncommon criminal at the time. "He was more than just an exceptional shoplifter," the officer remembered. "He was very intelligent. But I don't think he got smart enough to realize he was going to get caught."[9]

After the arrest and subsequent search of Blanchard's mother's home, the police reported finding equipment for printing fake price tags that allowed Blanchard to purchase items for a made-up low price, then return them for full retail. Blanchard served several months in jail for the crime, but as the mall security guard would say, "I guess that didn't stop him."[10]

After jail, Blanchard was released into his home-mechanics teacher's custody. His mentor still believed Blanchard could turn his life around and was willing to vouch for him. Surely the teenager's time in jail had scared him straight. But far from desiring to clean up his act, Blanchard was just getting started. There was no way he ever wanted to lead a mundane nine-to-five life. Not with his unique abilities.

On his own, Blanchard began obsessively studying the inner workings of mechanical devices and electronics, and he developed a penchant for cameras and computerized surveillance equipment. One day in the future, Canadian authorities would describe him as having "the best working knowledge of electronics in the country."[11] He also honed his mechanical skills, learning to take apart and reassemble complex Mas Hamilton and Lagard locks. According to Larry Levasseur, one of the Winnipeg investigators responsible for recovering the Sisi Star in 2007, "I took him a bag of parts of this lock. And it was like watching a person with a Rubik's Cube that could actually solve it," Levasseur said. "In a matter of a couple minutes, he put springs and screws all back together again. Spun the dial on that thing and it charged up. Never seen anything like it."[12]

Blanchard also learned to employ his wiry stature to get him out of sticky situations. On April 27, 1993, while being held in a police examination room past midnight on suspicion of setting a car on fire in Council Bluffs, Iowa, Blanchard decided it was time to wrap things up. When the interrogators turned their backs, "I managed to sneak into the next room and slip through the tiles into the ceiling," Blanchard said.[13] As the officers ran down the hallway frantically looking for him, Blanchard decided to just sit tight for several hours until the station was mostly empty. He then lowered himself down, stole police equipment, including a badge, gun, hand-held radio, hat, coat and duffel bag, then casually strolled past the front desk as if he worked there, but not before leaving a single bullet on the desk of the officer who had led the questioning—an unusually aggressive move for the mild-mannered Blanchard.[14]

Blanchard hitched a ride home on the back of a motorcycle for the nearly nine mile ride across the Iowa border to Omaha, Nebraska, all the while wearing the stolen police cap, then proceeded to hide in the attic of his mother's modest home. The next day, he was rooted out by a no-nonsense SWAT team who cleared out the middle-class neighborhood, then deployed flashbang grenades to extract Blanchard from his upstairs hiding place. He emerged with his hands up, was ordered down on the ground, then immediately handcuffed by the heavily armed men dressed in head-to-toe black, their faces obscured by balaclava masks. The authorities confiscated the police equipment Blanchard had stolen the night before, then stuffed him in the back of a police cruiser and carted him off to Central Police Headquarters. Remarkably, Blanchard wasn't ready to go quietly just yet and waited for the precise moment to take advantage of his uncommon dexterity yet again.

Once parked in the police station garage, Blanchard said the two officers got out of the car but left the keys in the ignition. That's when he made his next move. "I fiddled with the cuffs until I got my hands in front of me, locked the doors, slipped up front, and put it in gear," he said.[15] The startled policemen jumped in another waiting car and gave chase as Blanchard led them on a twenty-minute wild ride through Omaha. Blanchard eventually ditched the car at a downtown Omaha steakhouse and took off on foot until he was finally tackled by the aggravated officers. They hauled the two-time escapee back to headquarters under heavy guard this time, fitted him for an orange jumpsuit, and threw him in the Pottawattamie County Jail. Blanchard's mug shot did not betray any pride he might have felt for his cunning escapes; he scowled at the camera with the sign, "Sheriff's Department Pottawattamie County" held in front, and in back, the measuring tape that recorded him at sixty-six inches tall, or five-foot-six.

Blanchard was slapped with charges in both Iowa and Nebraska—arson, theft and burglary for the car-on-fire incident in Council Bluffs, and possession of a firearm by a felon, theft of property worth more than $1,500, assault of an officer, and escape from official detention for the Omaha arrest and police chase. Blanchard would eventually be sentenced to four years hard time for the crimes.

Two months into his jail stay, the twenty-one-year-old was ordered before a federal judge for something new—a deportation hearing. Prosecutors didn't just want to keep him behind bars; they wanted him out of the country. Blanchard's handcuffs and leg chains clanked vexatiously as he shuffled into the courtroom to stand before U.S. Immigration Judge Craig Zerbe. After the attorneys addressed the court, the judge ordered deportation back to Canada based not only on Blanchard's current convictions but also for his prior infractions of shoplifting and receiving stolen property. According to the judge, Blanchard had committed at least two crimes "involving moral turpitude,"[16] and the U.S. government wanted him off its soil. One assistant Pottawattamie County attorney was heard remarking that "anyone with Blanchard's abilities probably would have little difficulty in re-entering the United States once deported."[17] But first, he would have to finish serving out his time on U.S. soil.

At roughly the same age that most of his former classmates were heading to college or working their first real jobs, Gerald Blanchard was off to receive a very different kind of education. In prison he would learn to eat, shower, and sleep when he was told to; would be subject to strip searches, confiscations, routine bed checks, lockdowns and random head counts; and probably worked a prison job for pennies an hour. It may have been the first real structure that he had experienced in his life. Blanchard would also learn to play a role in the prisoner hierarchy that included keeping his head down and not making much eye contact. Blanchard was not a physically imposing figure, and the last thing he wanted was to run afoul of a large, irritable inmate.

Finally, in March, 1997, Gerald Blanchard was released from his oppressive prison cell. The shackles and jumpsuit were gone, but so was his U.S. Citizenship. Agents from the Immigration and Naturalization

Service immediately took custody and escorted Blanchard across international lines and back to his birth city of Winnipeg.

Far from learning his lesson, however, Blanchard returned to his native land with grandiose goals. He had used his time spent in U.S. custody mulling over his unique capabilities and realized he had just the right skills that could be used to pull off something big. But just what that something was wouldn't occur to him until he stood before the sparkling Sisi Star during his honeymoon trip to Europe one year later.

III

"I didn't know
anything about Sisi."

"No, not at all. I've just learned from what the news stories said."
—Gerald Blanchard, January 2014[1]

Gerald Blanchard had no idea who Sisi was when he took a private tour of Schönbrunn Palace in early June 1998, the same year the palace was designated a UNESCO (United Nations Educational, Scientific, and Cultural Organization) World Heritage site. He had just gotten married and was on a six-month grand European tour with his new wife when they decided to make a stop in Vienna. Schönbrunn is the most-visited attraction in the Austrian city, and tourists usually set aside half a day or more to tour the luxurious palace grounds begun in 1695, with the purpose of outshining Louis XIV's Versailles. Schönbrunn was named for the "fair spring" (*schöner brunnen*) on which the palace was erected and which provided drinking water to the Hofburg until water pipes were built in the eighteenth century.

The newlyweds were just in time for a special exhibit called "Elisabeth, Beauty for Eternity," to commemorate the one hundredth anniversary of Sisi's death. Blanchard's wealthy father-in-law had come along, too, and pulled some strings to get special access to the exhibit's high point, the Köchert Diamond Pearl, before the general crowds would be let in to see it several days later. The private tour guide told the threesome the story of how this last authentic Sisi Star once adorned the empress's hair, how she had donned an all-diamond version by Köchert in the famed 1865 Winterhalter painting, and how Sisi had been assassinated by an Italian anarchist. But Blanchard was no history buff and didn't care so much about the woman who wore the jewel as he did

41

about the object's value, which the guide said was priceless. Blanchard's mind immediately began to case the palace security—the motion sensors, the armed guards, the weight-sensitive pedestal holding the star itself.

And then he knew. He had finally found the challenge he had been looking for.

—⟶

Since first arriving in Vienna as a child bride, Sisi had found it virtually impossible to fit in with the haughty courtiers, and she no longer desired to try. Any interest she may have had in child rearing had been quashed by Archduchess Sophie, who was now managing all of the children's day-to-day activities. Sophie had tried in her own way to teach Sisi "how to be an empress," but had proven ineffectual. If Sisi wasn't willing to listen to her mother-in-law, however, she certainly could have turned to her immediate predecessor, former Empress Maria Anna, for instruction on how to conduct her life as a gracious imperial consort.

Maria Anna and her twin sister were born in 1803 in Palazzo Colonna in Rome, the daughters of King Victor Emmanuel I of Sardinia and his wife, Archduchess Maria Teresa of Austria-Este. At the relatively advanced age of twenty-seven, Maria Anna finally made her dynastic match, marrying Ferdinand, the heir to the Austrian throne, by proxy in 1831. When they finally met face-to-face, Maria Anna was taken aback by her invalid husband; in addition to suffering from epilepsy, Ferdinand also had hydrocephalus, or "water on the brain," that caused his cranium to swell. This affliction prompted daily seizures, slow movement, and a loss of balance that required assistance when walking. He also suffered from confusion that often precluded him from understanding important state documents or participating fully in political debate. But instead of abandoning her new responsibilities that required her to act as a nursemaid to her new husband, Maria Anna wholeheartedly put her imperial duties above her personal needs.

When Ferdinand's father, Emperor Francis II, was questioned whether his eldest son would make the best successor, Francis would not even consider deviating from the time-honored Habsburg law of primogeniture. Francis believed that whatever his first-born son's ailments, he had been chosen by God to succeed as Emperor of Austria, and God would see to it that Ferdinand had the strength to uphold his duties. When Francis II died from a sudden fever on March 2, 1835, Ferdinand took his rightful place as emperor with Maria Anna at his side. The couple would never have heirs of their own, however, as Ferdinand was probably unable to ever consummate his marriage. Ferdinand's brother, Archduke Franz Karl was next in line but was expected to renounce his claim in favor of his son, Franz Joseph.

Franz Joseph's time came in 1848, when an array of revolutionary factions threatened to tear apart the empire. Everyone at court, including Maria Anna, realized that Ferdinand may be an adequate peacetime emperor but that a younger, stronger ruler was needed to quell the uprisings and restore order. With urging from his wife, brothers, Archduchess Sophie and his faithful general Prince Winischgrätz, Ferdinand agreed to abdicate but had no precedence for his actions; no Habsburg ruler had ever willfully given up the throne, let alone outright skipped the next rightful successor for a second choice. But the small group of advisers had come to the conclusion that extraordinary measures were needed to keep the empire from crumbling altogether.

At 8 a.m. on December 2, a small group of imperial family members and government ministers had dressed in formal attire and gathered in the grand salon of the Vienna Bishop's Palace. Franz Joseph was the only one of his brothers present who understood the immensity of what was about to take place. Once everyone was assembled, Emperor Ferdinand read aloud the Abdication Act. He stumbled over the words as he read:

"Important reasons have lead Us to the irrevocable decision to lay down Our Crown in favor of Our beloved nephew, Archduke Francis Joseph..."

Following Ferdinand's brief statement, his brother Archduke Franz Karl's renunciation was read aloud by Austrian Prime Minister Schwarzenberg, who had been on the job for less than a month. Despite Archduchess Sophie's contention that her husband wanted nothing to do with the throne, Franz Karl actually felt some misgivings in the days leading up to the abdication. It was only after several anxiety-filled nights when he dreamed of his father giving his blessing that Franz Karl finally agreed to step aside.

Once the formalities were over, eighteen-year-old Franz Joseph knelt before Ferdinand to receive his uncle's blessing.

"God bless you, Franzi. Be good. God will protect you. I'm happy about it all," Ferdinand said.[2]

Following the private ceremony, a blare of trumpets on the steps of St. Stephan's Cathedral announced the transfer of power to astonished citizens. As news of Franz Joseph's accession spread throughout the empire, Ferdinand and his wife retired to Prague's Hradschin Castle to lead a quiet life where Maria Anna continued to devotedly care for her husband until his death in 1875.

Empress Maria Anna's life in the Austrian Empire was a prime example of *noblesse oblige*, the idea that royal privilege required responsibility and leadership. This was a concept by which Sisi did not abide. Although she occasionally visited hospitals and advocated for the poor during her reign, Sisi was much more concerned with protecting her privacy and living life on her terms. She created her own isolated world that focused on the things that were most important to her: equestrianship, language and literature, and cultivating her own beauty.

Sisi became known far and wide for her physical allure and for being a trendsetter rather than a follower. "The Empress of Austria, indeed, is not an advocate of French fashions—she mostly invents her own fashions," proclaimed one British publication.[3] These styles always emphasized her impossibly slender waist and were topped off with original hairstyles created from her extraordinary long, thick hair.

Sisi freely admitted that her hair dominated her life. One of the best sources of information on this mania came from the diary of Konstantine Christomanos, an unlikely fellow who taught the empress the Greek language each day as her hair was being washed and braided. Christomanos caused a scandal in 1899, one year after Sisi's death, when

III. *"I didn't know anything about Sisi."*

excerpts from his diary were published in *The San Francisco Call* newspaper.

Christomanos had spent three years tutoring Sisi before being dismissed, possibly once his sycophantic behavior became too much for even the empress to bear. He was then appointed reader in Greek at the University of Vienna and subsequently published the memoirs he kept while in the empress's employ in the city, onboard the imperial yacht, and on the Greek Island of Corfu. As San Francisco's leading morning newspaper, *The Call* was widely popular with the working class in the nineteenth century. The paper bragged of its journalistic coup since "never before has any royal lady so sincerely and fully expressed her thoughts." It cleverly warned its readers that Christomanos used little discretion in publishing Sisi's intimate reflections and speculated that "the Empress's sayings were certainly not intended for the world."[4]

Christomanos met the empress when she was fifty-four years old and had long since refused to sit for portraits or photographs that might reveal any hints of old age. He was a Greek national thirty years her junior, and suffered from a hunched back due to a childhood injury. As a result of his physical limitations, Christomanos made up his mind to become a cultivated scholar in the vein of his father, a professor at the University of Athens. He studied hard and became a poet and writer chiefly for the Greek theater. One of Sisi's biographers, Count Egon Corti, suggested that an affinity developed between teacher and pupil because they were both struggling with their shortcomings: Sisi's fading health and beauty, and Christomanos's deformity.

Christomanos had been living in Vienna for three years when he was asked to teach the empress Greek during her tedious hairdressing sessions each day. He recalled her explanation:

> To dress my hair ... takes two hours every day, and while my hair is busy my brain is idle, and I fear it passes out through the ends of my hair into the fingers of my hairdresser. That is why my head aches often. We will translate Shakespeare into Greek, while my hair is being dressed. I shall then have to hold my brain together.[5]

In addition to blaming her headaches on an "idle brain," Sisi also attributed her pain to the sheer weight of her hair. When a headache was unbearable, Sisi shuttered herself in her apartments for hours with her long curtain of hair strung up on a cord. The empress believed that this method allowed air to circulate around her scalp and significantly reduce her headaches.

It was just such an excruciating headache in 1875 that nearly cost Sisi her crowning glory altogether. After falling from her horse and knocking herself unconscious, Sisi's doctor suspected a slight concussion and remarked that if her head was not better within a day he would have to cut off her heavy hair to alleviate the pressure. In the nineteenth century, cutting a woman's long hair in times of serious illness was a common method used by doctors to aid recovery. Fortunately, Sisi's attendants Marie Festetics and Ida Ferenczy intervened, telling the doctor that, "no measure would be more calculated to retard" Sisi's recovery.[6]

—⟋ω⟍—

The first time Christomanos met the empress in her apartments, she was sitting at a table in the center of the room. The table was covered with a white cloth, and Sisi wore a white laced dress with her hair enveloping her slender frame all the way to the floor. One need only look at the Franz Winterhalter portrait, *Sisi in Morning Light*, to experience a younger version of the woman Christomanos saw that day.

As Christomanos began the Greek lesson, Sisi's hairdresser appeared wearing all black with a long veil and white apron. The Greek tutor then floridly described the "sacred act" of dressing Sisi's hair that followed:

> With her white hands she burrowed in the waves of hair, raised them and ran her fingertips over them as she might over velvet and silk, twisted them around her arms like rivers she wanted to capture because they did not want to run but to fly.[7]

Indeed, Sisi treated her hair as a sacred object that she worshipped daily. When an admirer—an Englishman named John Collett—once asked Sisi "for a lock of the hair she regarded as sacrosanct," a common practice of the day among intimates, she would not humor him and instead replied "that she had made a vow never to give any of it away."[8]

III. "I didn't know anything about Sisi."

In middle age, Sisi had begun wearing short bangs, or fringe, perhaps for fashion, perhaps to hide forehead lines that had stealthily crept onto her brow. According to a popular etiquette manual at the time, light fringe was very much a trend in the 1890s: "Very deep thick fringes coming down low on the forehead give an animal look to the face; but a few small light little curls on the top of the forehead are very becoming."[9] Christomanos described the hairdresser as using silver scissors to trim what he called "erring strings of hair" from the fringe to perfect the empress's style.

In his diary, Christomanos recalled a conversation he had with the empress about her hair:

> "I am aware of my hair," she told him. It is like a foreign body on my head." Christomanos replied, "Your Majesty wears her hair like a crown instead of the crown." Sisi answered, "Except that any other crown is more easily laid aside."[10]

Dressing Sisi's hair was one thing, but washing it was an entirely different matter. Once every two to three weeks, Sisi budgeted an entire day to cleansing. Her valet-de-chambre recalled, "washing the hair was an affair of state."[11]

In the 1800's commercial shampoos were not yet available and wouldn't become so until the dawn of the twentieth century, so Sisi experimented with different essences and concoctions. At the time, most women on a budget took soap shavings made from animal fats and potash lye, boiled them in water, and added various herbs for a more pleasing scent. In *Decorum: Treatise on Etiquette and Dress* published in 1877, proper Victorian women were advised to follow the soap wash with dilutions of vinegar or ammonia to remove any leftover residue.

For the empress to whom cost was no object, a more upscale Victorian remedy was in order: a concoction of protein-rich egg yolks beaten in warm water that was believed to cleanse and promote hair growth. Her valet-de-chambre reported that the empress used some forty eggs to wash her ankle-length hair, followed by a rinse consisting of twenty bottles of the best French brandy. Through the years, Sisi would add pressed onions and Peruvian balsam to the cognac, presumably to stimulate hair growth so she could maintain her lush curls as she aged. On wash day, these ingredients would have been delivered directly to her apartments, where a lady-in-waiting would have prepared them under the watchful eye of the hairdresser.

Hygiene was so important to Sisi that she became the first member of the imperial family to have a modern bathroom installed off her dressing room in the Hofburg. It included a tub of galvanized sheet copper, a porcelain toilet shaped like a dolphin, a small washbasin, and a ceramic stove heated with hot air pumped through adjoining pipes to warm the room. To prevent water damage to the expensive parquet flooring, linoleum was placed over top. But Sisi wasn't the first to have a toilet installed in her apartments; Archduchess Sophie had an "odourless convenience on the English model" installed in the Hofburg as early as 1835.[12]

Each day, Sisi rose between five and six a.m., and her personal bath maid helped with her toilette. First Sisi donned a bathing gown, possibly a lace-trimmed white linen chemise, then took a cold bath followed by a massage. After retiring from dinner in the evenings, Sisi took a special olive or almond oil bath to smooth her skin. On hair wash day, Sisi's hairdresser first detangled the empress's curls, then may have performed the washing in the bathtub or while the empress sat in a chair, draped in towels, with her neck bent backward as her hair was washed in a large bowl.

Following the cleansing, Sisi's ankle-length hair was wrapped in towels and gently patted to remove excess water. The hairdresser then began the immense task of carefully detangling the thick, curly mane with a carved horn or tortoise shell comb and possibly a touch of sweet almond oil to ease its passage. Once detangled, Sisi's hair was allowed to air dry, likely before an open window on a pleasant day. Finally, after hours and hours of drying time, Sisi's hair was brushed and sprinkled lightly with perfume essences, as heavy fragrances were something she never liked on men or women. The empress then chose which braided hairstyle she would like for the day, and the actual hairdressing would begin.

Over the years as her hair began to gray, Sisi tinted the color, possibly with mixtures of indigo and walnut shell extract. She also required her hairdresser to tweeze away extra gray hairs, but gave that up after the death of Crown Prince Rudolf in 1889. After that point, Sisi's hair was described as still thick, though streaked through with silver threads.

For her face, Sisi employed ancient Indian recipes, including treatments of crushed strawberries, the juice of twenty slightly moldy lemons, and even raw veal. She held these treatments in place with a leather face mask that she wore overnight. Sisi slept on a simple iron bed without a pillow, which she believed would ruin her posture. Instead, she wrapped cloths soaked in ionized water around her neck. Sisi's beauty treatments were created in batches for her in the court pharmacy or by a lady-in-waiting in her apartments. They included a simple cream called Crème Celeste that consisted of white wax, ambergris, sweet almond oil and rose water. Archived beauty recipes also show that Sisi repeatedly ordered a cold cream made from sweet almond oil, cocoa butter, beeswax and rosewater. This cream was popular with all of the court ladies because it luxuriously cooled the skin on contact. Sisi also used facial waters of rose, chamomile, lavender, and violet to remove impurities.

The one aspect of her appearance that caused Sisi embarrassment and that she tried to hide from public view were her teeth. Before Sisi's wedding to Franz Joseph, Archduchess Sophie mentioned that the young bride's teeth appeared yellowed, and she strongly suggested that Sisi pay them greater attention. Documents show that from that point on Sisi had regular visits from her dentist. But she may not have felt fully confident in the dental care and was never painted or photographed with anything other than a tight-lipped smile. Sisi also barely opened her mouth when she spoke, which made her difficult to understand, especially in a crowded ballroom. Rumors circulated that Sisi lost her teeth in later life and was forced to wear dentures, but doctors performing her postmortem examination recorded that her teeth were intact and in good shape.

In her youth, Sisi's beauty obsession worried both her mother and mother-in-law. However, there was a time when Archduchess Sophie actually encouraged Sisi to gaze at her own reflection. When Sisi was pregnant with her first child, the archduchess feared—in all seriousness—that the baby would be born resembling one of Sisi's beloved pets because the young empress stared at them too often. Sophie's fear stemmed from the story of her husband's youngest sister, Archduchess

Marianna, whose face was terribly disfigured at birth and who displayed signs of mental retardation. At the time, everyone believed Marianna's congenital defects were caused when her pregnant mother was startled by an orangutan who escaped from Schönbrunn's zoo. Wishing to prevent any future catastrophes, Sophie expressed her concerns to Franz Joseph in June 1854:

> I believe that Sisi ought not to concern herself so much with her parrots. If a woman is always looking at animals, particularly in the first months (of pregnancy), the children are apt to resemble them. It would be better if she looked at herself in the mirror, or at you. That kind of looking would please me.[13]

Later, however, the archduchess abandoned this suggestion. She felt that the time and energy Sisi spent gazing into mirrors and chasing beauty remedies could be better spent in service to the empire visiting hospitals and schools, and receiving the wives of high dignitaries. But Sisi was not about to lessen her grooming time, especially not the effort spent on her hair. She considered it a kind of magical protective cloak that shielded her from the coarse, intrusive world, and told Christomanos, "If I were to have my hair cut short to get rid of any unnecessary weight, the people would fall on me like wolves."[14]

The world might not have paid much attention to the eccentric empress's hair obsession had it not been for the Köchert stars immortalized on canvas in 1865. Souvenir copies of Winterhalter's painting circulated around the world, and people far and wide agreed that Sisi must certainly be the most beautiful royal they had ever seen. The empress became so enamored of the glittering effect the all-diamond Köchert stars created in her coiffure that she commissioned an additional twenty-seven with giant center pearls. The last remaining star of this set would come to be forever known as the Köchert Diamond Pearl.

Not to be outdone, court jewelers Rozet & Fischmeister created their own version of hair stars for the empress. Sisi now had two of the most talented and experienced goldsmiths in Vienna vying to decorate her hair, but the ones that would forever be linked to Sisi's romantic image were those that were first designed by Köchert.

IV

"I am a slave to my hair."

—Empress Elisabeth of Austria

As he stood before the Sisi Star display, Gerald Blanchard's mind began racing. He knew that if he successfully lifted the jewel it would be too hot to sell. Once authorities realized it was gone, they would immediately file a report with INTERPOL (the International Criminal Police Organization) and perhaps the Lost Art Register, the world's largest database of missing treasures. No buyer would want to touch it after that. But the challenge of taking the star was far too tempting, especially since he had cataloged the palace security flaws in his head and knew how possible this theft was. Perhaps he could use the star for some purpose in the future. But for now, Blanchard just knew he had to have it.

Just to be certain he would remember the setup correctly, Blanchard employed his video camera to tape every last security detail of the display: the glass case, the pedestal, and the motion sensors in the ceiling. All this despite a "No Cameras" sign posted near the jewel case. But he was a VIP on a private tour after all, and the guide didn't seem to notice or care.

Then Blanchard got to work. When his family accompanied the tour guide to the next room, Blanchard made some excuse to stay behind. He carefully removed his keys from his pocket, turned his back to the security cameras, and quickly loosened the screws that held the glass casing in place over the Sisi Star. He was committed now. On his way out of the room, Blanchard managed to unlock several of the huge palace windows that had been installed centuries ago to let in maximum natural light.[1]

Blanchard nonchalantly rejoined his private tour, then completed his prep work by purchasing a replica of the famous star in the palace gift shop under the guise of wanting a souvenir for someone back home. He turned the fake star over in his hand, wondering about its mass— would it be enough to fool the weight-sensitive alarm on which the real star rested? Would he need to alter it somehow? As these heady thoughts swirled in his mind, Blanchard's group said *danke* to their tour guide, then headed past the armed guards and out the palace doors.

After their Schönbrunn excursion, Blanchard, his wife, and her father posed for a photo on one of Vienna's 1,700 bridges overlooking the spectacular city. The newlyweds could have passed for brother and sister; both wore cerulean denim jeans, eyeglasses, and light weight jackets over T-shirts, while Blanchard's father-in-law sported a grey double-breasted suit and tie. Nothing appeared out of the ordinary in the photo—just a nice family on vacation. It was the same way they would appear on palace surveillance video as desperate officials scanned the tapes recorded between June 5 and June 26, 1998, trying to find a clue as to who could have stolen the priceless Sisi Star.

The imperial hairdresser's nimble fingers first expertly attached the Köchert Stars to Sisi's intricate braids in 1864. Sisi handpicked this hair artist, Franziska ("Fanny") Angerer, after seeing her work on Helene Gabillon, the lead actress of a comedy playing at Vienna's Hofburgtheater. The old theater was a convenient source of entertainment for Sisi and Franz Joseph since it was connected to the Hofburg Palace and was subsidized by imperial funds. To Sisi, this choice of an official attendant to dress her hair each day was of the highest importance, for if the empress didn't like the hairstyle created for her, she would go so far as to feign illness to get out of attending public events.

All of Vienna, it seemed, was interested in whom would be chosen to tend to the empress's ankle-length tresses. In April 1863, Berlin's *Morgenpost* answered that question in its "News of the Day" column:

> The question, pending for a long time, whether a man or a woman hairdresser would assume service with Her Majesty the Empress has finally been settled. Fräulein Angerer relinquishes the Order of Coiffeurs to Court

IV. *"I am a slave to my hair."*

Actresses and the honorarium assigned to it and receives instead a compensation of 2,000 (florins) a year to devote herself to the most exalted service as imperial hairdresser.[2]

Fanny was not high born like the rest of Sisi's ladies-in-waiting. Her mother had been a midwife, and her father's background is unknown. But it was her extraordinary hairdressing skills that allowed her to make her mark on the theater world and catch the eye of the empress. Fanny was said to begrudge Sisi's other ladies for their superior ranks and entertained a jealous streak when it came to Sisi's attentions. But this jealously may have been encouraged by the empress herself. One of Sisi's many Greek tutors, Frederick Barker, took note of Sisi's manipulative streak and habit of asking her closest attendants, "Who do you love most of all?"[3]

At 2,000 florins a year ($22,939), Fanny was soon making roughly the same amount as a university professor to wash and dress the empress's hair. One might argue that Fanny earned every penny, however, since serving as the imperial hairdresser was not a nine-to-five job. Fanny had to be on call twenty-four hours a day, seven days a week. She had to travel with the Empress even if that meant being overseas for months. And the new job nearly cost her the love of her life.

Shortly after attaining her exalted new position, Fanny fell in love with a bourgeois bank official. According to court rules, Fanny could not marry and still maintain her job at court, and Sisi wasn't about to let her leave—not after searching high and low and finally finding the perfect talent. So, Sisi intervened with the emperor, who granted an exception to the rule: Fanny was allowed to marry her love and keep her job, while her new husband was also hired into the imperial household.

Hugo Feifalik made the most of his court appointment by advancing to become the empress's private secretary and travel supervisor. Eventually, he became treasurer of the Order of the Starry Cross, a papal-sanctioned order for high-born ladies who agreed to lead a virtuous life and do good works of charity. Proving himself a faithful and capable employee, Feifalik became a trusted court councilor and ultimately received a knighthood for his service to the crown.

In 1863, Fanny developed a style of weaving the empress's hair into a crown on top of her head that made Sisi feel her most regal. The empress described it as her "characteristic hairstyle," or her trademark,[4] and it was this crest of braids that would become immortalized in sculpture after Sisi's death.

As a hairdresser, Fanny became indispensable to the empress, and as a confidante, she was an important part of Sisi's most trusted inner circle. Fanny held a kind of power over the empress and used her hairdressing skills to manipulate the trifling machinations of court politics. If she felt offended by any of the other court ladies, Fanny was known to "call in sick." She would send replacement hairdressers, even chambermaids, to tend to the royal coif, prompting Sisi to tell one of her confidantes, "After several such days of hairdressing, I am quite worn down. She knows that and waits for a capitulation. I am a slave to my hair."[5]

One of Sisi's ladies-in-waiting, Countess Marie Festetics, found Fanny to be insufferably self-important thanks to her natural talent and closeness with the empress. But Fanny's influence was undeniable; the styles she created for Sisi were being copied by fashionable ladies everywhere who attempted to wear their hair à l'imperatrice, or "in the style of the empress." That meant long, intricate braids held up with a profusion of hair pins. In 1881, Sisi was said to have set a new style that newspapers predicted "is likely to create a considerable sensation."

> She wears her hair falling in wavy folds upon her shoulders, fastened to the head by an agrafe of diamonds à la grecque. The Viennese ladies are all allowing their hair to fall down up on their shoulders and backs (the ends being cut even) in imitation of their imperial sovereign.[6]

Since most women didn't have hair nearly as long and lush as the empress, nor such a skilled hairdresser, they often used extra padding, called a cadogan, plus hair pieces to achieve the desired look. These additions required their own brand of upkeep and had to be consistently dyed the color of the owner's own hair as they faded over time.

Sisi made fun of women who turned to hair pieces to embellish their style. In an 1887 poem, *Family Dinner,* she wrote:

IV. "I am a slave to my hair."

The other one there in gaudy peacock splendour
and false hair,
Oh, how she laughs sarcastically,
with her leaning head!⁷

The empress's one-time favorite niece, Countess Marie Larisch, recounted her own introduction to the imperial style.

The first time I remember riding horseback in company with the Empress was as a little girl. My blonde hair flew wildly as I cantered with my adored aunt through the Prater, Vienna's Central Park. People stopped, lifted their hats or bowed deeply. Their eyes followed me and my fluttering mane. When we returned to the Hofburg—the Imperial palace—that day, Aunt Sissy [sic] issued the order that I was to wear my hair l'imperatrice in future. I have never changed my style of hairdress to this very day.⁸

The dressing of Sisi's hair took approximately two to three hours every day. Fanny was prohibited from wearing rings, even her wedding ring, lest they should catch on the empress's tresses. Fanny was also required to wear white gloves and to collect each hair that fell from Sisi's head in a silver bowl. At the end of the styling session, Fanny would present the combed-out hair to the empress for inspection. Sisi often became disconcerted at the sight of more shed hairs than she felt was necessary. Since little was understood about hair science in the 1800's, Sisi didn't realize that it was perfectly normal to lose around one hundred hairs each day as each follicle reached the end of its growth cycle and was replaced by a new hair. Instead, she saw it as a sign of careless combing, brushing, braiding, and pinning that must be reprimanded. In order to placate the nervous empress, Fanny turned to subterfuge; she hid a piece of adhesive tape under her apron and attached excessive loose hairs to it so she could avoid having to present them to the empress.

Most nineteenth-century women wore their long locks parted in the middle and twisted into a bun secured by pins during the day. At night, they would thoroughly comb or brush through their hair to stimulate the scalp and promote growth. Women collected the shed strands in a glass jar called a hair receiver and placed some of the saved bits in memento lockets or had it woven into "hair jewelry" like

Sculptor Hermann Klotz created this statue of Empress Elisabeth out of hard paste biscuit in 1906, eight years after her death. It depicts Sisi's famous crown of braids created by her much vaunted hairstylist, Fanny Feifalik, and is often referred to as the "Klotz hairstyle." Franz Joseph was so fond of the likeness that he gifted miniatures to family and friends (© The Metropolitan Museum of Art. Gift of Mrs. Stella Eisner, in memory of John Fitzgerald Kennedy, 1967. Art Resource, New York).

IV. "I am a slave to my hair."

bracelets or watch chains to gift to loved ones. Sisi obviously loathed the sight of her loose strands, preferring to keep them on her head. It's fairly safe to say that she never had any hair jewelry made from her fallen tresses.

Combing, braiding, and pinning Sisi's hair was such an arduous process that the empress once fainted while it was being dressed. Lady-in-waiting Countess Marie Festetics believed the fainting spell was due to the empress's poor diet and excessive exercise that was further exacerbated by the marathon hairdressing session. Marie sternly advised Sisi to stop starving herself before she had a stroke.

Fanny was expected to travel with the empress wherever her whims took her. Sisi's favorite mode of transportation was by steamer ship, but life at sea was no excuse for unkempt hair. As Christomanos observed, "Onboard ship the hairdressing took just as long and in stormy weather the empress allowed herself to be tied to a chair," ostensibly so she wouldn't slide away from her hairdresser while in rough waters.[9]

On one such overseas trip in 1885, Fanny's duties went far beyond hairdressing when she acted—on the empress's orders—as Sisi's own body double. While on a tour of Smyrna on the Aegean coast, Fanny took the empress's place in the boat of honor that sailed up and down the harbor, waving to the jubilant crowd. Since the people of Smyrna didn't seem to know the difference, Sisi heartily allowed Fanny to "act the empress" while the real empress went ashore to sight-see.

Another deception, this time at the Marseilles railroad station, was recorded in 1894 by Sisi's lady-in-waiting, Countess Irma Sztáray:

Under normal circumstances, Her Majesty felt extremely ill at ease, but this time she was entirely delighted, because the people's curiosity was fully satisfied—before she ever appeared ... Frau F., the Empress's hairdresser walked up and down the platform with a most stately bearing, thus playing the Empress to the best of her ability.... Her Majesty found this interlude very amusing. "Let's not interrupt my good F.," she said, and quickly and unnoticed, boarded the train.[10]

Christomanos understood why people could mistake the hairdresser for the Empress. He wrote in his typically flamboyant style that Fanny had "a very impressive appearance, traces of faded beauty on the

57

face and eyes full of somber features—reminding of a famous driven-away queen of secondary majesty in the European East."[11]

To show just how talented Fanny was and how intricate her hairstyles for Sisi really were, The Hofburg's Sisi Museum commissioned theatrical hairstylist Hannelore Uhrmacher in 2011 to recreate three of Sisi's looks. After researching Sisi's portraits and paintings, Uhrmacher used genuine human-hair wigs to bring Sisi's styles off the canvas and back to life in three-dimension.

The three styles were chosen to represent three different periods in Sisi's life. They included the Empress's famous crown of braids she wore in middle-age and beyond, now referred to as the "Klotz Hairstyle" after the famous life-size sculpture by Hermann Klotz in 1906, on display at New York's Metropolitan Museum of Art. Emperor Franz Joseph admired the artwork so much that he gave away miniature versions of the statue in biscuit porcelain to family and friends.

The second hairstyle was favored by Sisi in her thirties and forties: a half-up style that displayed some of her hair's extraordinary length. Fanny employed curling tongs that were heated on a fire to tame Sisi's waves and give a finished look to the hair that hung down her back. An example of this style can be seen in a portrait of Sisi in ruby jewelry by artist George Raab to commemorate the imperial couple's silver wedding anniversary.

The third hairstyle was taken from Sisi's youth. As a young bride, she wore her hair based on the fashion of the day but with an individual twist that utilized her uncommonly long, thick hair. According to the Sisi Museum, "although Sisi wore her hair parted in the middle and brushed backwards in a bow," like many young women of the day, Sisi's style "ended not in a knot at the nape of the neck but rather in plaits woven into a garland."[12] Each of the hairstyles on display took some two-and-a-half hours to recreate, lending credence to Sisi's claim that her hairdressing sessions lasted up to three hours each day.

The museum purposely chose not to recreate the Winterhalter portrait hairstyle with Köchert Stars precisely because it is so famous. To see a three-dimensional version of the coif that featured the brilliant Sisi Stars, one must visit Vienna's Madame Tussauds Wax Museum. The life-size figure of Sisi created in 2010 portrays her looking over her left shoulder with her coiled, star-studded braids reaching to the middle of her back, just as Winterhalter recorded on canvas in 1865. Observing this wax sculpture, one can imagine Fanny carefully pinning the Sisi Stars several inches apart around the circumference of the looped and pinned braids, giving the impression of a glittering halo in the candlelight.

V

"No one else
had one but me."

—Gerald Blanchard, January 2014

During his VIP tour, Blanchard had noticed that while the Schön-brunn Palace doors and hallways were heavily guarded, the palace roof remained alluringly vulnerable. Fortunately, one of the many useful skills he had picked up in his youth was skydiving, and he knew this aptitude would allow him to enter the palace grounds unnoticed.

Back in his hotel room after he had surveilled the Sisi Star and clan-destinely unscrewed the glass case protecting the jewel, Blanchard spent time thoroughly studying his videotape and committing the palace lay-out to heart. Now came a challenge; he would need to procure a plane and some equipment to finally set his plan in motion. He contacted a German pilot he had recently befriended, who agreed to find him a para-chute, and the conspirators plotted a course for Schönbrunn.

Since this was a night jump, Blanchard was careful not to turn on any white lights inside the plane in order to preserve his night vision. He and the pilot would have to examine their flight plan by red light only. When they had reached about 12,500 feet above the city, standard skydiving altitude, Blanchard cautiously leaned out the plane's open hatch and scanned the dotted lights of Vienna below. Recognizing the layout of Schönbrunn Palace, Blanchard signaled the pilot that this was the spot. The plane circled above the palace to establish wind speed and direction while Blanchard reviewed the landing pattern in his mind. Then he gave the thumbs up and took his leap. Blanchard free-fell at about 115 miles per hour for a minute before attaining "pull altitude."

Next, he reached around his lower back to release the pilot chute and a pin that would unfurl the main square chute behind him.

Once the rushing air snapped the parachute into a canopy above his head, Blanchard began gliding forward, steering toward the reddish-brown tiled roof just above the room containing the Sisi Star. He next determined his wind line, an imaginary demarcation running through his landing target so he could figure the current's direction. At 300 feet, Blanchard began his final approach. Now he would have to be wary of the "shadow effect" that has led to the demise of many an experienced jumper; the moon at a skydiver's back can cause a huge black shadow to loom on the ground, appearing as an obstacle. Panicking to avoid the mirage could prove fatal.

Blanchard homed in on the roof coming up fast beneath him. He pressed his feet and bent knees together, then pulled both toggles to lower his descent rate and forward speed. But he must have mistimed the chute flare that was meant to induce a precision landing; instead of coming to rest softly on the tiles, he began skidding uncontrollably toward the roof's edge.

He grasped for anything solid that would hold his weight. At the last second, he connected with a railing just inches from the precipice, narrowly avoiding a fall of some fifty feet to the ground below. His heart beating wildly, Blanchard lay silently for a moment, contemplating his nearly disastrous landing and making sure he hadn't been detected. Once he composed himself and believed he was clear, he unhooked his chute, rolled it into his body pack, and produced a rope to lower himself down to one of the towering windows he had unlocked the day before.

Blanchard carefully cracked the pane, just enough for his body to slip inside. He lowered himself down behind an enormous curtain that would act as a shield in case a guard was waiting on the other side. But the room was clear, and Blanchard made his way on tiptoe, painfully slowly toward the Sisi Star, careful not to set off the motion sensors that stared down menacingly from the palace ceilings above.

The imperial apartment was dark except for several track lights to help the guards see at night and the moonlight that shone through the soaring palace windows. Fortunately, Blanchard's impeccable memory of the setup allowed him to work as expertly in the dark as he did in the light. Reaching the display, he removed the pressure-sensitive screws he had loosened the day before and saw just what he expected: two long, thin rods that would set off the alarm if they were disturbed. He held them steady until he was able to slip a butter knife from his pocket and used it to hold the rods in place.[1] Now came the most crucial part of all, making sure the pedestal on which the Sisi Star rested wouldn't detect any change in weight. Like Indiana Jones replacing the Peruvian golden idol with a bag of sand in *Raiders of the Lost Ark*, Blanchard set to work swapping the real Sisi Star with the gift shop fake. Gingerly, he made the switch and waited. No alarm; Blanchard had judged the star's weight just right. Relief mingled with the cold sweat beading on his brow. Now, with the real star tucked safely inside his pocket, he left the same way he had come in.

Successfully reaching the outside wall and leaping to the ground, Blanchard took a deep breath of the cool Viennese air, then removed his used parachute from his pack and stuffed it in a palace trash bin before disappearing. He could easily haven taken the parachute with him, but perhaps leaving it behind was his small way of taunting the authorities. Schönbrunn guards would find the crumpled parachute in the dumpster within hours of the crime, but they didn't immediately catch its meaning. As INTERPOL explained to Blanchard later, "security didn't think anything of it. Other than someone threw away a parachute. But they didn't put two and two together."[2]

Once he was in a safe place, Blanchard was finally able to enjoy the fruits of his illicit labor. He held the jewel up to the light to see the twinkle of the thirty diamonds and the luster of the one extravagant pearl. He ran his fingers over the gems, felt its weight, and inspected the jeweled clip that had long ago attached the star to an empress's tresses. Asked what the experience was like, Blanchard said simply, "It was great. No one else had one but me."[3]

Some two weeks later, Schönbrunn Palace officials did something they rarely do: they agreed to open the glass case containing the Köchert

V. "No one else had one but me."

Diamond Pearl for a jewelry expert who asked to examine the piece and take a few photographs. Palace Director Wolfgang Kippes gave his personal consent as the guards shut down the security system and turned off the alarms. They carefully unlocked the showcase and stepped aside as the expert leaned in to get his view. On the surface, it certainly looked like the priceless jewel. But the expert knew upon closer inspection that you can't fake the craftsmanship of a master goldsmith like Köchert or the fire and luster of perfect stones cut specifically for an empress. To his trained eye, the jewel on the red velvet pad before him was quite obviously a fake. He also knew that as soon as he revealed the truth, palace officials would face a monumental public relations nightmare.

VI

"She worshipped her beauty like a heathen his idols."

—Countess Marie Larisch

Jakob Heinrich Köchert established his jewelry business in 1814 in one of the oldest buildings on Vienna's Neuer Markt. Eleven years later, Köchert would receive his first imperial order, a gold box for the Turkish ambassador. He would continue to design stunningly intricate pieces throughout the years for some of Vienna's wealthiest and most discerning clients. Then, some fifty years after the company's founding, the firm scored a major coup: Köchert was appointed personal jeweler to Austrian Emperor Franz Joseph and was permitted to display the "K.u.K" inscription on its storefront—for *Kaiserlich und Königlich* ("Imperial and Royal"). The distinction of purveyor to the court by royal and imperial appointment was highly coveted and seldom granted. Court officials monitored esteemed businesses like Köchert's to ensure imperial standards and quality were always maintained. A single customer complaint could cause the crown to withdraw the prestigious title.

But quite the opposite happened in the case of Köchert; The Emperor was so pleased with the goldsmith's work that he entrusted Köchert with the care of the entire imperial treasury and commissioned the firm to restore the Austrian Imperial Crown originally created for Habsburg ruler Rudolf II by Flemish goldsmith Jan Vermeyen in 1602. When Köchert was finished, the gold crown's circlet, high arch, and mitre boasted diamonds, pearls, spinels, zircons, and one spectacular blue-green emerald that shone with their original imperial splendor.

Alexander Emmanuel Köchert took over the business from his

64

VI. *"She worshipped her beauty like a heathen his idols."*

father the same year Franz Joseph married Sisi in 1854, and it was the Köchert son who oversaw the design and creation of the twenty-seven diamond Sisi Stars and the additional set featuring a lustrous center pearl.

The first occasion on record that Sisi wore the Köchert Stars was for the 1864 wedding of her brother, Karl Theodor, in Dresden, Germany. She appeared at the court ball in a white gown embroidered with matching gold stars designed by the "Father of Haute Couture," Charles Frederick Worth. She also wore a corsage of ivory camellias attached to the gown's bodice. According to Emperor Franz Joseph's brother, Archduke Ludwig Viktor, Sisi outshone the bride and caused a sensation. She was "stunningly beautiful," he wrote, and "the people here acted insane. I have never seen anyone having such an effect before."[1]

Sisi must have fathomed the impression she made that evening because she chose to wear the same white silk tulle dress with the diamond Köchert Stars instead of an old-fashioned tiara to pose for portrait artist Franz Xaver Winterhalter several months later. Winterhalter was famous for painting the crowned heads of Europe, including French Empress Eugénie, English Queen Victoria, and Queen Isabella II of Spain. To faithfully depict Sisi, the fifty-nine-year-old artist took up residence at Schönbrunn Palace for several months in the autumn of 1864 and became one of the only painters for whom the empress ever posed live since she found the process so tedious. Winterhalter's latest commission made news across Europe with one paper proclaiming, "The court portrait painter of the world par excellence, Winterhalter, has gone to Vienna, to paint a portrait of the Empress of Austria and has been received with all honours at the palace."[2] Franz Joseph had his portrait painted also, sporting his red, white and gold dress military uniform and his ever-constant Dundreary side whiskers, but his sitting didn't receive quite the same amount of attention as his captivating wife's.

By the time he met Sisi in 1864, Winterhalter was a favorite of both the British and French royal families. Queen Victoria, in particular, held Winterhalter in such high regard that she was reluctant to share his talents with any other court and had all but given up sitting for other portraitists.

"All these great artists ... cannot throw life and lightness and animation into a portrait that dear old Winterhalter could," she said.[3]

The queen was so devoted to his work that she once had to choose between several portrait sizes and subjects ("three half-lengths of Bertie, Alix and the baby or two full-lengths of Bertie and Alix"[4]) because the frugal monarch couldn't afford to have him paint everything she wanted at the time.

Franz Xaver Winterhalter was born in 1805, the son of a farmer from Menzenschwand, a small village in southwestern Germany's Black Forest. Early on, the village priest recognized Winterhalter's natural talent for drawing as did a local textile magnate who helped the fifteen-year-old obtain an apprenticeship with artist Karl Ludwig Schuler in the city of Freiburg im Breisgau. Schuler quickly realized that the boy needed proper art instruction and advised him to study at the venerated Royal Academy of Fine Arts in Munich.

During the early years, Winterhalter supported himself as a lithographer, spending long hours producing printed pages of text and artwork. His big break came at age twenty-three, when the young artist received the backing of Sisi's uncle, Bavarian King Ludwig I. With the king's money in his pocket, Winterhalter went on to study with self-taught portraitist Joseph Stieler, who had created a flattering portrait of Ludwig in his coronation robes in 1826. Winterhalter received his first royal portrait commission in 1833 when he painted British heiress presumptive Princess Victoria, who would become queen in 1837. It was the first of more than one hundred commissions with Victoria's royal family that would grow to include Prince Albert and their multitude of children.

Shortly thereafter, Winterhalter was appointed court painter at Karlsruhe Palace in Baden by Grand Duke Leopold and his wife, Princess Sophie of Sweden. Winterhalter found that he enjoyed being surrounded by the splendors of royalty and, while retaining his court appointment at Baden, took an apartment in Paris, hoping to attract the attention of the French king. Winterhalter's reputation for portraying his subjects in their most romantic, relaxed, and flattering light was cemented at his first Parisian exhibition in 1835, and a duly impressed French King Louis-Philippe retained his services. Over the next few years, the king would

VI. *"She worshipped her beauty like a heathen his idols."*

commission some thirty formal Winterhalter portraits of the French royal family.

When Victoria became Queen of England in 1837, Winterhalter was one of many artists who produced coronation portraits. By 1842, however, it was Winterhalter alone who was making regular visits to England to paint the British monarch and her family. Between July and September each year from 1843 to 1850, the queen invited Winterhalter to stay at Buckingham Palace and Windsor Castle to immortalize her growing family as well as to give the queen lessons in oil painting. Winterhalter was said to have relished the chance to be with so many German-speakers at a foreign court, Queen Victoria and Prince Albert among them.

Although Queen Victoria enjoyed time spent with Winterhalter enough to invite him to visit for up to three months each year, her nursery superintendent who looked after the nine royal children was not as enamored with the painter. Lady Lyttleton reported that she found him to be "one of the least agreeable, and most dry and half-sneering mannered men I have ever met." The queen agreed that Winterhalter had some odd idiosyncrasies but despite what she called his "peculiarities," the queen admitted that she "liked him so much."[5]

Queen Victoria was so comfortable with Winterhalter that she allowed him to paint the only known image of her as seductress. The portrait was a surprise gift for her consort Prince Albert's twenty-fifth birthday and depicted the queen with lips apart, bare neck and shoulder, and a long lock of hair reaching to the breast. She would say it was her husband's favorite picture of her, one that he kept in a treasured place in his writing room at Windsor Castle.

Winterhalter's court popularity aside, critics accused him of fawning over his privileged subjects and refused to take him seriously as an artist. He silenced them in 1853 with a rapturous subject painting depicting feminine beauty from the Spanish legend *Florinda*. But portraiture was his true calling, and the one that had made him a wealthy man, so Winterhalter returned to the genre to create his masterpiece, *The Empress Eugénie Surrounded by Her Ladies in Waiting*, in 1855. The portrait, depicting the French empress and her ladies collecting flowers, was presented that same year at France's International Exhibition. It was

Empress Elisabeth with Flowing Hair, painted by Franz Xaver Winterhalter in 1865, shows an informal Sisi with her long, thick hair hanging loose. Emperor Franz Joseph said Winterhalter's portraits were the first "which actually show a true likeness." He hung this portrait in his Hofburg study, where he spent much of each day on official paperwork (Kunsthistorisches Museum, Vienna. Photograph by Erich Lessing/Art Resource, New York).

Empress Elisabeth in a Star-Spangled Dress, painted by Franz Xaver Winterhalter in 1865. Sisi was at the height of her beauty, wearing a gown by Worth with diamond Köchert Stars in her hair. Winterhalter was one of the only artists for whom Sisi ever sat live, since she loathed the process. The painting garnered Sisi the title of "the loveliest crowned head in Europe" (Kunsthistorisches Museum, Vienna. Photograph by Erich Lessing/Art Resource, New York).

hailed for its "easy, fashionable insouciance" compared to the "chilly, academic 'correctness'" of other works on display.[6]

Winterhalter remained close with Eugénie and upon traveling to Paris in 1865, presented his first sketches of Sisi for the French empress's approval. Eugénie was so taken by the likeness that she immediately proclaimed her Austrian counterpart as "the loveliest crowned head in Europe."[7] The stylish Eugénie was twelve years Sisi's senior and it was she who had held the title of "most beautiful royal" until she passed the mantle on to Sisi.

The state portrait of Sisi, with its exquisite depiction of the waves of silk and tulle, became one of Winterhalter's most famous works while forever linking the public image of the empress with the sparkling stars in her hair. As was his practice, Winterhalter had paid as much painstaking attention to the texture of the dress, the folds of the fan, and the glint of the hair stars as he did to Sisi's alabastrine shoulder, the blush of her cheek, and the twists of her braids. Countless reproductions of the star-studded Empress with her knowing, half-smile spread throughout Europe, prompting travelers to Vienna to go out of their way to catch a glimpse of the glamorous and elusive Sisi on one of her walks through Lainz or Schönbrunn Park.

In addition to the ball gown depiction, Winterhalter painted two additional and more intimate portraits of the empress. *Sisi in Morning Light* is an oval-framed portrait of the empress in her dressing gown, with hair loose and crisscrossed over her folded arms. Although Winterhalter made his name on painting informal depictions of his subjects, the likeness of a half-dressed empress was considered too "familiar" for the day and somewhat scandalous. Regardless, it was said to have been Franz Joseph's favorite image of his wife. The third portrait, *Empress Elisabeth with Flowing Hair* depicts Sisi, wrapped in voluminous satin, looking wistfully over her right shoulder, her hair tumbling toward the floor. Franz Joseph hung the two intimate portraits opposite the Hofburg writing desk where he spent the majority of his days raking through reams of paperwork. Perhaps glancing at the portraits offered a gentle respite from the glaring reality of managing his troubled empire.

Of the experience of working with Winterhalter, Franz Joseph wrote to his mother: "The pictures he has painted of Sisi have turned out very

VI. "She worshipped her beauty like a heathen his idols."

charming and are the first portraits which actually show a true likeness."⁸ The emperor was so thrilled with Winterhalter's work, in fact, that he presented a copy of the state portrait to the artist's most ardent supporter, Queen Victoria. It was most likely painted by one of Winterhalter's assistants hired specifically to recreate the master's most popular royal commissions.

In 2014, one of the oldest auction houses in the world, the Dorotheum in Vienna, offered a reproduction painted by one of Wintherhalter's assistants as part of a lot of imperial court memorabilia. The portrait went for more than $110,000. It was nearly identical to Winterhalter's original ball gown portrait, apart from two aspects: the painting depicted Sisi from the waist up instead of full-length, and the artist changed the type of stars she wore in her hair. Instead of the ten-pointed all-diamond stars originally depicted by Winterhalter, the assistant portrayed the Empress wearing eight-pointed stars with center pearls. It remains a mystery as to why the assistant altered the work of his master instead of exactly copying the original. Furthermore, speculation abounds as to whether Sisi actually posed for Winterhalter wearing Köchert stars with center pearls with the master then deciding that the pearls were superfluous. He may have used his creative license to remove them, feeling that the pearl detail detracted from the overall affect of the finished work. One of Winterhalter's original sketches of Sisi that is published in Count Egon Corti's biography of the Empress appears to show the stars with center pearls. So, it is possible that the Köchert Diamond Pearl stolen from Schönbrunn in 1998 was actually worn by Sisi during her sitting with Winterhalter.

Winterhalter's private life remained much of a mystery. He had a brief engagement that came to nothing and constructed a home in Baden that he sold within a year because his professional popularity kept him constantly on the move. Winterhalter spent the rest of his life traveling between Great Britain and the continent, with his last official commission being the wedding of the Prince and Princess of Wales. Winterhalter died in 1873 after contracting the bacterial disease typhus during an epidemic that swept through Frankfurt, Germany. His death was said to have been a blow to Queen Victoria, who would outlive him for another twenty-eight years.

Two years after Winterhalter completed his work at Schönbrunn Palace, Madame Tussauds famous wax museum in London used the ball

71

gown portrait as a guide to create a life-size replica of the empress and her diamond stars.[9] Madame Tussauds sculpted and displayed wax figures of only the most famous people of the day, and the Baker Street location charged visitors a sixpence to view likenesses of Sisi, French Empress Eugénie, and other notable royals. In an age before mass media, Madame Tussauds finally gave average people a chance to witness a three-dimensional depiction of the enchanting empress they had heard so much about. Nine years later, Sisi visited Madame Tussauds with lady-in-waiting Marie Festetics during a sightseeing trip through London. The papers reported that the duo viewed a statue of Franz Joseph and commented that the wax displays were "Vastly amusing but very gruesome in parts,"[10] undoubtedly referring to the reproduction of scenes from the 1789 French Revolution. There was no mention, however, of whether Sisi observed her own wax figure. Today, the original wax sculpture of Sisi created during her lifetime is no longer in existence. Madame Tussauds often melted down old statues to make new ones, a fate that probably befell Sisi's replica.

If any doubted it before, the Winterhalter portrait cemented Sisi's reputation as an international marvel. The American envoy to Vienna at the time described her as "a wonder of a beauty—tall, beautifully formed, with a profusion of bright brown hair, a low Greek forehead, gentle eyes, very red lips, a sweet smile, a low musical voice, and a manner partly timid, partly gracious."[11] Yet the pathologically shy empress shunned the public attention her natural good looks brought her. She carried fans—some in the ornate Rococo style and others of simple leather—and lacy parasols to shield her face from onlookers who were hoping to catch a glimpse of the captivating empress in person. To Sisi, her physical allure wasn't solely for public consumption. She cultivated it to gain the self-confidence she needed to fulfill her imperial role as well to influence those she wished to manipulate. Although she didn't mind being considered one of the most beautiful women in the world, Sisi resented being gawked at by the masses, as expressed in her 1887 poem, *To the Starers:*

> It stirs my bile,
> When they stare at me so,
> I would like to creep into a shell
> And could die of rage.[12]

VI. *"She worshipped her beauty like a heathen his idols."*

Sisi deeply felt the sting of public criticism, and this may have contributed to her desire to hide. Two years after first wearing the Sisi Stars, a newspaper columnist wrote a particularly scathing review of the empress's love for quite literally "gilding the lily":

> A fashion has of late been introduced by the Empress of Austria which does not appear in good taste. It is to have a diamond representing a dew drop, fixed to a real flower. A few evenings ago the Empress had in her hand a bouquet of white camellias and on each in the centre was a large diamond. Fashion, with its hair powder and patches, hoops, high heels, pugs and paint, is so unaccountable and uncontrollable a power, that we may perhaps before long see a sparkling diamond fixed by a new plan to the cheek of beauty, to heighten its charms by thus representing a falling tear.[13]

Yet, for as much as Sisi deplored being talked about and stared at, she certainly didn't mind gazing at other women she found attractive. In 1862, Sisi began compiling an "album of beauties" with more than one hundred photos of women, including her own sister, Marie, the ex–Queen of the Two Sicilies.

Marie and her husband, the Bourbon King Francis II, had been exiled following the Siege of Gaeta in 1861. The couple had taken refuge in the coastal fortress town during the Second Italian War of Independence. And although Gaeta fell after 100 days and Francis and Marie were deposed, Marie was hailed as a pillar of strength for her resolute support of her husband and territory. The exiled couple moved to Rome, where they befriended American sculptor Harriet Hosmer. In 1868, Hosmer immortalized the ex-queen in stone; it would be the only portrait of a living woman Hosmer ever created. *The Times of London* described her hero's pose: "The Queen is erect and slightly defiant.... While the right hand rests upon the fold of the cloak where it is thrown across the breast and over the shoulder, the other points downward to a cannonball that lies close at her foot." Hosmer herself described the ex-queen's hair in the sculpture as forming "a natural crown as beautiful as any goldsmith's skill could supply."[14] Clearly the brave Marie had emulated Sisi's hairstyle for her dramatic representation. She was said to have been so alluring, in fact, that the sculptor became infatuated, referring to her relationship with the ex-queen as the romance of her life.

Also represented in Sisi's album were the French Empress Eugénie, a certain Madame Duz-Oglu from Constantinople, Sisi's lady-in-waiting

Caroline "Lily" Hunyady, and an assortment of Parisian circus artists and dancers. Class and social standing didn't interest Sisi; she was most concerned with unusual, striking features, not just conventional good looks.

Sisi wrote to her brother-in-law, Archduke Ludwig Viktor, requesting his help with her compilation: "I happen to be assembling an album of beauties and am now collecting photographs for it, only of women. Please send me whatever pretty faces you run across at Angerer's and other photographers."[15]

Ludwig Angerer (no known relation to Sisi's hairdresser, Fanny) was a Hungarian photographer who applied for and became imperial court photographer in December 1860. In that same year, he became the only person ever permitted to photograph the entire imperial family. The sitting included Emperor Franz Joseph and his brothers Maximilian, Ludwig Viktor, and Karl Ludwig; Maximilian's wife Charlotte; Sisi with her infant son Rudolf on her lap and her daughter Gisela; and Archduchess Sophie next to husband Franz Karl. It was also the only photograph in which Sisi ever appeared together with her husband and children. In an attempt to portray the family unit in additional photos, Franz Joseph permitted the following time-consuming, three-step process: Angerer would cobble together individual photos of Sisi, Franz Joseph, and their children that had been taken separately in his studio; the collage would be painted by an artist in monochrome; then Angerer would snap a final photo of the painting to distribute to the masses.[16]

Sisi may have gotten the idea for her album of beauties from her own uncle, King Ludwig I of Bavaria. Ludwig also appreciated beautiful faces regardless of class and compiled a famous "Gallery of Beauties" in the south pavilion of his Nymphenburg Palace in Munich. The gallery included some thirty-six women painted between 1827 and 1850, mostly by Winterhalter's teacher, Joseph Stieler. Among the portraits were middle-class women and even a few Wittelsbach relatives, including Sisi's adversarial mother-in-law, Archduchess Sophie, who had been considered beautiful in her youth. Ludwig also included a portrait of his paramour, Lola Montez, a commoner of Irish descent whose real name was Maria Dolores Gilbert and who gained fame as an actress and Spanish dancer. The king was sixty-one when he met the twenty-eight-year-old beauty, whose dance act had caused a commotion throughout

VI. "She worshipped her beauty like a heathen his idols."

Europe. Although he bestowed on her a mansion in Munich and the title of Countess of Landsfeld and Baroness Rosenthal after declaring her a naturalized citizen, both Ludwig and Lola maintained that their love never turned physical. But Lola was a polarizing personality, and the king was eventually forced to banish her from his life in order to save his throne. The gesture came too late, however, and, during the revolutionary fervor of 1848, Ludwig abdicated in favor of his son who became Maximilian II.

In addition to loving beautiful women, Ludwig was an enthusiastic patron of the arts, supporting the young Winterhalter and becoming good friends with Heinrich Heine. Heine was considered one of the greatest German writers of the era—excelling as a journalist, essayist, and literary critic as well as poet—and was known to tease Ludwig for the old king's notoriously bad verses.

Sisi enjoyed the presence of attractive people in her daily life and couldn't stand those she considered stout and ugly. In her 1887 poem *Family Dinner*, Sisi mocked one of her unattractive relatives:

> This one is just as fat
> as a Swiss cow,
> proudly thinking quietly so high of herself
> Right down to her stomach.[17]

In another poem written the same year, entitled *Court Ball,* Sisi turned her vitriol on the Viennese court establishment.

> The most noble names
> of our aristocracy are coming
> Medals of recognition—and palace ladies;
> (they are mostly fat and stupid).[18]

Even Katharina Schratt, the "dear friend" Sisi chose to provide companionship for the lonely emperor while she was away from court, was not immune to the empress's derision. Katharina was a comic actress at the Burghteater who had caught the emperor's eye one night during a performance. She was twenty-three years his junior and the opposite of Sisi in many ways—her body was short, soft and round, and her disposition jovial and uncomplicated. She was also unhappily married and had a young son.

Perhaps Sisi got the idea from Heine, whose own platonic relationship with a young woman later in life lightened his depression and encouraged his creativity. The budding relationship between the actress and the emperor made Sisi feel better that someone was there to console him while she was away on her extensive travels. What she probably didn't realize was that Franz Joseph had been having a relationship with a woman named Anna Nahowski, who was just fifteen when she met the forty-five-year-old emperor in 1875. Anna had been married the year before to an alcoholic businessman with burgeoning debts that the emperor gradually paid off. Anna had a child in 1885, Helene, who was rumored to be Franz Joseph's. The emperor finally broke it off with Anna some four years into his relationship with Katharina.

There is little evidence, however, that Franz Joseph's liaison with Katharina ever went further than deep friendship. The two wrote hundreds of letters over the years expressing their adoration for one other. Then, on Valentine's Day 1888, Katharina sent the emperor a letter where she appeared to offer to become his mistress. Franz Joseph replied that he was flattered but that their relationship "must remain for the future as it has been until now. I love my wife and do not wish to abuse her confidence and her friendship with you."[19]

Sisi commissioned court artist Heinrich von Angeli to paint a portrait of Katharina as a present for the Emperor. Even though she was friends with the actress and promoted the relationship with her husband, Sisi couldn't help but poke fun at what she felt were the actress's physical shortcomings. Katharina took on the role as Titania in Shakespeare's *A Midsummer Night's Dream*, the same play at which Sisi had first seen another actress with sparkling stars in her hair. Of her friend's portrayal, Sisi wrote:

> Imitation is her way
> In spite of pounds of fat.
> Titania she wants to play,
> Poor Katharina Schratt.[20]

The emperor's relationship with Schratt galled his children, especially Marie Valerie, who could never rectify the liaison—whatever its depth—with her staunch Catholic faith.

In the early 1860s, Sisi made no secret that she preferred the company of her lady-in-waiting, the beautiful Countess Lily Hunyady, above all others. Lily appeared in Sisi's album of beauties, and the two were inseparable, having a "magnetic rapport."[21] Sisi showed such favor to Lily that she neglected the other ladies at court and fostered petty jeal-

VI. *"She worshipped her beauty like a heathen his idols."*

ousies among them. Sisi also enjoyed being seen with her younger sister, Marie; the two were spotted gliding about Budapest, Hungary, in 1868, wearing matching dark silk dresses, plaid wraps, and pearl-gray silk hats.

Another Wittelsbach who captivated Sisi was her flamboyant, handsome second cousin, King Ludwig II of Bavaria, although his strange behavior and bloated appearance near the end of his life disturbed her, and she started to avoid him. Just like Sisi, Ludwig couldn't get enough of beautiful things—he was an enthusiastic patron of composer Richard Wagner, regularly attended the theater, and built the prohibitively expensive Neuschwanstein fairytale castle in the mountains above southwest Bavaria. As a young man, Ludwig was handsome, tall and had a certain "romantic flair" about him. When he and Sisi walked together, they captivated passers-by, "as if the Gods of Olympus had come down to earth."[22]

Sisi called him "The Eagle," and she was his seagull for her love of ocean travel. Ludwig was engaged for a time to Sisi's younger sister, Sophie Charlotte, but quietly broke it off nine months later. He was believed to have struggled with homosexuality all his life, trying in vain to deny his urges in order to stay true to his Catholic faith, and was said to be concerned that Sophie Charlotte would not be happy within the union. But rumors swirled that the engagement was broken after Sophie Charlotte admitted she had fallen in love with Edgar Hanfstaengl, the son of the man who had been hired to take the bride's pre-wedding photographs. Regardless of the reason, Ludwig would never entertain the possibility of marriage again.

Sadly, Ludwig's eccentricities and wild spending habits gave his enemies the ammunition they needed to have him deposed, and he joined his younger brother Otto by being declared insane. To Sisi, Ludwig was simply a sensitive soul like herself who preferred his imagination over the harsh reality of life. But he had lost his throne for good to the nearest Wittelsbach relative and heir presumptive, Prince Luitpold. Once in custody, Ludwig was confined to Berg Castle on Lake Starnberg, where he was threatened with ropes and a straightjacket under orders of Dr. Bernhard von Gudden, chief of the Munich Asylum. Following dinner one night, Ludwig asked the doctor to walk with him down to the lake. After the two failed to return, a search party found their bodies facedown in four to five feet of water. The chief of the British Legation in

Bavaria, Victor Drummond, postulated to Queen Victoria that Ludwig must have rushed into the water with the doctor chasing after him.

> Then the Dr. must have seized the King who I imagine retaliated by striking the Dr. a terrible blow on the forehead and by seizing his throat, and in

Crown Prince Rudolf shared similar liberal views with his mother, but the two were never close. He became disillusioned with the monarchy and suffered illness and addiction before taking his own life and that of his mistress in 1889. His death caused the line of succession to pass to Franz Joseph's ill-fated nephew, Franz Ferdinand (Library of Congress Prints and Photographs Division, George Grantham Bain Collection).

VI. *"She worshipped her beauty like a heathen his idols."*

fact mortally injured him. By so disabling his strength that falling in the water he was drowned, the King fulfilling at the same time his determination of suicide.[23]

Ludwig's official cause of death was suicide by drowning, although the autopsy report indicated no water in his lungs, while the doctor's body showed signs of strangulation as well as blows to the head and neck. Many Ludwig supporters believed he was trying to make his escape when a struggle ensued and Ludwig was murdered. Sisi blamed the deposed king's handlers for his violent end, saying, "They might have treated him more gently, and so, perhaps, spared him such a fearful end."[24] She could not bear to attend the funeral, but sent a bouquet of jasmine, Ludwig's favorite flowers, with orders that it be placed on his chest and accompany him to the grave. Sisi was shocked by the death of her once-beautiful cousin and feared even more for her own sanity now that the Wittelsbach curse appeared to have claimed another relative.

The empress's niece, Countess Marie Larisch, denounced Sisi's preoccupation with narcissistic aesthetics, writing,

She worshipped her beauty like a heathen his idols and was on her knees to it. The sight of the perfection of her body gave her aesthetic pleasure; everything that marred this beauty was displeasing and repulsive to her.... She saw it as her life's work to remain young, and all her thoughts turned on the best method for preserving her beauty.[25]

But Marie didn't always take such a bitter tone when writing about her aunt. In fact, Marie was a great confidante of the empress for many years, even though Sisi's lady-in-waiting, Marie Festetics, never liked her and wrote, "She is not sincere, nor straightforward, she is always acting a part."[26] Marie Larisch was considered the "morganatic niece," since her father, Sisi's brother Duke Ludwig, married beneath his station to an actress named Henriette Mendel. Morganatic marriages occurred when a person of princely blood married someone who did not hold an equal title. Often, the couple's children were denied rights to titles, properties, or succession.

Sisi, who eschewed judging people based on birth, took the girl under her wing and hoped to foster a devoted friendship. The empress even arranged her niece's marriage to Count Georg Larisch of Moenich in 1877 in order to secure the girl's future. Scandal tore aunt and niece apart, however, after Marie introduced Sisi's son, thirty-year-old Crown

Prince Rudolf, to one of her friends, seventeen-year-old Baroness Mary Vetsera. The teenager and the married Crown Prince became lovers, and Rudolf would go on to manipulate Mary's affections toward a tragic end.

—⟶⟵—

Once he was out from under the yoke of his repressive tutor Gondrecourt, Rudolf began to flourish. His new tutor, General Latour von Thurmburg, fostered Rudolf's interest in science, including a love of ornithology. The Crown Prince even attended a lecture given by a noted proponent of Darwin's Theory of Evolution, a move that garnered stern disapproval from members of the Catholic Viennese court. Rudolf also immersed himself in military history, of which he wrote prolifically and quite enjoyed his new military career as a colonel in the 36th Bohemian Infantry in Prague.

As a child, Rudolf wrote to his mother often during her copious overseas absences, but he was not especially close to her precisely because she was gone so much during his formative years. This fact was sadly ironic since both mother and son fostered ultraliberal ideas about the Viennese class system. Rudolf secretly condemned his father's conservatism and predicted that the monarchy was doomed to crumble before the century was out. He wrote scathing political articles under pseudonyms for the liberal newspaper *Neues Wiener Tagblatt* and told one Viennese journalist, "We live in a tottering, decaying age. Who knows how long things can still drag on?"[27]

At the age of twenty-three, Rudolf became engaged to fifteen-year-old Princess Stephanie of Belgium just two days after meeting her. Stephanie was the niece of Charlotte, wife of Archduke Max, Emperor of Mexico. The wedding was set for summer 1880 but had to be postponed for nearly a year when it was discovered that Stephanie had not yet begun her menstruation. Sisi was not impressed with her son's choice, calling his bride—and the assumed next Empress of Austria—a plain bumpkin. But with memories of the disastrous relationship with her own mother-in-law, Sisi made a conscious decision not to interfere. She took such a distant approach, in fact, that Stephanie arrived in Austria to bleak, unfinished palace apartments.

At first, Rudolf was extremely happy with domestic life, and Stephanie gave birth to a daughter two years later whom they named Elisabeth and called "Erzsi," short for the Hungarian, Erzsébet. But Stephanie was staunchly Catholic and loved the grand formalities of court life, which proved the exact opposite of Rudolf's personality. Slowly, the Crown Prince began to become disillusioned with his imperial position, the policies of the Catholic Church, and his father's conservative government. For comfort, Rudolf turned to numerous courtesans, from whom he contracted a "gonorrheal infection." He also passed it onto his young wife.

According to Stephanie,

> I myself did not suspect the cause of my complaint. Everything was hushed up upon orders from above, and the doctors were sworn to secrecy. Only later did I discover that the Crown Prince was responsible for my complaint. He too had been gripped by the terrible disease which never yet stopped at anyone.[28]

Rudolf and Stephanie were treated with medicines from the court pharmacy including zinc sulphate, copana balsam, and mercury, but she was cautioned not to try to have more children. That devastating diagnosis meant that the succession would veer to another branch of the Habsburg line after Rudolf's assumed reign.

This sexually transmitted disease marked the beginning of Rudolf's downward spiral into depression. He also suffered from a persistent cough and crushing headaches that he treated with copious amounts of alcohol and morphine. His health and state of mind deteriorated to the point that both Stephanie and Franz Joseph became exceedingly worried, and Rudolf was sent to an island retreat to recover. He never did rally and began to seriously entertain thoughts of suicide.

The despondent Rudolf had initially asked a twenty-four-year-old actress and courtesan named Mitzi Kaspar if she would be prepared to die with him. He suggested that they shoot themselves at the Hussar Temple near his hunting lodge at Mayerling, right in front of the a monument dedicated to the emperor. Mitzi initially laughed off his suggestion but was so disturbed by the Crown Prince's proposal that she reported it to the police. They declined to become involved in imperial affairs. Undeterred by Mitzi's reaction, the Crown Prince continued his search for a willing co-conspirator. He finally found what he was looking for in the teenaged Mary Vetsera.

Mary was besotted with the Crown Prince and was seen at a birthday reception with the imperial family at the German embassy the night before Rudolf left for his hunting lodge at Mayerling in the Vienna Woods. (Mary's own mother, Baroness Helen Vetsera, had made advances toward Rudolf herself when she was in her early thirties and he had just turned twenty.) Earlier in the day, Franz Joseph and his son were said to have had a heated argument with Rudolf storming out of the Hofburg. But father and son were cordial to one another at the embassy party. Rudolf left for his hunting lodge and, with the aid of his coachman, secretly summoned Mary Vetsera to join him there. Before she boarded the coach, Mary had written out a cryptic note for her mother: "By the time you read this I shall be in the Danube."[29] When Countess Marie Larisch was unable to find her friend, she, too, went to the police suspecting that Mary might be with the Crown Prince at Mayerling. But again, the authorities did nothing.

The bodies of Mary Vetsera and Rudolf were found at Mayerling on January 30, 1889. At first, strychnine poison was suspected, followed by an official report that the Crown Prince had died from a heart aneurism. Once foreign journalists descended on the hunting lodge, however, the truth was learned: Mary had been found shot in the forehead at close range and had been stretched out on a bed with a red rose in her hands. She had died some eight hours before Rudolf turned the gun on himself. He was found sitting up with a bullet wound to the skull and the gun at his feet.

Sisi was having her Greek lesson in her apartments when her Hungarian tutor Ida Ferenczy interrupted, informing her that Rudolf's hunting companion, Count Joseph Hoyos, had brought terrible news. The Count gently recounted the tragedy to the devastated empress, who had been so out of touch with her son and what was happening in his life that she was caught completely off guard by his fatal actions. Sisi had no idea that he had been depressed, let alone suicidal, and it remains open to conjecture whether Rudolf had waited for his mother to return to Vienna following one of her lengthy voyages before he pulled the trigger. Regardless, he now had her full attention.

Sisi managed to handle the calamity with great fortitude and first told her youngest daughter Marie Valerie, then asked to be alone with the emperor so she could tell him herself. But Franz Joseph became so distraught that Sisi ushered in his "beloved friend," the actress Katharina Schratt, to console him. At the same time, Mary Vetsera's mother, Baroness Helene, showed up at the palace begging the empress to help find her daughter. Sisi coldly informed the Baroness that both of their children were dead. But when the story hit the Viennese papers the next morning, there was no mention that anyone other than Rudolf had perished.

Mary's body was spirited out of Mayerling in secret, and even her mother was not permitted to attend the burial at the cemetery of the Shrine of Heiligenkreuz. Baroness Helene fled Venice under the direction of Minister-President Taaf to keep the involvement of her daughter and the Crown Prince quiet. Rudolf's body, complete with band-

Seventeen-year-old Mary Vetsera was good friends with Sisi's niece, Countess Marie Larisch, who introduced the teenager to Crown Prince Rudolf. Mary fell head-over-heels in love with the thirty-year-old married Crown Prince. Her body was found along with Rudolf's at his hunting lodge at Mayerling in the Vienna woods (Library of Congress Prints and Photographs Division, George Grantham Bain Collection).

aged head to hide the gaping gunshot wound, was laid in state in his Hofburg apartments where Sisi, Marie Valerie, and the rest of the imperial family knelt at the bed in disbelief and prayed for his salvation.

For a time, Franz Joseph would not accept that Rudolf died by his own hand; he believed it had been murder. But after his personal doctor performed an autopsy, the grief-stricken emperor acknowledged the truth and lamented that his son had died like a coward. The doctor comforted Franz Joseph by asserting that Rudolf's brain was "abnormal" and that he was not of sound mind when he killed himself. Thus the Emperor requested and received a dispensation from the Vatican declaring Rudolf in a state of "mental imbalance" during the incident, meaning the he could not be held responsible for taking his own life. Only then could the Crown Prince be buried on consecrated ground in the imperial Habsburg crypt in Vienna's Church of the Capuchins. Franz Joseph and his eldest daughter, Gisela, would attend Rudolf's funeral while Sisi and Marie Valerie sequestered themselves in a private chapel for prayer.

Rudolf had left his wife, Stephanie, a note before his death. It read, in part, "You are now rid of my presence and annoyance; be happy in your own way. Take care of the poor wee one [Erzsi], she is all that remains of me ... I now go quietly to my death, which alone can save my good name."[30] He also left a final letter for his mother, who ordered Ida Ferenczy to destroy it after the empress's death, and one for his youngest sister Marie Valerie. In his sister's letter, Rudolf mysteriously stated, "I do not die willingly."[31] He also advised her to leave Austria when the emperor died, predicting that the empire would soon be dismantled. Rudolf had no last words for his father with whom he had been so at odds in previous days.

Sisi partially blamed herself for Rudolf's death. She did not berate herself for being a mostly absentee mother who spent little time with her son during his formative years; she was convinced her sin had been to transmit the Wittelsbach tendency toward mental illness on to the Crown Prince. Sisi told one of her doctors, "The Emperor should never have married me; I have inherited the taint of madness! My son did too, or else he would never have treated me so!"[32]

It was Rudolf's wife, Stephanie, whom Sisi chiefly blamed for her son's demise. "If one comes to know this woman properly, one must excuse Rudolf for looking elsewhere for distraction and a narcotic to ease the emptiness of the heart in his own home," she said. "It is certain: Things would have been otherwise had he had a different wife, one who understood him."[33]

Stephanie recalled that she was interrogated by both Franz Joseph and Sisi in the moments after learning of Rudolf's death. She said she was submitted to a "crossfire of questions" and felt as if she were being accused of being an unfaithful wife. Marie Valerie remembered that Stephanie continually asked for forgiveness for her "lack of devotion" to the Crown Prince. Stephanie's parents, the King and Queen of Belgium, arrived shortly thereafter to comfort their daughter and five-year-old granddaughter.

Conspiracy theories abounded after Rudolf died. Among the rumors were that Mary Vetsera had been pregnant or that the Crown Prince had been assassinated by secret agents after he failed to carry out a *coup d'état* against his father in Hungary. One thing was for certain, however: Rudolf's death changed the course of European history by interrupting the line of Habsburg succession. Rudolf had long postulated that Austro-Hungary would soon fall apart along with the imperial family itself, and his death proved a catalyst in confirming the theory.

Sisi bitterly remarked on the fact that the succession would now pass to an alternate branch of the Habsburg family. "Now all these people who have spoken so much evil of me from the very moment of my arrival will have the consolation that I shall pass away without leaving a trace behind me in Austria," she said.[34] By "trace" she meant a son; in the imperial line of succession, her daughters did not count.

Sisi never forgave her niece, Countess Marie Larisch, for her role in the suicide of Crown Prince Rudolf. Shunned by the empress and the entire imperial family, Marie fled the court and moved to Bavaria, where she divorced the count in 1896. Following the death of her famous aunt in 1898, Marie began to write about her time at court, much to the chagrin of the remaining members of the imperial family. They reportedly paid her hush money, but she published her memoirs nonetheless: *My Past*, in 1913, followed by *Secrets of a Royal House*, and *My Royal Relatives*. Marie married twice more and spent time in America before returning to Germany, where she died in poverty in 1940.

After her son's suicide, Sisi went into deep mourning and was believed to have worn nothing but head-to-toe black for the rest of her life. But an item found at a Munich auction house in 2012 would debunk this long-held supposition. A moderately-sized dress box was presented with a label bearing the name of His Imperial and Royal Highness Archduke Franz Salvator, the husband of Sisi's youngest daughter, Marie

Crown Prince Rudolf's daughter and Sisi's granddaughter, Elisabeth (Erzsi), with her children (left to right) Rudolf, Stéphanie, Ernst and Franz Joseph. Erzsi married Prince Otto Weriand of Windisch-Grätz in 1902. Although Emperor Franz Joseph disapproved of her morganatic marriage and forced his granddaughter to renounce her right to succession, he gifted her the diamond Winterhalter hair stars as part of her trousseau (Library of Congress Prints and Photographs Division, George Grantham Bain Collection).

Valerie. Carefully folded inside was a stunning light blue and cream dress believed to have been worn by Sisi in Corfu in the 1890s—after Rudolf's death. According to the Hofburg's Sisi Museum, the dress contains a label at the back of the neck bearing an embroidered crowned dolphin, the same emblem on the dinnerware and stationery Sisi had created for her estate, on the Island of Corfu, the Achilleion.[35]

Sisi's jewelry, however, would remain plain and simple following her son's death: an electroplated watch with leather strap and buckle,

VI. "She worshipped her beauty like a heathen his idols."

her gold wedding band, and plain bracelets featuring jet or imitation gemstones. Never again would she wear the dazzling jewels of her youth. She began giving away all of her glamorous jewelry, including emeralds, pearls, diamonds, and individual Sisi Stars to her relatives and ladies-in-waiting. Some of the stars she even had specially made to hand out as gifts. One of the most valuable ornaments in the collection was a three-strand necklace of perfect natural pearls valued at 75,000 florins ($860,212.50) that Franz Joseph had gifted Sisi at Rudolf's birth. All-in-all, Sisi's jewelry collection was said to have been worth some five million florins ($57,347,500).

The original twenty-seven diamond Sisi Stars created by Köchert and depicted in the Winterhalter painting were kept on reserve, however, and Franz Joseph presented it to his granddaughter Erzsi, daughter of Crown Prince Rudolf, for her wedding on January 23, 1902. Erzsi married Prince Otto Weriand von Windisch-Grätz, who was beneath her royal rank, and a disappointed Franz Joseph declared the marriage to be morganatic. Erzsi was forced to renounce her right to the succession, although she was allowed to keep her imperial titles.

Despite the emperor's regret that his granddaughter had not made a dynastic match, he did not deny her any of her inheritance. The *Wiener Diarium* newspaper published a photo of her magnificent endowment with a description of the "very valuable collection of Jewellery [sic]" that made up the trousseau, including an exquisite diamond tiara, shimmering necklaces, jeweled hair combs, and gemstone encrusted rings. But the paper specifically mentioned the famous Sisi Stars, cognizant that its readers would be most interested in the "parure of twenty seven diamonds, which was a favorite ornament of the late Empress Elisabeth."[36]

The incomparable collection of jewelry was put on display in the Hofburg in the days leading up to the royal wedding, and Franz Joseph's administrators issued some 4,000 tickets for the empire's subjects to experience the grandeur. Despite the imperial guards' best efforts to keep order, pandemonium ensued as a far greater throng pressed through the doors, straining to get a look at the legendary diamond Köchert Sisi Stars in their velvet-lined box.

87

VII

"Who Has stolen Sisi's Star?"

—Kronen Zeitung

The headline "Who has stolen Sisi's Star?" greeted readers of Austria's largest newspaper, the *Kronen Zeitung*, on the morning of July 21, 1998. A photo of the Winterhalter portrait of Sisi with the Köchert Stars in her hair accompanied the compelling question. Far from a scoop, this news story was part of a carefully orchestrated effort by Schönbrunn Palace Director Wolfgang Kippes, the Vienna Police Department, and possibly the star's private owner and insurer, to root out the thief and bring the star home. It was an effort that would require careful deception on the part of palace officials.

"Yes, it's true. A security problem," Kippes explained to Viennese reporters. "But the star has already been recovered!"[1] The papers were told that once the jewelry expert had alerted him to the fake star, the Vienna police immediately began contacting local antique shops, where they miraculously stumbled upon the Köchert Diamond Pearl. Kippes said the antiques dealer in question had an alibi and was not a suspect, although, "getting the star back had its price," he improvised. The paper noted that Kippes "did not elaborate on the amount of money that was spent" in ransom. The news story speculated that the thief could be a Schönbrunn Palace employee, but Kippes expressed a lack of concern. "That's the investigators' job," he told them. "We only care about one thing: The star is back!"[2]

It was all an elaborate lie.

Palace officials hoped that falsely reporting the star as recovered would help root out the real thief by appealing to the criminal's vanity. Perhaps it would set the underworld abuzz with talk of who really had the star. Wolfgang Kippes has long since retired from his director post, but the current director, Franz Sattlecker, confirmed the strategy.

The plan was "to try to get some reaction from the thief and therefore to get some trace of who might have stolen the star," Sattlecker said.[3]

But there never was a reaction, and there's no telling if Gerald Blanchard ever even knew about the false reports. The paper was written in German, after all, a language Blanchard didn't speak. And besides, he had bigger fish to fry now that the Sisi Star was safely tucked away back in his home country.

—⁂—

Emboldened by his successful theft of the Sisi Star, Gerald Blanchard decided it was time to make some real cash by going where the cash was—banking institutions. If he could slip in and out of a well-guarded palace undetected, breaking into banks and ATMs would be a piece of cake. But first he would have to perform his due diligence. While working various house-flipping and rehashing schemes during the day to keep his cash flow steady, Blanchard spent his free time educating himself on the mechanics of ATM machines. Stealthily, he videotaped security guards opening and closing the cash dispensers at a local Winnipeg mall. Playing the tapes over and over again, Blanchard memorized everything about the procedure: what types of locks were used, how smoothly the cash drawers opened and closed, how the money was stacked, and where the dye pack sensors were placed.

Blanchard next did something that no other bank robber in Canadian history had ever done: He gathered up surveillance equipment that he planned to secretly install inside whichever bank he chose to hit. If he knew exactly what was going on inside the building at any given time, he would be able to pick the right moment to strike with a greater chance of success.

In 2001, some three years after the Sisi Star theft, Blanchard found the bank he was looking for, a new branch of the Alberta Treasury Bank in Edmonton. As the structure was being built, he tapped a collection of disguises he had been stockpiling and passed himself off as a workman to gain easy access to the building. No one gave him a second glance as he confidently strolled onto the property carrying a toolbox full of his surveillance equipment. Once inside, he made a beeline to the room that would contain the ATM machines. He carefully unpacked listening devices and pinhole cameras that he methodically planted behind the room's thermostat and electrical outlets. The devices would wirelessly broadcast to a monitoring station he had set up inside a van parked nearby, giving him a constant feed of information.

Before he left, Blanchard got a good look at the locks that secured each cash machine, then headed home, ordered the same models online, and took them apart to see exactly how they worked. Just before the bank was scheduled to open to the public, he listened in on his spy equipment to make sure the ATM room was empty, then sneaked in, picked the locks just as he had practiced, subverted the alarms and dye packs, and looted $60,000—not a huge score, but a nice start. Certainly a faster, more reliable way to make money than his rehashing scams had been, although he planned to continue those as well.

Feeling the same rush he had as a kid stealing the neighbor's milk, Blanchard knew he had found his niche. "I felt guilty to a certain extent," he would say, "but my reasoning behind it at that time was I'm not hurting individuals, I'm hurting corporations."[4]

Blanchard targeted six more banks in the next few years, breaking in through the air-conditioning ducts, picking locks or blocking the infrared motion detectors with a lead film bag.[5] He also started collecting fancier toys to make his work easier: night-vision goggles, police scanners, long-range camera lenses, and powerful antennas that would pick up bank chatter from miles away. Now he not only listened in on the bank employees; he was able to monitor the authorities discussing their investigations into his robberies.

"Everybody was talking inside the ATM room about where they're going with their investigation and what they're doing, while he was outside listening and watching," said one police sergeant who would investigate Blanchard's bank robberies.[6]

Blanchard set up a dozen different bank accounts in the Caribbean under various aliases and deposited cash in each of them in $10,000 increments. Back home in Canada, he invested in real estate. In Europe, he stashed cash for emergencies. Blanchard also had a little fun creating fake VIP passes and press credentials so he could hang out with celebrities like singer Christina Aguilera, world-champion race car driver Mario Andretti, and members of the Edmonton Oilers hockey team. He developed his different personas by researching fake baptism and marriage certificates and using those to obtain a collection of driver's licenses. According to Canadian Crown attorneys, "He would even go and take the actual driving test under the alias."[7] Blanchard became so good at searching records that friends told the press he used that ingenuity to seek out and meet his biological birth mother for the very first time.

Blanchard seemed to have everything covered to allow his life of high-tech crime and deception to flourish indefinitely. But the perfectionist was about to make a fateful mistake.

In 2004, his primary target was a brand-new Canadian Imperial Bank of Commerce (CIBC) in Winnipeg, and as always, he had done his research. Not only had he rigged the bank's locks and installed a pinhole video camera and a baby monitor in the ATM room; Blanchard had staged several run-throughs in a replica of the bank's floor plan he had built in a friend's machine shop. By the night of Saturday, May 15, Blanchard knew for certain he needed only ninety seconds after the alarm sounded to take the money and run.[8]

Winnipeg was still reeling from the worst May snowstorm on record that hit the city earlier that week. The squall had dumped nearly ten inches of snow and shut down the TransCanada Highway from Winnipeg to Saskatchewan for two full days. By Saturday night, heavy thunderstorms with hail and torrential rain helped melt some of the snow but made for poor visibility and slippery driving conditions. It was not the ideal evening to stage a bank robbery, but Blanchard felt he had no choice. The bank was scheduled to open on Monday morning, and the ATM machines were filled to capacity now.

Around midnight, Blanchard picked the bank's front door lock and made his way to the cash machines. He was pleased to find the door to the ATM room already unlocked. Before him stood seven ATMs, each chock full of $100,000 in cash in anticipation of the grand opening. Blanchard sprang the drawers on six of the machines, slyly leaving the last one untouched in a pre-planned bid to confuse the authorities. He could afford to do without the extra 100K if it kept the police guessing. Blanchard set to work stacking boxes of cash totaling more than half-a-million dollars on a dolly and wheeled it out to his waiting van. As he left, he snatched the hard drives from the bank's security cameras and locked the main doors tightly behind him.

Winnipeg Police arrived on the scene around eight minutes after Blanchard opened the drawers of the first ATM. But they found the bank's doors locked just as Blanchard had left them, and nothing seemed out of place. The police had experienced plenty of false alarms in the past and figured the bank's new system had simply malfunctioned. Radioing the "all clear" to dispatch, the officers headed back to their routine patrols.

Blanchard listened in the next morning as confusion ensued at the Winnipeg bank. Just as he had anticipated, the authorities couldn't figure out why there was no visible sign of a break-in and why money had been taken from every ATM machine but one. In an effort to cause further chaos, Blanchard dialed the bank manager's cell phone as well as police dispatchers, posing as a disgruntled accomplice who had been cheated out of his share of the take. He dropped fake tips about the "suspects" and the authorities took them seriously because the caller had insider information that only someone involved in the robbery would know.[9] While authorities slowly put the pieces together and decided how to best pursue the case, Blanchard was busy choosing which of his offshore bank accounts he would use to deposit his latest haul.

Once the case file landed on his desk, Gordon Schumacher, the Winnipeg Police superintendent in charge of the Criminal Investigation Bureau, immediately assigned a team of detectives to the CIBC robbery. Schumacher had spent a lifetime on the force, joining as an eighteen-year-old, then taking a leave of absence in the mid–1990s to attend law school before continuing his police career. He didn't yet realize that this would be one of the biggest cases he would ever oversee for the Winnipeg Police Service.

"It was initially being investigated as an isolated case," Schumacher said. "Some of the investigators were having trouble seeing the depth of the file."[10]

The officers presented their boss with a brainstormed list of suspects that included traveling gypsies. That theory was dismissed when detectives uncovered the pinhole cameras and other devices that had been planted by the clever thief. At first, the officers didn't know what to make of it all.

According to Winnipeg Police Sergeant Larry Levasseur, the CIBC heist was "by far, the most planning—and commitment—I've ever seen go into a crime."[11]

Superintendent Schumacher concurred: "I'd worked organized crime investigations for a significant part of my police career and as I was hearing the briefing information it seemed very unusual. Very seldom do you see meticulous planning and surveillance."[12]

But the officers hadn't yet discerned any patterns with the CIBC crime and past Canadian bank robberies, nor did they have any suspect names to go by. As fast as the investigation had gotten underway, it was now floundering.

That might have been the end of a perfect crime had it not been for an unlikely source. An astute Walmart manager had been monitoring a shared parking lot between his store and the new bank for people who parked their cars and left them overnight, a personal pet-peeve of his. The night of the CIBC robbery, the manager had spotted a sedentary blue van and wrote down the plate number. He reported his find to the police, who didn't jump on the tip right away.

"Initially it was just information, a bit of a fluke," Schumacher said. "Basically, it was just a suspicious vehicle parked in a parking lot. So, it took a while to get the attention of the investigators."[13]

But when they finally ran the numbers, the Winnipeg Police discovered that the Dodge Caravan had been rented by one Gerald Daniel Blanchard.

VIII

"I cannot conceive how anyone can love a number of people."

—Empress Elisabeth of Austria

At twenty-eight, Sisi's physical perfectionism paid off to her utmost advantage. She was finally able to exploit her reputation as "the most beautiful woman in the world" to manipulate the emperor in favor of her greatest—indeed her *only*—political cause: Hungarian sovereignty. It seemed as though Franz Joseph was so overwhelmed by his glamorous wife, so lost in adoration and afraid she would leave him again, that he could deny her nothing. His submission was evident in his letters to Sisi during this time signed, "your faithful little husband," "your lonely little one," "your loving and adoring little man."[1]

In her book, *The Lonely Empress*, author Joan Haslip looks to the Winterhalter portrait to explain Sisi's mysterious hold on Franz Joseph:

> The artist, whom the Emperor describes as "a strange independent man," appears to have pleased the Empress, and in pleasing her succeeded in capturing on canvas her shy mysterious smile, her almost magical charm. In a vaporous white ball dress, studded with stars, and diamond stars in her hair, she appears ethereally beautiful, elusive and intangible. Looking at this portrait one understands why Francis Joseph could refuse her nothing, why wounded soldiers in hospital begged for her picture to hang above their beds, and peasants in Hungary burnt candles to her image.[2]

But just as Franz Joseph was in love with Sisi, Sisi was in love with Hungary. The empress developed such fervent feelings for the Hungarian cause in part because she related to the Magyar freedom fighters and because her mother-in-law hated the country so much. Habsburg rulers had had a tumultuous and bloody relationship with the nation since the sixteenth century, when the Austrian rulers annexed the northwestern part of the country and styled themselves kings of Hungary. To counter mass demonstrations in 1848 in which Hungarian revolutionaries vowed to secede from the monarchy, Sisi's husband Franz Joseph asked for and received military assistance from Russia's Czar Nicholas I, leading to Hungarian surrender in August 1849. Many prominent Hungarian leaders were imprisoned and executed in the aftermath. One of those sentenced to death for his part in the rebellion was radical activist Count Gyula Andrássy, but he fled to London, then Paris, and the sentence was never carried out. Andrássy returned to Budapest in the 1860s to lead the moderate liberals in favor of a more conciliatory coalition with Austria instead of outright Hungarian independence.

Sisi had learned of the dashing, politically astute Andrássy from her Hungarian tutor, Ida Ferenczy, who was a confidante of the count's. With Andrássy's prompting, Ida encouraged Sisi's fervor toward Hungarian autonomy and appealed to the empress's romantic imagination by speaking of Andrássy as the hero of a just cause. Sisi finally met the man when his delegation traveled to Vienna in 1866 and greeted him wearing a full Hungarian national costume laced with diamonds and pearls. When she spoke to Andrássy in perfect Hungarian, he knew he had a staunch ally in the Viennese court that he could manipulate for the greater good of his country.

Ida delivered countless letters and messages between the empress and Andrássy, written in code in case they were intercepted, as the two strategized for the Hungarian cause. Rumors swirled that the unhappy empress had fallen in love with the forty-two-year-old Count, who considered himself an irresistible ladies' man. True or not, Andrássy obviously stirred some sort of passion in the empress since she religiously took up the politician's position to reconcile Hungary with the Habsburgs as long as Hungary received special rights within the empire. She wrote this poem, *Oh how I could give you the king!* in 1886:

> Oh Hungary, beloved land of Hungary!
> I know thee to be in heavy chains.

Stealing Sisi's Star

How I would like to offer my hand,
To rescue you from slavery![3]

Sisi and her children fled to Hungary during the short but devastating Austro-Prussian War in 1866, and from there she repeatedly wrote to Franz Joseph, zealously promoting Hungarian liberties. In one letter, Sisi wrote "so sharply as to approximate blackmail":

... if at this hour you refuse an unselfish counsel, then you will act dishonorably toward us all; ... then whatever will happen, I have no other redress but to comfort myself with the knowledge that one day I can say to Rudolf honestly: "I did everything within my power. Your misfortune is not upon my conscience."[4]

Finally, after seemingly endless negotiations with Andrássy and other Hungarian politicians, Franz Joseph gave in to the pressures of his unrelenting wife. He signed the Austro-Hungarian Compromise of 1867, called the *Augleich*, which divided the Habsburg domains into two parts with two equal capital cities, Budapest and Vienna. Archduchess Sophie and her Viennese contingent were appalled. Sisi had been so sure of her impending victory that she had an official photograph taken wearing her coronation robes and crown as Queen of Hungary in 1866 by court photographer Emil Rabending, before the

This nineteenth century postcard depicts Sisi in her coronation regalia as Queen of Hungary, a title she cherished above all others. The official portrait painted by George Raab in 1867 was then snapped by court photographer Ludwig Angerer, and copies were sold as souvenirs. The original is on display in the empress's small salon, now the Memorial Room, at the Vienna Hofburg (author's collection).

96

Augleich was even signed.[5] With the empress's continued support, the once-condemned Andrássy went on to become president of the Hungarian cabinet from 1867–1871 and foreign minister of Austria-Hungary from 1871–79.

Hungarian tradition called for the consort to be crowned separately from the king, but plans had been changed specifically for this coronation ceremony. Perhaps because Sisi had been so instrumental in bringing about the *Augleich*, she was crowned immediately following Franz Joseph on June 8, 1867. Franz Liszt composed his coronation mass for the occasion, and the celebrations lasted for four days. Sisi considered the ceremony at St. Matthew's in Budapest to be the high point of her life, and she said she felt like much more than a queen that day; she felt like a bride. She wore a gown by Worth based on a traditional Hungarian costume made from silver brocade trimmed with lace featuring a deep blue velvet bodice and pearl lacing.

Charles Frederick Worth was the only choice to design such an important gown in 1860s Europe. An Englishman who learned the art of dressmaking in Paris, Worth was a revolutionary who would completely change the way high-society women bought their clothing. He opened his exclusive French design business in 1858 and used the finest textiles, trimmings, and English tailoring techniques to design luxurious creations that perfectly conformed to women's bodies. One of his innovations was to drape linen or muslin patterns known as toile over a woman's form to ensure a perfect fit. Only then would he choose the proper fabrics and begin to craft the actual dress. Up until that time, even women who could afford the very best had to content themselves with relatively ill-fitting gowns.

Once his clientèle began to grow, Worth required that new customers present a letter of introduction from an established client. And instead of traveling to a woman's home to discuss what she would like to have made, Worth required ladies to visit his showroom on Rue de la Paix where he would consider her overall style then decide what colors, fabrics, and cuts would look best on her. Despite this air of pretension, English writer Charles Dickens described Worth as "...a perfect gentleman, always fresh shaved, always frizzled. Black coat, white cravat, and batiste shirt-cuffs fastened at the wrists with golden buttons, he officiates with all the gravity of a diplomatist."[6]

Instead of dress forms, Worth used live models, including his wife, Marie, called *demoiselles de magasin*, and recreated a single dress design in several different fabrics and colors to give women a range of choices for particular occasions. Since he aimed only to dress wealthy society ladies, one room in Worth's shop was lit solely by gas lamps so the client could better imagine how a gown would enhance her appearance at an evening ball. Due to these innovations and many more, Worth would come to shun the title dressmaker; he considered himself an artist who composed a woman's entire look.

But Worth wasn't content with dressing the *crème de la crème* of French society; he wanted to dress royalty itself. His goal was to appeal to French Empress Eugénie, the magnetic young wife of Napoleon III, who had ushered in a new era of glamour and prosperity to the French. In order to gain her attention, he decided he needed to dress a highly-ranked woman at court. She came in the form of Princess Pauline von Metternich, wife of the Austrian ambassador. (Her husband, Richard, was son of Prince Klemens von Metternich who played a defining role in the rule of Ferdinand I.) Pauline was described as "a person of the highest nobility and a very energetic and commanding personality, who was rapidly to become a dominant figure at the French Court."[7] Before Worth, dressmakers had always been women. This fact plus further Victorian constraints on royal personages meant Worth was unable to visit the princess himself, so he sent his wife with a book of his designs. Intrigued, Pauline commissioned a ball gown that Worth then created out of expensive silk tulle in white with silver stars, a precursor to Sisi's gold-spangled gown. But Pauline insisted that she pay just 300 francs for the gown, a pittance compared to the cost of the fabric alone. Although he lost a good deal of money on the deal, the dress had the desired effect, and Empress Eugénie asked to meet with him shortly after seeing the gown on Pauline at a court ball.

By 1864, Worth was one of the personal designers to the French empress and had begun collaborating with portraitist Franz Winterhalter. The artist and the dressmaker may have planned precisely how to bring out the best in their royal subjects with the proper fashions prior to the brush touching canvas. Sisi may have learned of Worth's sublime creations through Winterhalter's portraits of Empress Eugénie and

VIII. "I cannot conceive how anyone can love a number of people."

Princess Pauline from the 1850s and 60s. According to Worth, "Elisabeth, Empress of Austria, never came to Paris, but nevertheless ordered three or four dresses every year from us."[8]

Worth may have worked with Sisi much the same way he did with Empress Eugénie. First, he would present his sketched designs to the empress's ladies-in-waiting, who would make their suggestions. Worth would update the sketches then send them on to the empress for her approval. Next, Worth would create the garment from appropriate fabric using the empress's measurements, which had been taken by her ladies. When the gown was finished, he would dress Princess Metternich or another courtier in the frock and send her out in public. If the gown was admired by other fashionable ladies, it was deemed appropriate for the empress to wear.

Sisi wouldn't actually meet Empress Eugénie until two months after the Hungarian coronation. The August 1867 gathering in Salzburg had been arranged by Pauline von Metternich, and Eugénie's ankle-length skirts, designed by Worth to prevent them from dragging on the dirty ground as floor-length frocks tended to do, became a sensation. As had become her custom, Sisi tried to claim illness so she wouldn't be forced to meet Eugénie face to face, but to no avail. Sisi predicted correctly that the two empresses would be mercilessly compared to determine who was the more beautiful or stylish. It was the kind of microscope Sisi usually strove to avoid.

Although Sisi's iconic ball gown was first seen in silver on Pauline von Metternich, Worth also created a version in midnight black for Napoleon III's mistress, the flamboyant Virginia Oldoini, Countess Castiglione. The countess had a love affair with photography and often had her picture taken while dressed up in theatrical attire with a theme, such as the "Queen of Hearts." In 1858, Worth created an ebony ball gown that transformed her into the "Queen of the Night." The Worth gala gown featured four wide sashes overlapping a solid black bell-shaped skirt, studded with gold stars and dripping with fringe. Some seven years before Sisi would become famous for the jeweled stars adorning her braided coiffure, Countess Castiglione's own braids, looped in the exact same style, displayed some fourteen individual stars that are visible in her Queen of the Night photograph taken by

Pierre-Louis Pierson. Today, the countess's dark image appears as an eerie photographic negative of the Winterhalter portrait of Sisi all in white.

———ⱲⱲ———

Despite the momentous Hungarian celebrations for the new king and queen, all was not well for the House of Habsburg that June. The family tragedies began on June 6 when the eighteen-year-old daughter of Franz Joseph's cousin Archduke Albrecht was burned to death; she had tried to conceal a lit cigarette from her disapproving father when it caught fire to her ball gown. Large crinolines—light steel bands covered with horsehair and other padding—worn under dresses to produce up to six feet of width were known to be highly flammable, and Charles Worth would soon do away with the hazard in his future designs, replacing them with smaller, backward-facing padded bustles. Then, on June 26, Sisi's sister Helene's husband died at the age of thirty-six following a battle with chronic kidney disease. And on June 30, the imperial family finally learned of the execution of Franz Joseph's brother, Maximilian.

Maximilian had been in dire political straits since being crowned Emperor of Mexico just three years earlier. His nascent regime had been encouraged and backed only by French Emperor Napoleon III, who wished to establish a French foothold in the Americas, and remained unrecognized by the United States and many European governments. Empress Charlotte, who had been initially sent off to Mexico with trunks full of day dresses and ball gowns designed by Worth, had returned to Europe to plead for assistance for her husband. Maximilian was facing radical opposition from democratic reformer Benito Juárez and his followers. But her efforts failed, France abandoned Maximilian, and he was executed by firing squad just eleven days after the Hungarian coronation. Charlotte suffered a mental breakdown while trying to recruit military support and was reportedly never told of Maximilian's violent demise. She was eventually declared insane and lived the rest of her life in seclusion. After learning of Max's violent death, Archduchess Sophie refused

VIII. "I cannot conceive how anyone can love a number of people."

to travel to Salzburg with Sisi and Franz Joseph to meet with the French emperor and empress. Sophie considered them to be complicit in Max's assassination for failing to come to his rescue.

Despite the periods of mourning that went on for the lost family members, things were looking up for the Austro-Hungarian imperial marriage. Sisi had undoubtedly used her allure to convince Franz Joseph to accede to her demands for Hungarian autonomy, and she may also have blatantly used sex. It is highly possible that Sisi hadn't slept with her husband since Crown Prince Rudolf's conception in late 1857, some ten years earlier. Sisi obviously agreed to return to the marriage bed around the time Franz Joseph conceded to her demands regarding Hungary, with the evidence in the form of their fourth child, Archduchess Marie Valerie. She was born just ten months after the imperial couple were crowned King and Queen of Hungary. Two years after the baby was born, Sisi and Franz Joseph officially moved into separate bedrooms, and the emperor was forced to ring a bell to announce himself before visiting his wife's apartments.

Sisi insisted on giving birth to her baby in Hungary, where no royal child had been born for hundreds of years. The Viennese courtiers whispered that Count Andrássy was the child's true father, but those notions were permanently dispelled as Marie Valerie grew to look more and more like Franz Joseph. Back in Vienna, the court was relieved at the birth of a girl. According to Sisi biographer Brigitte Hamann, a boy could have caused serious implications for the future of the dual monarchy, as he would have the possibility of being crowned king of a future breakaway Hungary. But the birth of a girl nullified talk of true Hungarian independence, and the future of a stable Austria-Hungary seemed intact.

Courtiers secretly referred to Sisi's youngest daughter as the "only child," since Sisi seemed to suddenly develop a new fervor for parenting, much to the detriment of her other two living children. She insisted on speaking to Marie Valerie only in Hungarian in an effort to coerce her daughter to love the country as much as she did. Sisi's efforts backfired, however, as they caused Marie Valerie to feel alienated from her father, brother, and sister, who spoke German to one another. But Sisi wasn't willing to share; she regarded Marie Valerie as her very own, the one child that her mother-in-law couldn't take away from her, and this ardent passion threatened to smother the young archduchess. Sisi wrote, "Now I know what happiness a child means—now I have shown the courage to bestow her with my love and keep her by me."[9]

Throughout her life, Marie Valerie admitted to feeling overwhelmed by her mother's affections and embarrassed that neither Gisela nor Rudolf received the same attention. In her diary, Marie Valerie referred to her mother's "vast, indeed crushing, love" and she recorded Sisi's fanatical words:

> I really love nobody but you. If you leave me my life is at an end. One can only love like this once in one's life. All one's thoughts are of the beloved one, it is entirely one-sided—one requires and expects nothing from the other person. And for that reason I cannot conceive how anybody can love a number of people.[10]

As the years passed, however, not even her beloved Hungary or youngest daughter could keep Sisi in one place for long. The empress resumed her wanderings in the 1870s, traveling all over Europe, England, and Ireland. Thanks to the empire's railway companies, Sisi traveled in style. They gifted the empress a luxurious set of coaches consisting of a saloon car and a sleeping compartment that boasted all of the modern conveniences: electric lighting, steam heating, a wash basin and a lavatory.

Sisi's absences were now being actively perceived by her children. Highly intelligent and precocious at twelve years old, Rudolf wrote a letter to Archduchess Sophie that was possibly meant to pander to her own thoughts on the matter: "So in these difficult days poor Papa must be separated again from darling Mama. I am only too happy to accept the noble duty of being the sole support of my dear Papa."[11]

Franz Joseph compliantly financed Sisi's extravagances, tripling her allowance to 300,000 florins ($3,440,850) a year with another two million florins ($22,939,000) as capital to purchase art and thoroughbreds. Her entourage included some ninety people, yet Sisi thought she was being deceptive by traveling under one of her lesser titles, such as the Countess of Hohenembs, so as not to draw public attention. Despite her best efforts, it wasn't unusual for news stories of the day to begin, "The Empress of Austria, traveling incognito..."[12] or "The Empress of Austria, traveling under the incognito title of Countess of Palfry..."[13] No matter how much Sisi tried to stay under the radar, onlookers always tracked her down. The one person who never seemed to catch up with her was her husband, who rarely saw his wife anymore.

Sisi's eldest daughter, Gisela, announced in 1872 that she would wed another Wittelsbach, her second cousin Prince Leopold of Bavaria. Gisela was just fifteen, the same age Sisi had been when she was betrothed. Sisi had spoken disparagingly of marriage at such a young age, calling it "a ridiculous institution. When I think of myself, sold as a child of fifteen and taking an oath which I did not understand and could never undo."[14] On Sisi's urging, the family agreed to extend the engagement for one year. Archduchess Sophie was thrilled with the idea of another Wittelsbach-Habsburg match regardless of the bride's age, but Sophie's health would fade before she had the opportunity to witness her granddaughter take her vows. At the age of sixty-seven, Sophie developed a consuming cough that severely weakened her until it became apparent she would not recover. It was Sisi herself—the defiant daughter-in-law of years past—who sat vigil for eighteen hours beside the dying Archduchess until Sophie breathed her last on May 28, 1872.

Gisela married one year later and would go on to give birth to four children. She was not a pretty girl, which may have been part of the reason Sisi was never close to her, but Gisela was philanthropic and much loved by the people of Schwabing in northern Munich, where she lived with her family at Palais Leopold. During World War I, Gisela turned her palace into a military hospital and became known as "The Good Angel from Vienna." Gisela's marriage was also successful, and she celebrated her golden wedding anniversary in 1923.

Sisi did not enjoy visits to Gisela's growing family, writing to Ida Ferenczy how glad she was when another day was over and how bitter and lonely she felt in her eldest daughter's company. When Gisela's second daughter was born, Sisi wrote to Rudolf, "The child of Gizela [sic] is unusually ugly, but amuses Valerie..."[15] Rudolf was especially close to Gisela since both had been so outwardly neglected by their mother while she lavished attention on Marie Valerie. Sisi's cruel words must have hurt him deeply, and he probably never shared them with his favorite sister.

The Vienna World's Fair of 1873 featured Emperor Franz Joseph promoting the arts, technology, and industry. The emperor was a stickler for military discipline and duty, and never could relate to Sisi's sensitive nature. Nonetheless, he stood in awe of his wife's beauty, denied her nothing, and always referred to her as "my angel" (Library of Congress Prints and Photographs Division, George Grantham Bain Collection).

Franz Joseph was exceedingly grateful to his normally flighty wife for her dedication to his mother at her deathbed. She proved that she could be supportive and dependable when she wanted to be. Thinking she was now more amenable to official duty, Franz Joseph asked Sisi to accompany him on a trip to Russia in February 1874 to discuss Austria-Hungary's Balkan policies, but once again, Sisi declined to support her husband. She was apparently annoyed that the imperial family would be gone from Vienna for the pre–Lenten festivities, and it was then that she and her Hungarian reader, Ida Ferenczy, hatched a plan to attend *Karneval* in disguise.

Sisi had just become a grandmother at the age of thirty-six and perhaps felt the need for some youthful excitement. On the last day of carnival when the entire household was asleep, Sisi and Ida secretly arose and dressed for the masked ball. Sisi donned a loose, cloak-like domino fashioned from heavy yellow brocade along with an auburn wig and mask. Her name for the evening would be "Gabrielle." Once at the ball, Sisi pointed out an elegant young man and requested that Ida escort him up to the gallery where the empress was observing the festivities. Assuming he had no idea who she was, Sisi began to cautiously flirt with the handsome stranger and ask his feelings on the emperor and empress and the politics of court life. Sisi learned his name, Fritz Pascher, and that he was a twenty-six-year-old civil servant. She also obtained his mailing address and wrote him coquettish letters for weeks following the ball ("Are you dreaming of me at this moment, or are your songs full of longing going forth into the stilly night?"),[16] always signed "Gabrielle" with a return address of the General Post Office in London. Sisi's sister Marie in England played along and collected Pascher's return letters, posting them on to Vienna. Sisi naively believed that Pascher never knew her true identity, and like a perfect gentleman, he never exposed the empress's secret in her lifetime. Pascher finally shared the letters with Sisi biographer Count Egon Corti shortly before his death in 1934.

The clandestine yellow domino affair ended as abruptly as it had started, and Sisi fondly tucked the romantic encounter away in her memory. She wandered from country to country for another five years until she decided to come through for the emperor once again. In 1879, the now forty-two-year-old empress returned to Vienna at her husband's request for the imperial couple's silver wedding anniversary celebrations. She would pull out all of the glamorous stops for the three-day event, and the ruby jewelry she wore would become the object of another mysterious disappearance along with a full set of diamond Sisi Stars, some eighty years before Gerald Blanchard would steal the last remaining Köchert Diamond Pearl.

IX

"The diamonds and rubies … sparkle like fire."

—Journalist's account of Sisi's ruby parure

By 1879, Sisi had a lamentable reputation for canceling appearances due to illness or simply because she felt her hair wasn't cooperating that day. The Viennese called this "shamming sick," and the term was closely associated with their empress. But the imperial couple's silver wedding anniversary was a different occasion altogether. Franz Joseph had implored his wife to support him for this extravagant, three-day event, and she had agreed, although she wasn't happy about it: "It's already enough to have been married for twenty-five years without also having to celebrate the fact," she complained.[1]

Despite her true feelings, Sisi appeared as a vision of royal grandeur and acted the gracious monarch, standing for hours and accepting congratulations from countless ambassadors. The highlight of the celebration was an evening court ball at the imperial palace with 5,000 guests. The empress was radiant and glittered with jewels, as recorded by journalists:

> The empress's outfit was charming. The monarch wore a pearl-grey, high atlas dress with a white gauze plaid and long train. Rich embroidery adorns the robe. The train displayed elaborately stitched palm leaves. The diamonds and rubies on the vest sparkle like fire. The empress wore the same stones in her belt and in her necklet, comprised of three rows of diamonds and rubies. The tiara also had alternating large diamonds and rubies.[2]

The forty-two-year-old Sisi's appearance that evening was immortalized by painter Georg Raab and became the last portrait for which she ever sat. (The very last likeness for which she sat was a bust depicting her as Queen of Hungary created that same year by sculptor Victor Tilgner.) The Raab painting is arguably the most famous portrait of Sisi

besides the Winterhalter ball gown painting created fourteen years earlier. In the Raab likeness, the empress wore her hair long and flowing down her back with the ruby tiara at her crown and a light crop of fringe peek-ing out beneath. She also donned a matching ruby necklet and wrist corsage. The jewelry set called a *parure* was part of the Austrian Crown Jewels. As such, they belonged to the empire and would be passed on to the next empress; they were not Sisi's to bequeath as the Sisi Stars were.

The parure's origins dated to 1770, when then Austrian Empress Maria Theresa gifted it to her daughter Marie-Antoinette (Franz Joseph's great-aunt) for her ill-fated marriage to future French King Louis XVI. Before her arrest and ultimate beheading, Marie-Antoinette gathered up her jewelry in the presence of her lady-in-waiting, Madame Campan,

Nineteenth century souvenir postcard features George Raab's painting, *Empress Elisabeth with Ruby Jewelry*, for her silver wedding anniversary in 1879. As part of the crown jewels, the ruby set passed to Sisi's successor, Zita, but disappeared under mysterious circumstances as the Habsburg dynasty crumbled. The original portrait is in the Hofburg's Sisi Museum (author's collection).

who recalled in her memoirs: "Her Majesty shut herself up with me in a closet in the entresol, looking into the garden of the Tuileries, and we packed all the diamonds, rubies, and pearls she possessed in a small chest."[3] The story goes that the jewelry chest was sent to the care of Marie-Antoinette's nephew, Austrian Emperor Francis II, in Vienna for safekeeping. But when the French queen's daughter traveled to Austria to reclaim the gems, she found they had already been added to the Habsburg collection of crown jewels.

After Sisi's death, the ruby parure remained safely locked away with the rest of the crown jewels until the fall of the House of Habsburg in 1918. Before that year, however, the succession had passed to several potential heirs. First, Franz Joseph's brother, Karl Ludwig, was named heir after Rudolf's death, but he treasured his carefree life as an archduke devoid of many responsibilities and harbored no ambition for the crown. Karl Ludwig was expected to step aside in favor of his son, Franz Ferdinand, if Emperor Franz Joseph died first. But Karl Ludwig was the first to go; he contracted typhoid and died while on a pilgrimage to the Holy Land. This opened the door for Archduke Franz Ferdinand to officially become heir presumptive, meaning that as long as Emperor Franz Joseph had no further legitimate sons, the throne would go to him.

Franz Ferdinand immediately began acting the part of heir apparent, attending official engagements and state visits along with the emperor. But the more time he spent with his nephew, the more Franz Joseph grew troubled over Franz Ferdinand's anger issues and prejudices against the diverse nationalities that made up the Austro-Hungarian Empire, especially the Magyars of Hungary. Franz Joseph had a difficult time picturing the future of his empire under his nephew's rule. In addition, Franz Ferdinand was known to have weak lungs and suffered from tuberculosis, a fact that left the fifty-nine-year-old Emperor wondering if his nephew would even live to succeed him.

Franz Ferdinand then caused great consternation for the emperor by insisting on marrying a woman beneath his station: Bohemian aristocrat Countess Sophie Chotek. Since she was not from a reigning dynasty of Europe and not entitled to marry a Habsburg Archduke, Franz Joseph refused to attend the wedding and stipulated that it would be a morganatic marriage, precluding Sophie from enjoying the same rights and privileges as her husband. This meant she would be unable to appear beside him at court functions, would never hold the title empress, and would never see their eldest son succeed to the throne.

Things would never progress that far, however. On June 28, 1914, Yugoslav national Serb Gavrilo Princip assassinated both Franz Ferdinand and Sophie as their motorcade wound through the streets of Sarajevo. It was the second attempt on the Austrian heir's life that day; earlier, a political radical had lobbed a grenade at the car, but the bomb had missed its intended target. Princip shot the couple dead as they drove to the local hospital to console those who had been injured in the initial grenade attack.

Although shocked and saddened by his nephew's violent death, Franz Joseph admitted to his daughter, Marie Valerie, "For me it is a relief from a great worry."[4] Franz Joseph had far greater confidence in his grand-nephew Karl and began to initiate him into affairs of state. When Franz Joseph died in 1916 at the age of 86, Karl became the last emperor of Austro-Hungary, inheriting not only the crown jewels, but a world war as well. His wife, Zita, the new empress, was bequeathed a full set of diamond Sisi Stars that were most likely created by jewelers Rozet & Fischmeister and left to her in Franz Joseph's will.

Karl was condemned by his critics for being far too weak and politically inept to handle such a devastating conflict. Even his chief of staff complained, "He can't even write properly," while one of his advisers griped, "He is 30 years old, looks 20, and thinks like a 10-year-old."[5] Despite the naysayers, Karl was said to be a very moral and pious man. According to one of his relatives, "If one does not know how to pray, he can learn from this young gentleman."[6]

Morality is tricky in warfare, and Karl may best be remembered for turning his back on the Germans during World War I and secretly trying to broker a separate peace with France. When the subterfuge was discovered, Karl denied any involvement. But the French prime minister published letters signed by the Austrian Emperor as proof, and Karl was forever branded a liar.

As the empire collapsed around him, Karl refused to abdicate but agreed to "renounce participation in state affairs" on Armistice Day, November 11, 1918. His dream was to one day return to Vienna to reclaim

KAISER FRANZ JOSEPH

Franz Joseph attended the wedding of his grand-nephew Karl and bride, Princess Zita of Bourbon and Parma, on Oct. 21, 1911. The emperor had not attended the morganatic marriage of his heir, Franz Ferdinand, to Countess Sophie Chotek. When Franz Ferdinand and his wife were assassinated in 1914, Karl became the new heir apparent. Karl and Zita ascended to the throne when Franz Joseph died in 1916 (Library of Congress Prints and Photographs Division, George Grantham Bain Collection).

the throne. But for now, he took his growing family, the ruby parure, a full set of diamond Sisi Stars, and the Hungarian coronation jewels with him into exile. The family stopped first in Switzerland, then finally on to Madeira—the Portuguese Island where Sisi first sought refuge as a young wife. In her memoirs, Karl's wife, Empress Zita, insisted that the jewels were stolen on Madeira. But a Swiss jeweler told a very different story.

In his memoirs, Alphonse de Sondheimer claimed that while in Switzerland, Karl contacted the gem dealer with the intention of selling the jewels because he never received the 20,000 ($1,374,118) yearly stipend he was promised by the Western powers. Sondheimer described the jewelry in detail and said the sets were broken up and the gems sold individually to finance the imperial family's life in exile. Sadly for Karl, that life did not last long; he died of respiratory failure at thirty-four in Madeira, where he was also buried.

Although he tried to reclaim the Hungarian throne twice, Karl never became emperor or king again. Yet in death, the Vatican sought to bestow on him a new title: that of saint. Despite authorizing the use of poison gas during World War I, the church considered the exiled emperor to be a great pacifist and the only leader during the Great War to pursue peace, e.g., the separate peace debacle with France. Then in 1960, a miracle was credited to Karl when a crippled nun in Brazil prayed for his beatification and awakened able to walk for the first time in years. In 2008, a church tribunal recognized a second miracle attributed to Blessed Karl, whereby a Florida woman who prayed for his intercession was cured of terminal cancer. With two miracles now attributed to Karl, the path is clear for the pope to declare him a saint.

Shortly after Karl's death, Zita gave birth to a baby girl whom she named Elisabeth, after her predecessor on the Austrian throne. Zita now had eight children to look after with no country to call home and little money to the Habsburg name. The young family bounced from the politically unstable Spain to Belgium, where her eldest son, Crown Prince Otto, would attend university.

In 1933, there was talk of a Habsburg restoration with Zita positioning her family as a beacon of hope against the rising National Socialist German Workers' Party and their boisterous leader, Adolf Hitler. Zita decreed that any European power against fascism must support the imperial restoration. But in March 1938, all hopes of a Habsburg reclaiming the throne were dashed when Hitler invaded and annexed Austria in what was called the *Anschluss*. Shortly thereafter, the Nazis issued a warrant for Otto's arrest for the crime of high treason. Once Great Britain declared war on Germany and the Nazis moved to take Belgium, Zita and her children fled to France, then Spain, before settling in North America. There, Zita released a strongly-worded statement against the Nazis: "The empress, who holds firmly to the cause of democracy in Europe, is convinced that freedom and Christianity will triumph over barbaric totalitarianism."[7]

Zita was right; the Allies prevailed, but the Habsburg restoration would remain just a dream. She spent the years following World War II advocating for Austria to be declared a Nazi occupied state and not a collaborator. Finally, due to her incessant lobbying, Austria received monetary support for rebuilding through the Marshall Plan. Zita eventually settled back in Europe, calling Luxembourg and then Switzerland home. In 1982, the ninety-year-old Zita was granted one of her greatest wishes: permission from the Austrian government to return from exile. She traveled back to her former homeland several times over the next few years.

Zita maintained her right to the Austrian throne until the day she died in Switzerland in 1989, at the age of ninety-six. Her body was taken to Vienna, where she was interred in the imperial Habsburg crypt as "Zita, Her Majesty the Empress and Queen." In 2008, the Vatican's Congregation for the Causes of Saints opened the beatification process for the last Empress of Austria. Zita and Karl's first-born son, Otto, was buried in the Habsburg crypt in 2011. He is expected to be the last Habsburg ever to be interred there.

The ruby parure worn by Sisi and secreted away by Zita exists today only as a Swarovski crystal reproduction on display in the Hofburg's Sisi Museum. Replicas of the diamond Sisi Stars Zita inherited, as well as the Köchert design with pearls, are available in the museum gift shop, a fact not lost on Gerald Blanchard.

X

"It's only priceless
if you have to have it."

—Schönbrunn Palace Director Franz Sattlecker

The tour guide leading Gerald Blanchard and his wife around Schönbrunn Palace said the Köchert Diamond Pearl was priceless. But when it comes to imperial jewelry, "priceless" is a subjective term. Schönbrunn Palace Director Franz Sattlecker defined the word this way: "Priceless? Well, there's a sentimental value because of Elisabeth," he said following the theft in 1998. "But it's only priceless if you have to have it."[1] Austria definitely had to have it back.

Not only was the Sisi Star of historical importance and national pride, there was also the private owner to consider—the one who had lent it to the museum for the display commemorating the empress's assassination. According to palace officials, the Köchert Diamond Pearl did, in fact, have a price—it had been insured for $9,500. Unfortunately, we don't know how much Sisi originally paid when she commissioned the Köchert Stars. We do know that price was never an object for the empress.

When they were first married, Franz Joseph gifted his new bride a gift of 100,000 florins ($1,130,000) in addition to the $240,000 "morning gift." She also received 100,000 florins yearly from the treasury for "costumes, hats, and other small purchases."[2] Her toilette of beauty preparations alone cost 20,000 to 30,000 florins a year ($226,000 to $339,000). Franz Joseph also gifted Sisi a magnificent jewel case, approximately four-feet across, designed in the shape of a castle and encrusted with semi-precious gemstones. It came up for sale in a New Orleans auction

114

X. *"It's only priceless if you have to have it."*

house in the twenty-first century and was reportedly valued at between $300,000 and $1,000,000.

Then, in 1875, the abdicated Emperor Ferdinand I died, leaving his vast fortune to his nephew, Franz Joseph. Ferdinand's financial advisers had tucked his personal funds safely away, refusing to invest in the stock market. It turned out to be a wise move, and Ferdinand's money remained intact even after the stock market crash of 1873. Overnight, Franz Joseph became one of the wealthiest rulers in Europe, telling his assistant. "From now I am a rich man."[3]

And yet, despite the lavish gifts and allowances, Sisi never seemed to have enough. Again and again, throughout their marriage, Sisi asked Franz Joseph for more money, and he always complied. After her death, it was learned that Sisi had hidden away a fortune of millions of florins that no one knew about. It seemed she was convinced, as her son had been, that one day the empire would fall, forcing her into exile. She wanted to be prepared.

Following the short but costly 1866 Austro-Prussian War (it lasted just two months, nine days, although it was called the Seven Weeks' War), the Austrian government started drastically cutting costs; written decrees were shortened so they could be issued on single sheets of paper, envelopes were turned inside-out and used more than once, and even army coats were tailored to be single-, not double-breasted, in order to save cloth and buttons.

As a good faith measure, Franz Joseph cut back on family expenses. He announced that the imperial household must lead by example, before slashing the Hofburg's food budget. Franz Joseph wrote to his wife in Hungary, imploring her to be more frugal and asking her not to buy the 136-room Gödöllő Palace. Gödöllő would eventually be gifted to the imperial couple as a coronation present by the Hungarians, but at the time it was being used as a military hospital for soldiers wounded in Königgraz, the decisive battle of the Austro-Prussian War.

If you wish, go to Gödöllő and pay a visit to the wounded. But don't inspect it as if you were considering purchasing it. I have no money at present and in these hard times we have to be very saving. Even our family estates are terribly devastated by the Prussians and it will take years before they can recover. For next year I have reduced the court budget to five mil-

115

lion, which necessitates a cut of two million. Almost half the stable must be sold. We must live modestly.

Your sad little fellow[4]

But Sisi was unfazed by his plea. She was not about to give up her lifestyle, especially not her beloved horses. Once Gödöllő was formally presented to the imperial couple, Sisi created a palace riding school where she took her equestrian passion to new heights, deciding that the world's most beautiful empress-queen would also become the world's best horsewoman. Sisi's hunting stable consisted of twenty-six of the finest thoroughbreds, and she hired the most accomplished riding instructors to teach her *haute école*, or classical dressage, whereby the horse and rider perform a series of jumps and ballet-like movements in tandem. She also learned circus stunts and took part in steeplechases and fox hunts with other members of the Hungarian aristocracy. It was understood that "with the Empress of Austria hunting and horse-riding is not the least a fashion, but a passion."[5]

As always, vanity took precedence even when riding. Sisi had herself stitched into her riding costumes to ensure a perfect fit, and in the words of her niece, Countess Marie Larisch, "her costume looked as if it had been moulded to her." In addition, Sisi wore high, laced boots with spurs and three pairs of gloves to protect her hands from chafing on the reins. Her most important feature, her hair, "lay in heavy plaits upon her head, above which she wore a top hat."[6]

Not everyone appreciated Sisi's trend-setting look, however. According to one newspaper columnist:

> One fault only has this illustrious huntress. She sets a bad example in her costume. She does not paint, she does not dye her beautiful hair, but she insists on having her habits made so tight that her imitators wonder how she can breathe at full gallop. They cannot, and are obliged to moderate their pace or let out their corsets or habit bodies.[7]

Despite her restrictive costume, Sisi rode hard and was often one of the few to finish a fox or stag hunt, leaving dozens of talented male equestrian experts in her wake.

It took a vast amount of preparation for a country to host the empress for her lengthy riding vacations. For one winter trip to Ireland in 1878 that was to last six weeks, planning began in late summer with the securing of a residence fine enough to host an empress with her forty tons of luggage and ninety-person entourage.

The *Irish Times* reported,

We understand there was great difficulty in producing a suitable hunting residence in Ireland for her Imperial Majesty, for although there are several fine mansions within the desired area, the owners were not to be tempted "by woman or gold." It so happened, however, that it suited the noble proprietor of Summerhill to dispense with the use of his princely abode for a time.[8]

Lord Lanford at Summerhill, County Meath, finally agreed to lend his home, and the Empress graciously allowed him to remain in residence along with her retinue. One room of the mansion was turned into a chapel for her daily prayers, while a telegraph was installed so she could communicate directly with Franz Joseph in Vienna. Stables also had to be procured, with a Mr. Danbar eventually loaning his. The empress's thoroughbreds and carriage horses were shipped ahead of time, as were several members of her household to make final preparations for Sisi's arrival in January. Each of Sisi's hunters was valued by the contemporary British press at £500 ($69,138), and many of them would perish on the dangerous steeplechase course.

For one trip to England, the Crown also paid for tanks of Welsh seawater to be delivered each day for Sisi's baths meant to reduce the pain of sciatica and swollen joints that became a hazard of her hard riding and meager dining. The empress knew no moderation on her hunting excursions; in one trip alone she managed to hunt for twenty-two out of thirty days. Just one of her English voyages was documented at having cost 106,516 florins ($1,203,000) while one trip to Ireland cost 158,337 florins ($1,789,000).

The Crown did not have to pay much for Sisi's food, however, since during these riding trips, she ate like a jockey: A typical day consisted of a cup of tea and a biscuit early in the morning, a mug of beef broth and an egg for lunch, and at dinner, chilled milk with egg whites whipped in port.

For safety, Franz Joseph stipulated that Sisi's groom, a man named Bayzand, should always ride beside her on these excursions. But Sisi broke that rule in 1876, when she replaced her captain of the hunt with a rugged redhead named George "Bay" Middleton. Middleton was equerry to England's Fifth Earl Spencer, who asked him to pilot the empress during rides at the country estate at Althorp, the same estate that would one day become home to Lady Diana Spencer. At first, Middleton refused, telling the earl, "What is an empress to me? How can I look after her? I'll do it, of course, but I'd rather go my own way."[9]

But after matching him jump for jump over the course fences and even plunging into a ditch before remounting her horse, Sisi won the seasoned horseman over. Middleton led the Empress on nearly every British Isle hunt over the next five years, sometimes forcibly preventing her from taking jumps he felt were too dangerous, much to her consternation. He even attended the empress at the Gödöllő hunting course where he was the guest of honor at Sisi's dinner parties.

Lady-in-waiting Marie Festetics wrote in her diary of the danger of Sisi's riding:

> The drops are so high, the ditches and Doubles so deep and also the Irish banks and walls and God knows what else to break your hand, foot and neck. Never do I hear so much about broken limbs as here and every day I see somebody carried … really, my hair often stands on end.[10]

Middleton, who was nine years younger, was said to have fallen in love with the daring and elegant empress. Although she enjoyed flirting with the horseman and relished his attention, she never acted on any feelings she may have had toward him. Yet, she did act with a certain sentimentally when Middleton announced he would marry the wealthy Charlotte Baird, possibly to pay for the exorbitant sums he had racked up piloting the empress all those years. Following their final hunt together in 1882, Sisi held a private dinner for Middleton and spent several minutes alone with him before presenting him with a ring to remember her by. Only after she had finally lost Middleton's attentions to a younger woman and was racked with sciatica pain from years of hard riding and falls did the forty-four-year-old Sisi decide to give up riding for good. The passion that propelled her over dangerous courses and through demanding dressage routines had finally abandoned her.

During the five years of hunting and reckless spending, Count Franz Folliot de Crenneville, commander of the Austrian Gardes du Corps Regiment in Vienna, expressed his dismay at Sisi's extravagances and the emperor's refusal to put his foot down:

X. "It's only priceless if you have to have it."

I do not understand how, at this time of general hardship, it is possible to think of a trip to Ireland, and how she can be allowed to do it. What an effect would it have made if the expenses of the trip … had been distributed to the monarchy's aid organizations, how much hunger would have been assuaged, how many blessings would heaven have sent the benefactress? Has the master renounced all influence, all power to express a veto in his position?[11]

But Sisi understood little about the value of money and may not have fully grasped such criticisms. Countess Festetics wrote a diary entry illustrating the fact: While on an excursion to Pest, Sisi asked the countess if she had any money. Marie replied, "Not very much, twenty florins ($226)." To which Sisi answered, "But that is a great deal." The two walked to Kugler's, a world-famous Hungarian confectioner, to buy candy for Sisi's favorite daughter, Marie Valerie. Once there, Sisi picked item after item until a very large parcel was wrapped up for her. When she asked if the purchase would cost twenty florins, the startled shopkeeper answered that it was more like 150 ($1,695).[12]

Sisi's extravagances caught the attention of both the foreign press and the burgeoning German Socialist Party. One working-class merchant wrote to the empress, complaining that he could finance his entire business on what she spent in just one day.[13]

And yet, despite her lavish spending, Sisi considered herself an anti-aristocratic liberal and champion of the people. She seemed to have a promising common touch when, as a sixteen-year-old new to the throne, she met with delegates and petitioners from Germany's Ore Mountains. According to the *Wiener Zeitung* newspaper:

… when the President movingly described the poverty of the mountain people, the beautiful eyes of the lovely sovereign filled with tears, and Her Majesty was hardly able to master her inner emotion. What a deeply affecting impression this new proof of her angelic gentleness had on those present is indescribable, it was a solemn moment.[14]

Sisi used this ability to connect with commoners sporadically throughout her reign. Death and insanity fascinated her, and she was known to visit injured soldiers and insane asylum patients. When in London, she visited Bethlehem Hospital, which is most famously known by its slang name "Bedlam," England's first hospital for the mentally ill.

Her Majesty, after seeing over the different wards, and having had explained to her the different regulations governing the institution, expressed her admiration at the care bestowed upon the unfortunate persons confined there. Her Majesty's visit to the hospital extended over two hours, and she made a thorough scrutiny into all the arrangements.[15]

Much to her ladies' horror, Sisi also visited the poor souls dying of dehydration due to cholera infection at a Munich hospital. At the time, little was understood of the disease, which modern medicine says is spread through contaminated food and drinking water and very rarely from person to person. In the nineteenth century, public health officials believed cholera to be a disease of the poor and morally depraved. To prevent further infections, they advised against drunkenness, urged people to "sweep out their rooms daily and wash the floors at least twice a week," and to "leave the windows of their bedrooms open during the whole of the day."[16] Instead of encouraging rehydration, doctors of the day often turned to opium or bleeding to treat patients already showing symptoms of severe diarrhea and vomiting.

After greeting and offering kind words to the cholera patients she encountered, the empress returned home to change her clothes, bathe, and dispose of her gloves. But panic ensued at the palace a few days later when Sisi complained of not feeling well. Several tense days passed before the empress fully recovered, and her "courageous, selfless act" was noted throughout the city. The emperor, however, gently admonished his wife for taking such a risk.

Sisi also took up women's causes, specifically the appalling conditions of working women in Vienna. Austria experienced a great economic boom in the late 1840s to 1870s, referred to as its *Gründerzeit,* or industrial revolution. The population of Vienna would more than double in those years from 440,000 to 900,000, and factories sprang up throughout the city. Housing shortages and low wages crushed the lower classes, and the average life expectancy for laborers was just thirty-three.

Sisi wrote to one government minister, "My heart bleeds when I think of the misery of those poor women and girls, who work like the slaves of ancient times, without ever being able to earn enough to feed themselves properly." In the competitive Vienna embroidery trade, women ruined their fingers and eyesight by sewing thousands of stitches per square inch for twelve to fifteen hours a day to produce the finest embroidered cloth in the world. They earned no more than one hundred eighty florins a year ($2,000). And in the brick-making and house-building trades, Sisi wrote to officials, "They are obliged to draw carts filled with great loads of mortar, to carry heavy buckets up the scaffolds, and to endure cold and heat during a working day of sixteen to seventeen hours, labouring away as true martyrs up to a motherhood that brings them no joy and allows them no rest."[17]

According to biographer Brigitte Hamann, Sisi's "liberalism ... anti-clericalism, her enthusiasm for the constitutional state ... was the antithesis of the demands for divine right, absolutism, and aristocratic thinking espoused by Archduchess Sophie."[18] Thus, unlike her mother-in-law, Sisi was "for the little people" in theory, but the empress certainly enjoyed the lifestyle her rank afforded her and never seemed willing to live by example.

Around 1888, at the age of fifty-one, Sisi first wrote Franz Joseph about starting her most expensive project to date: building the Achilleion Palace on the Greek Island of Corfu. Sisi ardently admired Greek culture and fluently spoke both ancient and modern Greek, thanks to years of study on her long walks and while her hair was being dressed. She also loved the weather and the stunning seascape that Corfu offered. Sisi had the palace built on Corfu's highest point and designed it with the mythical hero Achilles as its main theme. Neptune was also represented in the form of a dolphin wearing the Austrian imperial crown. This became Sisi's new emblem, and all of the place settings, furnishings and stationery were marked with the image. She called her new palace, "my sanctuary, where I may belong to me."[19]

Sisi commissioned a famous German sculptor to surround the palace with works depicting Greek mythology and hoped the finished product would represent "a royal palace of the golden age of the Phaeacians" as mentioned in Homer's *Odyssey*.[20] In the elaborate gardens, not finished until after her son's suicide in 1889, she built a monument to Crown Prince Rudolf as well as a temple to Heinrich Heine. The entire project cost Franz Joseph millions—up to five million dollars ($125,000,000) according to one contemporary American newspaper report. Knowing well the Viennese opinion of the empress as a reckless spendthrift and neglectful monarch, Franz Joseph paid for the construction out of his own pocket instead of public funds in order to avoid a scandal.

Heinrich Heine had become an obsession by this time in Sisi's life and was a dominant subject of conversation when she met with Romanian Queen Elisabeth, an award-winning writer who went by the literary name of Carmen Sylva. Carmen's writing career was prolific: She published poems, plays, novels, short stories, and essays in German, Romanian, French, and English. She was particularly well-known for her aphorisms like this one that could easily have applied to Sisi's life: "Duty knits her brow only when you fly from her. Follow her, and she smiles."[21]

Carmen Sylva was one of the few people outside of Sisi's inner circle whom the Austrian empress trusted enough to discuss subjects that were particularly important to her. While visiting the Romanian spa town of Băile Herkulesbad, Carmen told Sisi that she no longer admired Heine because she found some of his more cynical poems to be disturbing. But the Romanian queen understood Sisi's fascination with the German poet because she believed they both shared a bitterness and despair of the world's duplicity. The next morning after their conversation, Sisi swore that Heine's apparition had visited her in her bedroom overnight and had initiated a struggle to draw her spirit from her body. When the vision faded, Sisi said she was disappointed that she remained alive but was still grateful to God because, "He sanctioned the intercourse between my soul and that of Heine."[22] Sisi enjoyed time spent with Carmen and visited her several times during her lifetime but felt that the Romanian queen could never fully understand her true nature. As it turns out, Carmen Sylva was far more perceptive than Sisi allowed.

"People have tried to harness the fairies' child," Carmen said of Sisi, "to the torture of etiquette and still, dead forms, but the fairies' child cannot endure bolts and bars, restraint and servitude. The fairies' child has hidden wings, which it spreads and flies away whenever it finds the world unbearable."[23]

During one of Sisi's flights to Greece, perhaps in a bold attempt to reclaim her life and body as her own, Sisi had the image of a ship's anchor tattooed on her shoulder. Tattoos were frowned upon by nineteenth century polite society, who believed the practice to be the sole domain of prostitutes and sailors eager to display tribal markings from New Zealand and North American. But some members of the monarchy were known to indulge in the art form; in 1882, England's George V reportedly received a large blue and red dragon tattooed on his left arm during a visit to Japan. Many members of Russia's royal house were also believed to have had tattoos, including Catherine the Great. Franz Joseph, however, was not amused by Sisi's antics. He believed the marking to be the cause of Marie Valerie's distress when he walked in on the two women crying tears of joy over the youngest daughter's engagement.

"Papa came in and asked me whether I had been crying about the dreadful shock of finding out about mum having had an anchor burnt into her shoulder, something I found very original and really not that shocking..." Marie Valerie remembered.[24]

Sisi's tears of joys dissolved into something quite different after that happy scene, however. Marie Valerie wrote in her diary, "Mama said, if I ever marry she will never be glad to see me again, she is like some animals who abandon their young as soon as someone touches them."[25] Sisi was apparently still not ready to share her youngest daughter with anyone.

—⁂—

For a time Sisi was pleased with her Corfu palace and while standing on the terrace observing the ocean below, told Marie Valerie that this would be her preferred resting place. But the empress eventually changed her mind and expressed a desire to be with her son in Vienna's Church of the Capuchins.

"I feel such a vast longing to lie there in a good large coffin and simply find rest, nothing but rest," she told her daughter two years before her death.[26]

Shortly after the Achilleion was finished, Sisi's restless spirit would not allow her to enjoy it any longer. For her, it had become a destination, something she despised. She once told Christomanos, "The destinations are made desirable only by the traveling in-between. If, on arrival some-where, I knew that I would never leave, my stay in a paradise would be hell."[27]

Sisi wrote to the emperor with what she felt was a plausible excuse: She should like to sell the Achilleion so Marie Valerie could spend the money on her growing family now that she was married to her cousin, Archduke Franz Salvator. Franz Salvator was from the less-than-wealthy Tuscan branch of the Habsburgs, a fact that rankled Franz Joseph. The emperor fostered dynastic ambitions for his daughter and had wanted her to marry a European heir apparent, but Sisi was adamant that if Marie Valerie had to marry, she should follow her heart. The couple would eventually have ten children, and Franz Joseph saw to it that they were well provided for. He knew that selling the Achilleion was just one more of Sisi's excuses to prevent settling down.

Archduchess Marie Valerie was Sisi's self-professed favorite child, born in Buda just ten months after the Austro-Hungarian Compromise. Sisi insisted that her youngest daughter speak fluent Hungarian and love the country as much as she did. When Marie Valerie married her cousin, Archduke Franz Salvator, Sisi felt she had lost her "Hungarian Child" for good (Library of Congress Prints and Photographs Division, George Grantham Bain Collection).

"I had cherished a secret hope that after building (the Achilleion) with so much pleasure and zest, you would remain quietly in the place which is your own creation for at least the greater part of the time which you unfortunately spend in the south," he wrote to his wife. "Now even that is to come to nothing, and you will only go on traveling and roaming about the world."[28]

Nonetheless, Sisi got her way, and in 1897–98, negotiations began for the sale of the Achilleion to the Byron Society of London. But the society considered the price of two million florins ($22,600,000) far too high and discussions came to a halt. Despite the setback, furniture from the Corfu palace was shipped out to Vienna, where it was stored in the Hermes Villa. The Achilleion would never sell in Sisi's lifetime, and she bequeathed the behemoth to her all-but-forgotten eldest daughter, Gisela.

In 1907, some nine years after Sisi's death, the pompous Kaiser Wilhelm II purchased the Achilleion from Gisela. The kaiser probably got quite a bargain since the palace had long stood empty and stripped of its former splendor. Its value was estimated at just 60,000 florins ($678,000). Wilhem, the last German emperor and zealous anti–Semite, tore down the temple to German-Jewish poet Heinrich Heine, whose prescient line from the 1821 play *Almansor*, "Where they burn books, they will also burn people," would so aptly predict the future actions of Hitler's Third Reich. In its stead, Wilhelm commissioned a bronze Greek Achilles statue to take its place. At the statue's base was Wilhelm's own epigraph: *"To the Greatest Greek from the Greatest German."*[29]

Wilhelm was shocked and offended by the assassination of his friend, Austrian Archduke Franz Ferdinand, in 1914 and vowed to back Austria in what would become the First World War. Austria and Germany made up the Central or Axis Powers, while the United Kingdom, France, and Russia formed the original Allies. Trench warfare, machine guns, and poison gas contributed to the deaths of some nine million combatants. Germany ended up fighting a losing war on two fronts, and Wilhelm was forced to abdicate in 1918. At the Treaty of Versailles, Article 227 called for the prosecution of the former kaiser "for a supreme offence against international morality and the sanctity of treaties." His English cousin George V called Wilhelm the greatest criminal in history.

Wilhelm was never prosecuted and lived out his life in exile shuttling between Norway and Corfu, where he spent his time excavating Greek ruins. He threw his support behind the German Nazi Party and hoped Adolf Hitler would be his ticket to restoring the German monarchy. Although they never met, Hitler loathed Wilhelm and, like other top-ranking Nazi Party members, blamed him for Germany's greatest defeat.

Wilhelm died in June 1941 at Norway's Huis Doorn, aged eighty-two, just weeks before Hitler was to invade the Soviet Union. After Wilhelm's death, the Axis Powers took over the Achilleion as a military headquarters in the Ionian Sea. Four years later, after Germany's second great defeat, the Hellenic Tourist Organization acquired Sisi's old palace on Corfu. Upon inspection, they found that Wilhelm's inscription on the statue of Achilles calling himself "the Greatest German" had been erased.

XI

"The file started to get even more interesting."

—Police Superintendent Gordon Schumacher

Gerald Daniel Blanchard, the master thief of the Sisi Star and robber of various Canadian banks, had actually used his real name when renting the Avis getaway van for the CIBC robbery. It seemed a sophomoric mistake, especially since Blanchard had created at least thirty different aliases over the years. Perhaps he had just been careless. Or maybe he was overly confident, having gotten away with so many robberies over such a long period of time. Regardless, his oversight finally gave investigators in Winnipeg's Major Crimes Unit their first real lead.

"Even when the connection was made, it still took a while before people started to understand who this guy was," said Gordon Schumacher. "As we learned more about Blanchard we started to understand how he was doing business, how he was basically walking into banks ... and identifying weaknesses that he could exploit."[1]

Also on the police docket, Avis Car Rental had reported the van stolen after Blanchard dumped it post-robbery. Once investigators tracked it down, they were able to sweep for fingerprints. They got a match, plus an unwelcome bonus: Blanchard had left two used adult diapers inside. Police now wanted to question Blanchard, but they had to find him first.

Using his surveillance system to listen in on the police, Blanchard learned he was a suspect and decided to lay low. He was divorced by this time and living with a new girlfriend, Lynette Tien, a beautiful model and actress. Blanchard couldn't help but snap a photo of a scantily-clad

Tien wearing knee-high black stiletto boots and rolling around in a pile of $100 bills. He also captured his black and white pet spaniel sprawled out on the cash just for good measure.

In addition to plenty of cash, Blanchard also had a plethora of aliases and was able to lead what investigators would call a "jet-set lifestyle," without much trouble and without alerting police to his movements. Since patience was one of his greatest attributes, Blanchard was able to stay off law enforcement radar for two whole years.

By 2006, it was evident to Police Superintendent Schumacher that the initial CIBC task force investigation was going nowhere fast. That's when a new group of investigators, including Inspector Tom Legge and veteran Sergeants Mitch McCormick and Larry Levasseur, was brought in. Eventually, the second Winnipeg-based task force would gain momentum, swelling to twenty-three full-time investigators and computer experts from the Edmonton and Vancouver Police Services as well as from the Combined Forces Special Enforcement Unit of British Columbia.

"This new team was re-energized," Schumacher said, "and it was after that the file started to get even more interesting."[2]

The new task force was dubbed "Project Kite" after the slang term for bank fraud. Soon, the investigators started to see a pattern among the Winnipeg bank robbery and similar heists at banks in Ontario, Alberta, and British Columbia. Then they reviewed Gerald Blanchard's criminal past and deportation and his stockpile of identities, and they read that he was even a person of interest in the Austrian Sisi Star heist from 1998 where he had been spotted as a tourist on Schönbrunn Palace video. Somehow, Austrian officials had matched Blanchard's face with a name and researched his robbery and fraud transgressions in the United States. But the star was an anomaly and nothing the Canadian police ever expected to recover in Winnipeg. They were after a bank robber, plain and simple.

Mitch McCormick recalled to journalist Josh Bearman that his budget was tight in the first days of Project Kite. "We got no resources and had to put together a task force out of thin air," McCormick said.[3] In fact, McCormick said the budget was so small, that the officers spent their own money on office items including note paper.

XI. "The file started to get even more interesting."

But Gordon Schumacher, chief in charge of allocating funds among other things, remembered the situation differently. "There's nothing that they needed that they didn't get. They flew all over the country, they got everything they needed," Schumacher said.[4]

As Schumacher made high-end decisions and coordinated the joint forces operations, it was Tom Legge, commander of the Criminal Investigations Bureau, plus McCormick and Levasseur who pursued the ground-floor investigation.

During his career as both a general patrol and plainclothes officer for the Winnipeg Police Service covering everything from homicides to drug offenses and robberies, Mitch McCormick had attended two ten-day career development courses offered by the Canadian Police College: Major Case Management and Major Crime Investigative Techniques. The lessons he learned in the programs, including how to take the lead in major crime investigations, how to best conduct undercover operations, and how to manage multi-agency investigations, may have provided the foundation and impetus for McCormick to pursue a complicated case like Blanchard's. McCormick already had plenty of experience with wiretapping and working with multiple agencies to investigate organized crime. By the time he first heard the name Gerald Blanchard, McCormick had attained the rank of sergeant in charge of the Winnipeg Police Major Crimes Unit in the Criminal Investigation Bureau and was poised to be a major asset in just such an investigation.

Levasseur was a wiretap expert and a sergeant in charge of the Winnipeg Commercial Crime Unit, where he had spent the majority of his career covering check and tax fraud, counterfeiting, and money laundering, among other commercial crimes. His advanced training included designations of Certified Forensic Investigator from the Association of Certified Forensic Investigators of Canada, and Certified Protectional Professional through ASIS International, the top organization for security professionals. Levasseur had led several task force investigations during his police career and was rewarded in 2002 with the Excellence in Law Enforcement Award from the Manitoba Attorney General. The honor specifically cited his work combating credit card fraud and uncovering major crime rings throughout Canada.

The seasoned officers decided that phone surveillance was the best way to find out what Blanchard was really up to. Tom Legge approached Gordon Schumacher with the idea during a weekly briefing, and together they decided to include "some specialty guys from the training academy" to help out.

The Project Kite team presented a judge with some hundreds of pages of evidence and were granted a warrant to tap Blanchard's many phone lines. "The investigation really started to take off once we were wired up," Schumacher said.[5]

Almost immediately, the detectives were blown away at how chatty Blanchard was about his upcoming projects. McCormick and Levasseur listened in as Blanchard directed a crew of people in a rehashing scheme at Best Buy appliance store, the same type of scheme he started out with when he was a teenager in Nebraska. They also heard him making real estate transactions, planning his next bank heist, and keeping tabs on his underlings. Thanks to the wire taps, the officers now knew that Blanchard wasn't just a lone criminal; he was a crime boss. From that point forward, they would refer to his camp as the Gerald Blanchard Criminal Organization.

And then, "Out of the blue, Gerald got a phone call from a guy in London and referred to him as 'The Boss,'" Levasseur said. "And basically The Boss asked him, how quickly can you get your crew together? I have a job for you to do in Cairo."[6] Another surprise courtesy of the wire taps: Blanchard's criminal enterprise had gone international.

McCormick and Levasseur listened intently as Blanchard made call after call, recruiting a five-person team to head to Egypt and telling them they were all going to make a lot of money. "I was dealing now with a guy that was traveling the world and crafting his crimes on a level that most police officers don't ever get to investigate," Levasseur said.[7]

When the detectives presented Gordon Schumacher with the wiretap information at their weekly briefings, he was dismayed by what he heard. "At first I did wonder if (Blanchard) was just blowing smoke, but once we started to compare our notes against his own words we realized that maybe he was for real."[8]

Schumacher said that once his team realized Blanchard's relationship with The Boss was legitimate, they contacted London's Metropolitan Police, who sent two of their own officers over to Canada to investigate.

XI. "The file started to get even more interesting."

The London police spent about a week reviewing the wiretaps before flying home to confer with Scotland Yard.

This was not Blanchard's first dealing with The Boss. The two had reportedly met in London at an earlier date where they bonded over similar interests in surveillance equipment and fraudulent activities. The Boss then had a test for Blanchard: earn the Londoner's trust by taking twenty-five pirated debit cards to Canada, then bring the spoils back to Great Britain. Blanchard reportedly went home, ripped off his countrymen, then returned to London with $60,000 cash.[9] It was the beginning of a lucrative friendship.

Investigators would learn later that The Boss was from northern Iraq and planned counterfeiting and bank fraud schemes throughout Europe, Africa, and the Middle East. He was also believed to be funding Muslim extremists by funneling a good deal of the stolen money back to Kurdish separatists. Iraq is home to up to four million ethnic Kurds, a Sunni Muslim people with distinctive linguistic, tribal, and ethnic lines. Traditionally nomadic, the Kurds settled after World War I in portions of northern Iraq, northwestern Iran, northeastern Syria, and eastern Turkey. The ethnic Kurds who made up one-fifth of Iraq were targeted for eradication by President Saddam Hussein in the late 1980s. Following Saddam's capture by American troops, he was charged in 2006 with genocide for attempting to annihilate the race through death squads and poison gas in attacks that killed at least 50,000 people. Saddam was executed for other horrific human rights violations before he could face the charge of Kurdish genocide. Kurdish groups have been fighting ever since to create an independent sovereign Kurdish state, while others fight for full Kurdish autonomy within Iraq, Iran, Syria, and Turkey, host nations that consider the separatists to be outright terrorists due to suicide attacks and well-armed militias. The Boss was thought to be funneling his stolen money to at least one of these separatist groups, and now Gerald Blanchard appeared to be expressly involved.

Directing the operation from London, The Boss put Blanchard and his crew to work in Cairo stealing money from bank accounts all over the world. He provided the group with hundreds of credit and debit cards that he had created with stolen numbers. The Boss may have obtained the pirated data using "skimmer equipment" attached to ATMs, gas station terminals or even handheld devices. When a victim swiped his card at a tainted ATM, for example, his card information was stored on a computer chip while a pinhole camera hidden in the kiosk recorded his movements as he punched in his PIN number. That information would be later retrieved by thieves like The Boss. In the case of handheld skimmers, a corrupted restaurant employee might run a credit or debit card through a secreted skimmer device before using the actual card reader to charge for a meal. Or, The Boss may have set up fake discount Wi-Fi hotspots near hotels and airports that would record credit card data once an unsuspecting victim took the bait and logged in. In all cases, the stolen credit and debit card data would be passed on to someone with an electronic card printer and a stash of blank plastic cards. The thief would print the stolen numbers onto a fresh card that could then be used at legitimate ATMs to withdraw the victim's cash.

Armed with their share of pirated cards, Blanchard's crew dispersed through the Middle Eastern streets to target ATM machines and withdraw the maximum amount of cash allowed. Since his fair hair and pale skin made him stand out, Blanchard donned a woman's body-concealing burka as the perfect disguise. The crew worked twelve-hour days withdrawing cash and stuffing the bills into backpacks or beneath their traditional Muslim costumes. In a one-week period, Blanchard's crew had stolen around a million dollars.

The detectives back in Winnipeg couldn't believe their ears, not when they heard about the scope of the fraud nor the Egyptian pound notes piling up in the crew's hotel suites. McCormick and Levasseur were working eighteen-hour days, but they couldn't stop listening in on Blanchard. They knew the future payoff would be huge. They just had to pick the right moment to strike.

According to Gordon Schumacher, "As far as the average person who lost money from their ATM or credit card, in most cases the bank will restore their money; that helps some but not all. Getting your money back is part of the battle but depending upon how much of a person's identity and credit was corrupted will dictate the inconvenience, frustration and physical or emotion trauma to follow."[10]

Then the detectives listened in as the international skimming scheme turned sour. One of Blanchard's crew members, Congolese-born Balume Kashongwe, was traveling from Cairo to sub–Saharan Africa to continue the thefts when he called Blanchard to say that the airline had lost his luggage. In the bag were diamonds, $50,000 in cash, and several hundred stolen credit cards, all belonging to The Boss. That was the last Blanchard would hear from his crew member, who then disappeared from radar. Police heard Blanchard frantically calling Lynette Tien back in Canada, trying to get in touch with one of Kashongwe's relatives, but no one could pinpoint him; Kashongwe had simply vanished.

Back in London, The Boss made it clear that Blanchard himself would be held responsible for the missing loot. Armed henchmen were sent to Blanchard's Cairo hotel room to make sure he didn't leave town without recovering Kashongwe's spoils. But Blanchard still had no idea where his crew member went, and through numerous phone calls, Blanchard used his soft spoken charisma to get The Boss to agree to a face-to-face meeting in London. Once there, Blanchard was able to talk his way out of a very volatile situation. The two men finally agreed to forget about the missing diamonds and cash and to continue skimming on Blanchard's home turf of Canada. According to Blanchard, "After all, why fight when there was more money to be made?"[11] Before departing, Blanchard handed over The Boss's take of the Cairo scam, then walked away with $65,000 and his life.

After ten days overseas, Blanchard's plane touched down on a rain-soaked tarmac at Vancouver International Airport on December 3, 2006. Now that he was home, Blanchard immediately returned to his old tricks by researching another new bank under construction, this time in Chilliwack, that he believed was good for a whopping $800,000.

"The bank was all by itself in the middle of nowhere," Blanchard said. "At the time I felt like it was asking, 'Come and take my money from me.'"[12]

The Chilliwack bank would be a considerable payday in case The Boss changed his mind and demanded the money Blanchard owed him from the missing crew member's lost luggage. Blanchard drove the hour and twenty minutes to Chilliwack, then employed his time-tested methods of infiltrating the bank. First, he chose a new identity as a construction worker that would allow him to waltz onto the building site like he was in charge. Once inside the new structure, Blanchard grabbed the blueprints right from where they rested on a dusty work bench. He then headed over to an adjacent drug store, made photocopies, and returned the originals before anyone noticed they were gone. From the printed plans, Blanchard learned the exact locations of the bank's dye pack sensors, motions detectors, and panic alarms.

Once the legitimate construction workers went home for the night, Blanchard got to work on the new bank vault's lock mechanism. First he dismantled it, then carefully cut hairline fractures in the tiny pins that held the lock together. When he was ready to make his move, all he would have to do was push hard enough on the vault door so the ruptured lock pins would allow it to swing right open.[13] Now it was up to the planted pinhole cameras and radios to tell him when the bank would be vacant and the ATMs stocked with cash.

Blanchard himself admitted that what made him a great bank robber was his level of surveillance, patience, and attention to detail. But with The Boss on his mind, he found himself losing his once laser-like focus. Blanchard was also being very loose-lipped about his projects, and the police were recording it all. On the way to case the Chilliwack Bank, Blanchard had phoned The Boss to discuss the arrival of a skimming team in Montreal planned for the next day. The investigators were now ready to make their move.

As the team members touched down in Montreal, the authorities were waiting for them and seized all of the tools needed to rip off millions of Canadian dollars: blank credit cards, a card writer, and computer hard drives. One of the hard drives even contained amateur video taken by Blanchard of the Cairo operation, something the thief had a habit of doing at each of his crime scenes. According to one Canadian official, "Blanchard had a proclivity to record his whereabouts by taking photos of himself in his hotel room, wherever that might be, holding a package of matches to identify the hotel and city where the photo was taken."[14]

But Blanchard remained oblivious to the sting that was going down more than 3,000 miles away; he was up to his neck in executing the Chilliwack job.

XI. "The file started to get even more interesting."

At 12:30 the next morning, The Boss placed an urgent phone call to Blanchard at the very moment the Canadian was crawling through the bank's ceiling vent system toward the ATM room. McCormick and Levasseur listened as Blanchard answered in a hushed tone and politely explained that he was a little busy and unable to talk. Not to be deterred, The Boss informed Blanchard that the skimming team had just gotten pinched at the airport, and he wanted to know how it could have happened. Blanchard thought for a moment, said he suspected the phones had been tapped, then added in an earnest whisper: "I'm looking down. There's a security guard down there right now. I have too much invested in this job ... I have to go."

But The Boss got in one last word: "We have to fix this, Danny," he said.[15]

Nothing would get fixed, however, before a SWAT team descended on Blanchard's condominium at 4 a.m. on Tuesday, January 23, 2007. The Project Kite leaders, Schumacher, Legge, and Levasseur, had flown in to Vancouver specifically for the show. They watched as SWAT took Blanchard and his girlfriend unawares, even though the master criminal had rigged a security system so he could monitor anyone approaching his home from blocks away. Unfortunately for Blanchard, he was sound asleep at the time of the raid.

While authorities were apprehending Blanchard, they were also executing some sixteen search warrants across British Columbia, Alberta and Manitoba. They scoured four separate homes connected to Blanchard, as well as his red BMW and a self-storage unit. All-in-all, police confiscated 60,000 items, including a cache of high-powered weapons, several dozen cell phones, computers, night-vision goggles, sonic ear enhancers, pinhole and underwater cameras, $10,000 cash in various currencies, plus tens of thousands of damning documents including fake police and secret service IDs. In addition to all of the high-tech guns and gear, authorities retrieved a blood-stained towel with a hotel key from the UK and what had apparently become indispensable tools for long nights surveilling banks: boxes of adult diapers.

"When we came back from Vancouver, we had to procure a warehouse to put all the seized evidence and equipment: computers, hard drives, documents. We had so much it was ridiculous," Schumacher said.

"For us to actually go through every piece of evidence would have taken an extremely long time."[16]

As for the guns they uncovered, police said they never suspected that Blanchard planned to use them; rather, authorities felt that the six high-velocity firearms, including a "rocket-propelled device," plus 60,000 ammunition rounds, two silencers, and equipment to manufacture weapons, were part of a new business opportunity Blanchard was working on at the time of his arrest.

Although Blanchard was meticulous at planning his crimes, he may not have been as fastidious about managing his finances. During the raid, police found dozens of unopened letters from various banks and credit card companies. They also discovered "various papers and phone numbers" for local Hells Angel president and one of its longest serving members, Dale Sweeney.[17] Sweeney and ten other suspects with ties to the outlaw motorcycle gang would be taken down by Winnipeg SWAT in 2012 in connection to "high-level drug sales throughout the province."[18] But police said they didn't believe Blanchard was involved in the drug trade and postulated that his relationship with Sweeney was out of friendship, not business.

Three years after Gerald Blanchard first crept up on Canadian police radar, he and seven other people were in custody thanks to an observant Walmart employee.

At the time of the arrests, Schumacher recognized the high-tech pioneers for what they were and gave a nod to their sophisticated ability to gather intelligence and gain access. "These guys are leading the charge in the new wave of organized crime," he said. "It's not just handguns anymore. It's computer crime."[19]

By the end of the sting, the eight members of the Gerald Blanchard Criminal Organization had more than one hundred charges pending against them stemming from identity theft and money laundering to fraud and forgery. Blanchard himself had forty-one, including a new charge leveled against him once he was in custody: conspiracy to kidnap and murder his girlfriend, Lynette Tien, who was cooperating with authorities. But Blanchard had a reputation for being a non-violent, gentleman thief, and the kidnapping and murder conspiracy charges didn't seem to fit. Blanchard maintained that the "plot" was completely made up by two prison inmates he had come in contact with at Manitoba's Headingley Correctional Center so they could use the information as a bargaining chip in their own cases.

"The police quickly realized it wasn't true," Blanchard said, and those charges were dropped for lack of evidence.[20] In fact, far from wanting Tien dead, Blanchard told the press that he planned to marry her while still in custody.

Following his arrest, Blanchard hadn't even bothered to apply for bail (or a "judicial interim release" as it's called under the Canadian Criminal Code) through the Manitoba Provincial Court. He would spend nearly a year locked up at Headingley, Manitoba's largest prison, while he decided whether to plead not guilty or try to negotiate a plea deal. The red-brick facility, with wings designed to hold the entire range from minimum to maximum security prisoners, was situated on twenty acres near the Assiniboine River and, in 1996, had been the scene of the province's worst ever prison riot. The trouble began when a group of drug-addled inmates overpowered guards as the officers performed a search. Authorities estimated that 321 inmates then became involved over a twenty-four hour period, mercilessly beating other prisoners and guards, setting fires, and destroying equipment. When it was all over, dozens were left injured and the destruction totaled more than eight-million dollars. In 2000, the medium and maximum security wings received an 18 million dollar makeover. The medium wing was enlarged to 32,000 square feet and the maximum swelled to 42,000 square feet. The entire facility was given a unique new feature designed to prevent future rioting: The guard stations were relocated in a central position with the inmate's cells radiating outward from the core. The guards were now able to keep an eye on prisoners like Blanchard at all times without having to rely solely on electric surveillance to show them who was doing what.

Blanchard had phone privileges at Headingley, and Mitch McCormick and Larry Levasseur were sure to listen in when he used them. The officers were pleasantly surprised one day when The Boss phoned his old associate behind bars. The mysterious Londoner wanted to know how Blanchard had managed to upset the Canadian establishment so much that the legal machine staged such a massive takedown of his criminal enterprise.

Blanchard answered that it wasn't the establishment that targeted him: "It was these Keystone Cops out here in Winnipeg."[21]

—⁓—

Blanchard's dim view of the police would change, however, once he sat across the table from Sergeants McCormick and Levasseur. In fact, the interrogators developed a sort of fondness for Blanchard's quiet, congenial nature.

"He's a personable guy," Gordon Schumacher said. "He was an unassuming, weakling type who was likable—as much as a cop can like a criminal. So, I think it made it a little more difficult for the frontline investigators once they got to know him. I'm not saying their objectivity had changed, they just looked at him differently."

Although Schumacher had a hard time viewing Blanchard as anything more than a villain, the police superintendent did give his foe points for persistence and ambition. "This guy is smart, there's no question about that," Schumacher said. "Not only was he sophisticated and daring, he was committed and intelligent. Committed, meaning that: 'I see a bank, that's my target, and if it takes me six months to get to the end, well then it takes me six months and a lot of hard work to get there.' You very seldom see that in the criminal world."[22]

At first, Blanchard may have contemplated escaping from custody again, but he knew that the authorities had too much on him this time and had seized too many of his assets to really make it work. So he did the exact opposite. He decided to be highly cooperative, hoping his insight into the banking system's security flaws would gain him a lighter prison sentence.

"Never in policing does the bad guy tell you, 'Here's how I did it, down to the last detail,'" said Mitch McCormick. "And that's what he did."[23]

XI. "The file started to get even more interesting."

But just to solidify his chances that prosecutors would recommend the lightest sentence possible if they offered him a plea agreement, Blanchard decided to put his biggest and most extraordinary chip on the table: the whereabouts of the missing Sisi Star.

Nobody, especially not Gordon Schumacher, took the offer seriously.

XII

"Thoughts of death encircle her incessantly now."

—Irma Sztáray, Sisi's maid of honor[1]

Sisi would spend the rest of her days on the open seas sightseeing and visiting health spas throughout Europe, searching for relief from the excruciating sciatica caused by her poor diet and extreme exercise. She believed that bathing in ocean water twice each day eased her pain and had herself wrapped in sea-soaked sheets at night, instead of the perfumed vinegar of her youth. But Sisi wasn't solely looking for a cure for her physical complaints; she was also running as fast and as far away as she could from any remaining responsibilities at court. Sisi now attended only the largest official functions that she was absolutely unable to avoid. Invariably, Sisi would suffer from what Marie Valerie called a "court-ball headache" that would be the empress's excuse to take her leave. Sisi wrote about her disdain for such events in 1887:

> Sighing before the tired head-in-the-clouds
> I remove the crown;
> How many good hours has
> the ceremony robbed me of today![2]

Once her official duties were over, Sisi made her escape via the imperial yachts *Chazalie* and *Greif*. But her true floating home was the *Miramar*, built in England in 1872 and based in Trieste, Italy. The vessel was described as a fast iron-paddle ship of 1830 tons and 2,500 horse-power that measured 269 by 32 feet.[3] Sisi had this yacht altered to her specifications: Her favorite spot on the quarterdeck behind the main mast was fitted with an awning to shade her from the sun, the top deck

XII. "Thoughts of death encircle her incessantly now."

was reconfigured so she could continue her long walks while at sea, and she had a glass pavilion assembled so her view of the ocean was never impeded. When in port, Sisi did her best to avoid calling on local royalty and became adroit at politely turning down their invitations. On the *Miramar,* she received no important guests and hosted no formal dinners. It was her pleasure ship, and her greatest pleasure was solitude.

While at sea, Sisi's prime source of entertainment was the wrath of Poseidon. She loved nothing more than a good storm blowing off the Adriatic, tossing her ship about like a child's toy. She would command her anxious servants to tie her by her slim waist to one of the ship's masts so she could feel the storm's unrelenting power, imagining herself as Odysseus on his way home to Ithaca. She expressed her love for the freedom of the sea in 1885:

> Ah, greatly do I love thee,
> Thou harsh tempestuous sea,
> Thy wildly tossing billows,
> Thy storms that rage at me.
> But love endures no fetters—
> Must needs go wandering,
> To nothing constant ever—
> Palace or wedding ring.[4]

Sisi may have relished the pitching and rolling, but her attendants found it unbearable. They languished below deck, miserable and wracked by seasickness. Following one particularly harrowing storm, Sisi's butler Leopold Alram wrote in his diary: "The sea was dreadful, our ship was tossed around like a nutshell ... we thought we'd be fish bait."[5]

Sisi was aware that her voyages upset her attendants but brushed their discomfort off to a lack of a firm constitution. She wrote to Marie Valerie that her new Greek tutor, Alexis Pali, was a "mollycoddle," too weak to keep up with her on her walks and travels. "He is now trembling at the prospect of the voyage and saying it would be better to stay here till the wind drops."[6]

Due to her delicate health, Sisi's Hungarian tutor, Ida Ferenczy, did not accompany the empress on her excursions but remained safely home at court. There, Sisi instructed her to set up a small dairy where special cows would be raised to provide the empress with the pure whole milk she now subsisted on. Marie Festetics wrote to Ida often, complaining of Sisi's troubling behavior. Of one particularly strange incident, she wrote:

> We had bad weather yesterday morning, but she still set sail. It started to pour down at 9 in the morning, accompanied by thunder until 3 in the afternoon. During the whole time she sailed around us, sitting on deck, holding the umbrella above her and was very wet. Then she alighted somewhere, called for her carriage and wanted to stay the night in a stranger's villa!"[7]

Showing up unannounced on strangers' doorsteps had become another of Sisi's bizarre habits in the 1890s. During one incident in Nice, France, an old woman chased Sisi off her property when the unanticipated stranger dressed all in black tried to enter the Frenchwoman's house. Franz Joseph wrote he was glad that Sisi "did not also get a beating from the old witch but sooner or later that is exactly what will happen, for one does not simply push one's way uninvited into people's houses."[8]

As if the storms and turgid seas weren't bad enough, the ships' cramped quarters intensified the already burgeoning tensions amongst the travelers. In particular, Sisi's ladies-in-waiting complained about the haughtiness of Greek reader Christomanos and found Sisi's irreplaceable hairdresser, Fanny Feifalik, to be simply overbearing.

Marie Festetics wrote, "On board it is becoming more intolerable every day, the hairdresser growing more and more insolent and giving herself the airs of a great lady. The yacht is so small that one cannot escape from her."[9]

In addition to the hairdresser, Sisi's main companions for the last years of her life, the people she confided in and was closest to, were her maids of honor, Marie Festetics and Irma Sztáray, Hungarian compatriots who proved their complete loyalty to the empress. These high-born women willingly gave up the possibility of marrying, having children, and running their own households for a life of service to the Crown.

Raised in the family palace in Keszthely, western Hungary, Countess Marie Festetics had originally been maid of honor to a Habsburg relative of Franz Joseph's. When another of Sisi's ladies resigned her post in order to be married as was the requirement at the Austrian court, Sisi requested that Marie join her retinue. Marie was hesitant at first, put off by malicious rumors about Sisi being spread by the empress's detractors. But Hungarian Count Gyula Andrássy urged her to accept, saying, "It is your duty to make this sacrifice for your country. A person whom God has endowed with plenty of intelligence ought to show gratitude for it, and the Queen stands in need of someone faithful."[10] Marie filled this role fastidiously, devotedly serving the empress for twenty years before Sisi's incessant sea travels and hikes took their toll. Although two years younger than the empress, Marie was worn out by 1890 and was replaced by the younger and more athletic Irma Sztáray.

Irma was one of seven children of Count Viktor Sztáray of Sztára. She was appointed temporary maid of honor when she was thirty and Sisi was fifty-six. Despite her relative youth, Irma had to prove her physical fitness in order to keep up with the empress on her strenuous walks and limitless excursions. In the one-year period of 1895 to 1896, Irma accompanied the empress on visits to the Hermes Villa outside Vienna in May and June; the Hungarian spa of Bartfeld in July; Bad Ischl in August; Territet in September; Gödöllő in October; Vienna in November; Cap Martin from December through February; and Cannes, Naples, Sorrento, and Corfu in March. Irma would be by the empress's side when Sisi took her final breath outside Switzerland's Beau-Rivage Hotel in a just a few year's time.

Occasionally, Franz Joseph would meet his peripatetic wife in Switzerland or for her brief visits back home to Austria or Hungary, but for the most part, Sisi relied on their mutual friend, Katharina Schratt, to keep the emperor company. Even so, he missed Sisi desperately and would pensively drift through her empty apartments, running his fingers over the covered furniture and reminiscing over a previously shared meal or conversation. In his mind, he had been permanently backed into a corner of extreme loneliness and had no means of escape except through Sisi's good graces. Sisi often petitioned the emperor to visit her on her layovers, but political conditions within the empire precluded his leaving for any serious amount of time.

Throughout his long reign, the much-respected monarch had nonetheless watched his vast empire undulate with discord. He had a falling out with the Russians over the Crimean War, lost most of Lombardy to France during Italy's Second War of Independence, saw Austrian dominance over the Germanic states shift to Prussia, and felt the wrath of the Czechs and Romanians following the Austro-Hungarian Compromise. Eventually, his annexation of Bosnia-Herzegovina and subsequent tensions with the Serbs would be the catalyst for the First World War. He had lost his sole heir to suicide and fostered an uneasiness toward his new heir, Franz Ferdinand. Clearly, this was a man under enormous stress who struggled daily to keep his crumbling empire and marriage together.

Despite his overwhelming responsibilities and broken heart, Franz Joseph continued to support Sisi's actions even through the harshest criticisms. A contemporary newspaper article commented that "that strange woman the Empress" preferred to be anywhere other than Vienna. This observation did not please the emperor, who told a group of journalists he hoped the press would cease to concern itself with Sisi's private life.[11]

Sisi's father, Duke Max, also had a habit of criticizing his daughter and went a step too far in 1888 when he read a book passage to family members gathered for his diamond wedding anniversary: "The nervousness of those who do not work can be cured only gradually—not until, that is, the dukes, counts, and barons teach their children that work is the best occupation for the nobility and at the same time the surest road to a long and happy life."[12] Sisi felt the passage was aimed directly at her and she essentially ended her relationship with him that evening; she would not attend his funeral in Munich later that year after he died following a prolonged illness.

The 1890s ushered in two notable personal tragedies for Sisi. First, her mother Ludovika died suddenly of pneumonia at the age of eighty-four. And second, Sisi's younger sister, Sophie Charlotte, once engaged to their flamboyant cousin Ludwig II of Bavaria, died in a fire that shocked all of Paris and made headlines around the world.

After her broken engagement, Sophie Charlotte had married Ferdinand d'Orléans, Duke of Alençon, at the Wittelsbach family summer home of Possenhoffen Castle. On May 4, 1897, the fifty-year-old Sophie attended the annual Bazar de la Charité in Paris, an event organized by the French Catholic aristocracy, where she was the highest-ranking royal.

The occasion featured a newfangled motion picture projector that ran on a combustible system of ether and oxygen. A curtain caught fire during the film demonstration, and the ensuing conflagration rapidly tore throughout the wooden venue with its cloth and papier-mâché decorations. The crowds of mostly women and children trampled one another as they tried to escape the advancing flames. As rescuers helped individuals to safety, many of the aristocratic women declined their efforts, insisting that the festival workers be saved first. Sophie was remembered as famously saying, "Because of my title, I was the first to enter here. I shall be the last to go out."[13] But there would be no second chance. When it was all over, the dead were estimated around two hundred, and the devastation was so complete that many victims had to be identified through dental records. Newspapers reported that among the ashes was discovered an engagement ring bearing the names of both the Duke and Duchess of Alençon as well as the gold brooch she had been wearing. Her remains were finally identified several days later.

Sophie Charlotte was remembered as a heroine who sacrificed herself in the interest of allowing others the chance to escape the inferno first. One romantic version of the tragedy recounted how a group of nuns of the Order of St. Vincent de Paul vowed to remain with the Duchess through the ordeal. While they knelt around her praying, Sophie Charlotte was said to have loosened her long hair and donned it as a protective cloak while the flames ultimately engulfed the remaining women. The Chapel of Notre Dame de Consolation was finished in 1901 on the Rue Goujon as a monument to all of the victims who perished that day.

Several months after Sophie Charlotte was killed, Sisi turned sixty, and her zest for life was visibly all but gone. Two of the most important aspects of her life, her health and the extraordinary beauty that she had fought so hard to maintain, had finally abandoned her. Her once-smooth skin was now weathered and wrinkled from hours spent riding or hiking in the elements and was covered with an angry eczema that would not clear, her body was stiff and swollen, and her eyes had dulled. Spending so much of her life trying to achieve physical perfection, Sisi had ignored the irrefutable fact that age would finally and relentlessly overcome her. She had failed to cultivate the familial relationships and deep friendships that so often add meaning to life in older age. And, according to Lady Walburga Paget, a confidante of Queen Victoria, Sisi was finally reaping what she had always sewn: "Having led a life of unalloyed selfishness, worshipping her own health and beauty as the sole objects in life, she has nothing to fall back on now … she will become a ghost in her own lifetime."[14]

Few people knew what Sisi really looked like any longer since she had stopped sitting for photographs in her thirties and portraits in her forties. At her last official public appearance at Hungary's Millennial Celebration of 1896, people were taken aback at how aged and sad their queen appeared. A Hungarian newspaper reporter described her as a *mater dolorosa*, or mother of sorrows, clad all in black, hiding her face behind her dark fan. He described her still-magnificent hair, "waving round her brow like a silken fringe, and above this her luxuriant braids, the loveliest of all crowns." Her overall visage was still the same, he wrote, "but as though shrouded in mist."[15]

When out in public, Sisi was intent on hiding herself from the world behind her parasols and fans. Frustrated court photographers, prevented from capturing her real image any longer, had taken to altering earlier prints of the empress to give the public some inkling of how she might look in the present. Still, occasionally, an astute observer would catch a fleeting glimpse of the elegant woman dressed all in black with her attendants trailing behind and recognize her as the aging empress. She had become a curiosity.

One such observer was Prince Alfons Clary-Aldringen, who was a young boy when he and his sister came across the empress in Territet, Switzerland, about a year before Sisi's death. He remembered offering a great bow while his sister curtsied and that the empress did not cover her face with her fan but offered a friendly smile instead. When he told his grandmother of the meeting, she exclaimed, "Children, do not forget this day, when you saw the most beautiful woman in the world!" But with an honesty only children can seem to muster, he answered back,

"But Grandmama, her face is all wrinkled!" For his insolence, the boy received his grandmother's derision in the form of a hefty slap.[16]

A Parisian newspaper correspondent who recognized the empress out on one of her walks described Sisi as having lost her the "flexible elegance" and grace of her youth: "The face betrays infinite suffering and has the drawn expression of dry-eyed grief, which is the worst of any. I was also struck with the darkened colour of the hair and the pale reddish streaks—certain signs of silver grey.... Her step is now unelastic, and she seems not to feel the ground under her feet, walking as if they were 'asleep.'"[17]

Sisi's family was well aware of her increasing depression over the years and her talk of welcoming death. She spoke of envying Rudolf for being at rest and claimed that she had no fear of departing this world and often longed for it, although, "It is the moment of passing and the uncertainty that make me tremble."[18] Such talk particularly worried Marie Valerie, as did Sisi's intermittent bursts of hysterical laughter when she spoke of one day being dragged off to the madhouse. Sisi's elder daughter, Gisela, cautioned Marie Valerie to keep an eye on their mother when walking by the waterfall at a spa town near Salzburg where Sisi was traveling to take the cure. Gisela's warning implied a fear that Sisi might just jump if given the chance.

Sisi had been raised a devout Catholic, believing in the holy trinity of the Father, Son and Holy Ghost, and the power of intercessory prayer. Taking one's own life was verboten, and Sisi had witnessed the dilemma Rudolf's suicide had caused when it came time to have him buried on consecrated ground in the Habsburg crypt. Instead of the God of her Catholic faith, however, Sisi now turned more toward deism and began referring to the Almighty as "Jehovah," a terrible entity who did not intervene in the concerns of man on earth. Marie Valerie worried for Sisi's immortal soul, especially when her mother told her, "I often feel as though Rudolf's bullet had killed my faith."[19]

Shortly after Rudolf's death, Sisi toyed with the supernatural in a desperate attempt to contact her son's spirit. Five nights after his burial, she sneaked out of the Hofburg alone to visit the imperial crypt at the Capuchin monastery. The startled monks hurriedly lit torches beside Rudolf's grave, then left the empress alone at her request. Twice, she called out her son's name, expectantly waiting for his apparition to appear before her and answer back. But all she heard that night was her own echo reverberating through the draughty chamber. Sisi would continue to try to contact her dead son's spirit, possibly through mediums and séances, which gained popularity in the nineteenth century. But her desire to ask her son why he took his own life would remain unfulfilled.

Sisi never directly tried to end her life, but she did act out recklessly by tempting the elements on the open seas, refusing proper nourishment, and declining to accept bodyguards while out walking. Perhaps these were her ways of hastening her own end in a way that would be acceptable in the eyes of her creator.

Franz Joseph was particularly struck by his wife's dispirited state on a stop at the Bavarian spa town of Kissingen in April, 1898. He was overcome by how slowly and wearily she moved as they travelled on to Bad Ischl, the place where Franz Joseph had first fallen in love with Sisi forty-five years earlier. But the emperor knew immediately by Sisi's lethargy that she would be unable to join in the upcoming Golden Jubilee celebrating his reign. To prepare the public for his wife's absence, he issued a proclamation on her health, explaining that her anemia, inflammation of the nerves, insomnia, and dilation of the heart would require treatment at the salt springs of Bad Nauheim and that she must leave straightaway. Sisi left Ischl and Franz Joseph on July 16. It would be their final farewell.

XIII

"I gave the diamond back voluntarily."

—Gerald Blanchard, January 2014

The phone call Gerald Blanchard made to his grandmother on a spring day in 2007 was one of the most gut-wrenching conversations of his life. There may have been some strained pleasantries, but Blanchard knew he had to get right to the point.

"I need to come to the house and I'm bringing the police," he told her.[1]

Minutes later, a law enforcement vehicle wound through western Winnipeg, arriving at an unassuming residence in the middle-class neighborhood of St. James-Assiniboia. Blanchard's grandmother was waiting for them.

Mitch McCormick and Larry Levasseur escorted the handcuffed Blanchard to the front door, where he received his grandmother's hug. Then Blanchard led the officers down to the basement where he said the Sisi Star was concealed. The detectives still weren't sure Blanchard would actually produce the long-lost Köchert Diamond Pearl.

"Who would have thought that a guy from Winnipeg, Canada, was in Austria and stole the Sisi Star out of a museum?" asked an incredulous Mitch McCormick.[2]

But Blanchard delivered, and when they finally reemerged, the investigators carried with them the fabled star, extricated from behind a piece of Styrofoam that had been tucked into a crawl space. It was a place no one would have ever thought to look for a missing nineteenth century jewel, and the Sisi Star might well have been lost forever if it

Winnipeg Police Detective Mitch McCormick presents the recovered Köchert Diamond Pearl to the press in June 2007, along with cash and weapons recovered from the sting on Gerald Blanchard. In explaining who Sisi was, McCormick echoed the popular belief that the empress's unhappy life mirrored that of Britain's Princess Diana (photograph by Jason Halstead/QMI Agency).

hadn't been for thorough police work and Blanchard's self-professed magnanimity.

"I gave the diamond back voluntarily," he said.[3]

Not wanting to take any chances on another of Blanchard's famous escapes like those in Iowa and Nebraska, the investigators immediately locked him back up at Headingley, then got to work on the enormous amount of paperwork they would need to complete for this sparkling new piece of evidence.

"Right to the very end, to be honest, there was still some doubt that [Blanchard] actually had this thing," Gordon Schumacher said. "It was like, this is a Tom Cruise movie, this isn't real. I mean, we know he's really smart, and we know he did all these interesting things as a criminal, but, really? And so, when Tommy (Legge) came to me and said 'I think we've got it,' it was almost surreal. It was like, OK, I'll believe it when it's right in front of me."

Schumacher wouldn't have to wait very long for the detectives to present the star. "It was Larry who brought it up … it was just in his hand encased in a homemade Styrofoam container. [It] looked like it was made out of the same insulating material used on the inside of walls, between the foundation and the wall studs. " Schumacher said. "He put it on my desk, we opened it up, and we had a little chuckle about it."

Although Schumacher said he didn't find the star as magnificent as he had expected a celebrated imperial ornament to look, "I realized the historical significance of it. There was certainly some enthusiasm on actually seeing the royal jewel in front of me and realizing that this was pretty much a wrap up to the entire investigation," he said.

Then there was the matter of a small wager to be settled. According to Schumacher, "One of the guys, when we were in Vancouver said, 'I think we're gonna find it.' I'm like, 'We're not gonna find that thing, I'll bet you a bottle of wine.' And at the end of the day, we found it."[4]

The star's brief moment back in the sunlight would come to an abrupt end as it was once again shuttered away, this time in a secure exhibit locker at the grey limestone and steel fortress that was Winnipeg's Public Safety Building.

Later, following his day in court, Blanchard would contact the local *Winnipeg Free Press* to get something off his chest. He told the paper how ashamed he was of involving his grandmother in his criminal enterprise and said he wanted to make amends to everyone he hurt.[5]

Shortly after the Köchert Diamond Pearl was catalogued and assigned its exhibit number, Schönbrunn Palace Director Frank Sattlecker received a phone call that he wasn't sure he could take seriously. It was nearly nine years to the day that the Sisi Star had first gone missing, and every couple of years since a hodge podge of con artists had dialed the palace to say they were willing to give up the Star for a ransom.

"We've had a few calls all these years where people claimed to have found it, and it came to nothing," Sattlecker said. "We just accepted the fact the Star had been stolen." But this time, it was no ruse; on the other end of the line was the Royal Canadian Mounted Police liaison officer saying that a special task force had recovered the long-lost Köchert Diamond Pearl in a basement crawl space a continent away. It was so astonishing, perhaps it had to be true.

Once Sattlecker was convinced, the two officials discussed how and when the Sisi Star would be coming home to Vienna.

"We are happy that it's back," the understated Sattlecker would tell the press. "It's an important piece and it was such a long time ago."[6] Despite his reservedness, champagne corks were undoubtedly popping in Vienna that evening.

After much negotiating, Gerald Blanchard had struck a plea deal with prosecutors and would begin his criminal atonement by taking the fall for all seven of his partners in crime. Appearing in Manitoba's highest ranking trial court, The Court of Queen's Bench, on November 7, 2007, in jail-issued sweat pants and sweat shirt, Blanchard pleaded guilty to sixteen charges of bank robbery, credit card fraud and heading up a criminal organization. Regarding the Köchert Diamond Pearl, Blanchard admitted only to possessing it. He was never charged by Canadian authorities with outright stealing the Sisi Star because the actual crime had been committed outside of the country. If the Viennese authorities had gathered enough evidence to charge Blanchard in Austria, they could have applied to have him stand trial there under an official extradition treaty formalized between the two countries in October 2000. Canada's minister of justice would then decide whether to proceed with an extradition hearing. But so far, Austrian authorities had kept mum on the subject.

Superintendent Schumacher believed Blanchard took the plea deal in order to keep his secrets safe. Among the warehouse full of confiscated evidence, "There was tons of information that was just never seen. And that is, in part, why the guilty plea, why the deal," Schumacher said.

"The reality is, had he pleaded not guilty, and was throwing his dice on the table, we would have gone through much of the documents and computer data that we had and likely would have found more evidence against him. I think it was probably a very smart move on Blanchard's part to take this very light sentence ... and at the same time understanding that all that equipment would not be looked at. You know, from Blanchard's perspective, it was a pretty sweet deal."[7]

—⟋⟍⟍—

As Senior Associate Chief Justice Jeffrey Oliphant presided over Blanchard's sentencing hearing and closely examined the Sisi Star for the first time at his bench, Crown Attorney Sheila Leinburd gave Blanchard credit for revealing its hiding place to police. "The police would not have been able to find the diamond if not for the cooperation of Mr. Blanchard," she told the court.[8]

Although, like Gordon Schumacher, he wasn't particularly

impressed with the star itself ("I thought it was rather ordinary looking. Aside from its provenance, it would not have attracted my attention") Judge Oliphant had come to court this day completely prepared for what he was about to hear regarding Blanchard's complicated case. In an unusual move, Defense Attorney Danny Gunn had agreed to allow the judge to preview a massive binder known as a "show and tell" prepared by Crown Attorneys detailing all of the particulars of the case. Normally, the judge would have had to wait until the day of Blanchard's plea to learn the minutiae. But Gunn, whom Oliphant called, "an excellent defense counsel," knew that allowing the judge ample time to study how Blanchard's infractions progressed from Austria to Canada, then Egypt and back to Canada would help assure the fairest possible sentencing.

"The lawyers knew that I always read whatever was provided to me and in this case, my having the 'show and tell' book saved an immense amount of time in terms of the submissions counsel would have to make," Oliphant said.[9]

Prosecutor Leinburd then had some choice words about Blanchard as she addressed the court: "Cunning, clever, conniving and creative. Add some foreign intrigue and this is the stuff movies are made of," she said before explaining how Blanchard had defrauded his way from Canada to Cairo over an eight-year period.[10] Leinburd told the court about Blanchard's numerous aliases, fake press cards, and doctored security passes that identified him as a member of law enforcement and even the U.S. Secret Service.

Regarding Blanchard's dealings with The Boss in Cairo, Leinburd said the stolen ATM money was used to fund terrorism and Blanchard knew it, even though he had not faced terrorism charges. The evidence was in the form of a phone recording of Blanchard discussing how the money was being used by The Boss. "His lawyer said the money went to the Kurdish freedom fighters in Iraq—those were his exact words," Leinburd told the court.

"It was a large scale operation" she continued. "It was going on in Spain and other European countries at the same time. This was not the only cell that was operating."[11] Leinburd went on to say that Scotland Yard knew The Boss's identity and were on to him even though they hadn't shared that particular information with Canadian authorities.

XIII. *"I gave the diamond back voluntarily."*

According to Gordon Schumacher, "As it turned out that they did subsequently identify The Boss and many of the players on their side of the pond and made arrests. Unfortunately wire tap evidence cannot be used at trial in Great Britain, it's only used for intelligence gathering which pretty much left The Boss free and clear. He never dirtied his hands but one of his cells was arrested and the money they gathered was tied directly back to rebels in Northern Iraq."[12]

Danny Gunn said Blanchard may have known about The Boss's terrorist connections but that his client cut ties with the Londoner as soon as Blanchard learned how the scammed money was being used. "It was at this point he realized he'd gotten himself involved in something pretty serious and with people who didn't abide by the same code as he did," said Gunn.[13]

Judge Oliphant believed Gunn's story, telling Blanchard, "I'm satisfied you really weren't aware of where the majority of money you were stealing was going. I guess this just says something about the world we now live in," he said.[14]

In addition to giving up the Sisi Star, Blanchard had explained to authorities in detail exactly how he had circumvented such state-of-the-art security systems when robbing the Canadian banks. He never went into detail, however, on how he got by the Schönbrunn Palace security.

Blanchard provided so much useful information, in fact, that Sergeants Mitch McCormick and Larry Levasseur were able to assemble a lengthy presentation for the banking industry on Blanchard's ingenious methods. When the judge suggested the banks should hire Blanchard as a security consultant and pay him millions of dollars, Crown attorney Leinburd responded that the possibility had been discussed.

All-in-all, Blanchard faced 164 years in prison but had been so forthcoming about his crimes that prosecutors agreed to reduce his sentence to just five years. But the Crown attorneys also wanted prison time for each of Blanchard's seven cohorts, and that's when the ringleader decided to give authorities everything they wanted.

"I took an eight-year prison sentence instead of a five-year sentence, I forfeited eight properties that I own in Vancouver, three-and-a-half million dollars in cash that I had in a storage locker, and gave the Sisi

Star back in return that nobody else would be sent to prison except for me," Blanchard said.[15]

Blanchard's eight-year sentence would immediately be reduced to six, however, due to time already served. Canadian law in 2007 stipulated that a prisoner would be given two-day's credit for every day served in custody prior to being convicted.

Inspector Tom Legge expressed an admiration for the way Blanchard stepped forward to take the fall for his people. "The things that came out in court ... that Blanchard seemed to care very much about the people he was involved in—we saw that, as well. He's not of the same ilk as a lot of the criminals that we normally deal with," Legge said.[16]

In addition to prison time, Blanchard was ordered to pay $500,000 in restitution to the banks he stole from. According to him, that was all that was left of the millions he had taken in. The other twenty-five charges against him were stayed, or set aside.

But before dismissing Blanchard, the judge couldn't help but poke fun at the gaffe that had put police onto Blanchard's trail in the first place.

"Pretty dumb leaving that car sitting there in your name," Oliphant said, referring to the Avis rent-a-car spotted by a Winnipeg Walmart employee. Oliphant's comment caused the packed courtroom to erupt into laughter.[17]

Judge Oliphant then recognized Blanchard for taking responsibility for his crimes by pleading guilty and helping Manitoba avoid what could have been one of the longest trials in its history.

"You're no hero, Mr. Blanchard, but you could have made things a whole lot more difficult," Oliphant said.[18]

Blanchard did not address the court himself but had his lawyer issue a statement that surprised everyone present. Blanchard had apparently developed a newfound respect for the officers he once referred to as "Keystone Cops."

"My client wishes to recognize that this huge lie that he had been living could now finally fall apart," Gunn said. "He recognizes that the men and women of the Winnipeg Police Service made that all possible."[19]

But Superintendent Schumacher wasn't buying Blanchard's contrition. When asked how long he would like to have seen the master thief locked up, Schumacher replied, "Double digits for sure."

That's because Blanchard's financial crimes had the potential to devastate all segments of the population, including those who could least afford it. Blanchard justified his ATM crimes by saying he believed he was only hurting the financial institutions and not everyday people.

"I could have copied their personal information and made more money than just taking the money from the ATM machines," he said.[20]

But according to Schumacher, the losses suffered by the banks and merchants were ultimately passed on to consumers in the form of higher retail prices, financing charges, bank fees, and insurance costs. Schumacher explained that society loses billions of dollars each year to financial fraud, and the people who end up paying the price are often the working class, the elderly, and those on low fixed incomes. What's more, businesses that can't afford the insurance hikes can be wiped out altogether, leading to worker layoffs. Clearly, financial fraud is not a victimless crime.

"He was probably more dangerous to society than a guy with a machine gun," Schumacher said. "It is clear, the man in the dark jacket standing in the shadows with a gun can impact a small group of the community significantly, but people like Blanchard, who permeate and exploit the financial integrity of ordinary and honest people can impact thousands more with a few simple keystrokes."[21]

The Canadian Bankers Association reported that losses from debit card fraud alone reached a high of $142 million in 2009, two years after Blanchard was caught, but dropped to $29.5 million in 2013, thanks to better technology, thorough investigations and diligent prosecutions. Out of twenty-three million active debit cards in circulation in Canada, the association reported that less than half of one percent were involved in skimming incidents in 2013.[22]

Closely examining Blanchard's crimes and learning exactly how he perpetrated them undoubtedly helped the Canadian banking system tighten the reins on future scams. Blanchard had opened up a whole new world of possibilities for fraudulent activities with his surveillance systems and credit card printing machines. Authorities would study his ingenious methods for years to come.

"The way he looked, the way he thought, the way he planned, that's why he was successful," Schumaker said. "Of course, even the smartest criminals get caught in the end."[23]

—⁓—

The members of Gerald Blanchard's criminal organization now had their day in court. Appearing together on April 8, 2008, were twenty-two-year-old Angela James from Edmonton and Blanchard's thirty-six-year-old cousin, Dale Fedoruk from Winnipeg. Fedoruk pleaded guilty to accepting credit cards and other mail at his home that was addressed to one of Blanchard's aliases. Fedoruk also accepted a weapons shipment that included an assault rifle, two handguns, and 1,000 rounds of ammunition. The court handed Fedoruk a twenty-one-month conditional sentence that included twenty-four hour house arrest with breaks that would allow him to seek employment. "You got yourself in quite a jackpot with your involvement with Mr. Blanchard," Provincial Court Judge Kelly Moar told Fedoruk.[24]

Twenty-two-year-old Angela James pleaded guilty to participating in the criminal organization by accompanying Blanchard to Egypt for the Cairo credit card scam. She had been present in the hotel room with Blanchard when The Boss sent armed henchmen to collect the money that had gone missing when Balume Kashongwe disappeared somewhere in Africa. Blanchard had negotiated James' release with The Boss, and she had been safely allowed to leave the hotel.[25] For her part in the whole affair, James was given a two-year conditional sentence.

"Mr. Blanchard was the ultimate con man and it seems both you [Fedoruk] and Ms. James were conned just like other people—but you didn't suffer financial loss," said Judge Oliphant.[26]

Blanchard's now ex-girlfriend, twenty-three-year-old Lynette Tien, was in court on September 25, 2008. She admitted that she had returned stolen goods to electronic stores using fabricated receipts in conjunction with Blanchard's rehashing scheme and pleaded guilty to three counts of fraud and one charge of participating in a criminal organization. The court did not consider her to be a major participant in the crime ring, however, and spared her any jail time as well. Tien was permitted to serve a one-year conditional sentence in British Columbia while continuing her acting, modeling, and university studies.

"She's learned a big lesson and is going to be a lot more careful with respect to what she does and who she becomes affiliated with," Tien's lawyer said.[27]

The man whom police initially believed directly helped Blanchard with at least one of his bank robberies, twenty-six-year-old Aaron Syberg, had all of his twenty-five charges stayed and was permitted to leave court a free man. So was the oldest member arrested in connection with the Organization, eighty-three-year-old Carl Bates, whose five charges were also stayed. Police believed he was used as one of Blanchard's mail drops to receive illicit shipments. In Canada, when charges are stayed, the accused's prosecution is essentially over. If the defendant runs afoul of the law within one year, however, the stayed charges can be reinstated and prosecution may go forward. That meant that Syberg and Bates would have to stay out of trouble for at least one year to the day they last appeared in court if they wanted to forget they were ever involved with Gerald Daniel Blanchard.

Police finally caught up with thirty-three-year- old Balume Kashongwe, the Congalese man who had disappeared in Africa with the London Boss's ill-gotten gains, and charged him with five counts of conspiracy and participating in Blanchard's criminal organization. He pleaded guilty and was sentenced to six months time served plus one extra day in custody. That one-day sentence made Kashongwe the only member of Blanchard's gang, besides Blanchard himself, to do any extra time at all.

Forty-year-old businessman Lance Ulmer was the last of the Blanchard Criminal Organization to be sentenced. Ulmer pleaded guilty on April 9, 2009, to allowing Blanchard to use his Edmonton shipping company to perpetrate his financial crimes. Among other things, Blanchard had guns and ammunition delivered to Ulmer's business, arranged money orders there, and used the photocopy machine to fabricate false sales receipts. Ulmer's lawyer said Blanchard "seduced" his client into helping him and that the business owner was "willingly used." The judge agreed that Ulmer didn't realize the depth of Blanchard's criminal dealings.

"They were looking for a gullible, good guy they could dupe and that's what they found," said Judge Kelly Moar.[28] Ulmer received an eighteen-month conditional sentence.

In every case against the accused gang members the legal opinion was the same: Gerald Blanchard had manipulated otherwise law-abiding citizens into getting involved in criminal activity they neither sought out nor fully understood.

"He didn't have everybody in one meeting room sitting around saying, 'This is the plan.' Not all of them knew each other, either," said Gordon Schumacher. "He was using the people that he needed to accomplish what he had to get done. He had all the cards held pretty close to his chest. He was the guy that educated himself criminally to a level that was pretty impressive by the end."[29]

Fortunately for the seven accomplices caught in Blanchard's web, the nightmare would soon be over. They would be in the clear as long as each member obeyed the conditions set forth by the judge or remained out of trouble for one year until the stayed charges were finally withdrawn.

—⚄—

Judge Oliphant wouldn't hear Gerald Blanchard's incredible story of how he claimed to have stolen the Sisi Star until many years after sentencing. In fact, the judge wasn't even sure if Blanchard had been the one to take the star in the first place, and it hadn't been his job to find out.

"There was nothing in the information provided to me to indicate that Mr. Blanchard had actually stolen the star," Oliphant said. "I had no facts presented to me in the 'show and tell' book or the submissions of counsel that led me to infer he did take it."[30]

If Canadian officials had gathered evidence that Blanchard had actually stolen the star, they probably would have mentioned it in court documents or during the sentencing hearing, just as Crown Attorney Leinburd mentioned a terrorist connection with The Boss even though Blanchard wasn't charged with terrorism. At the time of the hearing, however they apparently had nothing.

XIII. *"I gave the diamond back voluntarily."*

One of the most intriguing aspects of Blanchard's story was not how he later claimed to have dismantled the Schönbrunn Palace display and a multitude of security features, nor how he said he tip-toed through the imperial apartment undetected; Blanchard had proved time and again that he possessed a singular skill to subvert any security system he wished. What was so incredible was that he claimed to have parachuted onto the palace roof under cover of darkness, a feat that few very experienced skydivers ever have a chance to tackle during their careers.

The director of sport promotion for the United States Parachute Association, a non-profit organization with more than 36,000 members, explained what it would take to pull off such a dangerous jump. "For a night jump, you need a 'B' license, which is a minimum of fifty jumps," said Nancy Koreen who has a twenty-year history with the sport. "A regular night jump is over open fields, same as jumping during the day. For a tight space into a city or stadium or something like that, you need to have what we call a 'Professional Exhibition Rating,' which requires a minimum of 500 jumps along with a series of other accuracy landing qualifications."[31]

Koreen herself has some 7,000 jumps under her belt, yet she has never landed on a city roof, during the day or night. "That's really more of a stunt that a skydiver might do for a movie or other special project," she said. "It's not something skydivers do normally."[32]

And yet, Gerald Daniel Blanchard isn't exactly known for doing normal things.

"That is a pretty incredible story, but Blanchard has done some pretty incredible things," Judge Oliphant said. "Perhaps Blanchard has been caught up in his own publicity and is embellishing what is an already interesting story. With Blanchard, it's kind of hard to tell, but it makes a good story ... a great story."[33]

XIV

"I wished for my soul to escape to heaven through a tiny hole in my heart."

—Sisi to Baroness Julie von Rothschild, September 9, 1898.[1]

The empress was running late. She downed a last glass of milk before Countess Irma Sztáray hurried her along from her suite at the Beau-Rivage Hotel to the dock where a public steamer was preparing to sail from Geneva to Montreux at 1:40 p.m. on September 10, 1898. Sisi's other attendants had already boarded along with the luggage, and the two ladies dressed all in black had just said their goodbyes to the hotelier and porter. Carrying her customary parasol and fan, Sisi and Irma hastily made their way along the deserted Quai Mont-Blanc alone. The ship's bell rang a five-minute warning, and Sisi tried her best to calm the nervous countess.

"We shall still be in time," Sisi assured her.[2]

Suddenly, a powerfully-built man of medium height with dark, curly hair rushed toward the unattended women, who stopped short to allow him to pass. But the man did not veer to either side; he kept to his course and made direct contact with the empress. Silently, Sisi fell backward with only her thick, coiled hair to cushion her head as it hit the pavement. The man ran off as quickly as he came, and both the shaken countess and a cab driver helped the empress to her feet. Sisi immediately tried to collect herself and began to arrange her disheveled hair, all the while asking what had happened and insisting that she was fine. She suspected the man was a jewelry thief and supposed out loud, "Perhaps he wanted to take my watch?"[3]

XIV. *"I wished for my soul to escape to heaven..."*

The hotel porter insisted that the two women return immediately to the hotel, but Sisi had no intentions of missing the boat to her next destination. Upright again, she made her way under her own power to the steamer that was approximately one hundred yards from the attack site. Once on board, her strength finally gave way, and she fainted from what was thought to be a heart attack caused by the shock of the ordeal. Countess Sztáray unbuttoned Sisi's bodice to make it easier for the empress to breathe. But when she parted the stiff black fabric, Irma noticed a tiny hole in Sisi's camisole that was stained a brownish-red. It was then that she realized: the perpetrator was no mere thief. He was an assassin.

—ϡ—

Luigi Lucheni was a twenty-five-year-old workman of Italian descent who deeply resented Europe's aristocracy and who dreamed of attaining everlasting glory by killing one of its members. How he came to target the Empress of Austria was a story of desperation and happenstance.

Born to an indigent single mother who abandoned him at a Parisian hospital, Lucheni grew up in a children's home before being taken in by a foster family. He had started work as a railway laborer by the time he was nine years old and traveled throughout Europe thereafter seeking temporary jobs. As a young man, Lucheni was drafted into the Austrian Italian army, where he saw battle in the First Italo-Ethiopian War of 1896. He was considered a loyal and honorable soldier and thrived under the discipline of military command. When his service came to an end a year later, however, Lucheni found himself with few prospects and went to work as a manservant for his squadron commander, Prince Raniero de Vera d'Aragona. It was while in the prince's employ that Lucheni developed a deep resentment for the ruling class; they seemed to have everything without having to work, while he, the manservant, was forced to do the household's dirty jobs for a pittance. After just three months on the job, Lucheni purportedly requested a raise, which was refused, and he hastily quit the prince's employ. Later, Lucheni thought better of his actions and begged to be reinstated, but the damage had been done and he was sent packing. Lucheni was destitute once again, and he set off wandering, eventually finding his way to Switzerland, a haven for anarchists in *fin de siècle* Europe.

By 1891, Switzerland was a constitutional republic, surrounded by imperialist nations such as Russia, Austria-Hungary and Germany that were ruled by firm autocrats. As a free republic, Switzerland attracted dissidents from all over Europe and appeared to look the other way at the political plotting that took place within its borders. Each time Sisi and Franz Joseph visited Switzerland, Vienna held its collective breath fearing an anarchist might turn his sights on the sovereigns. These fears were exacerbated by the fact that Sisi refused to entertain a police escort anywhere she traveled, leaving her vulnerable to anyone who might cross her path. Sisi was well aware of the dangers and had even written disparaging remarks about how readily Switzerland embraced anarchists. But she seemed to enjoy placing herself in dangerous situations later in life as evidenced by her behavior at sea, and this was perhaps one more chance for Sisi to tempt fate.

Lucheni was hired on to help build a new post office in Lausanne, and it was there that he fell in with the revolutionaries who spoke vehemently against the ruling class and blamed the aristocrats for the extreme poverty forced upon the common man. Lucheni absorbed their rhetoric and decided that he would bring down a member of the monarchy himself for the fame and "for the sake of example."[4]

He wasn't picky about which aristocrat he would kill. It all came down to convenience. He traveled to Geneva after hearing that the Orléanist claimant to the French throne would be in town. Lucheni had fashioned a dagger with a triangular point from an iron file he found in a Swiss market, but the Prince of Orléans failed to show and Lucheni found himself without a target. Thanks to the local newspapers, however, Lucheni didn't have to wait long for a new victim.

As usual, Sisi was traveling under a pseudonym when she checked into the Hotel Beau-Rivage on September 9. She and Countess Sztáray had spent the day having lunch with Baroness Julie Rothschild at her magnificent Pregny estate before traveling back to Geneva to buy ice cream and a gift for Marie Valerie. Despite registering as the Countess von Hohenembs, someone at the Beau-Rivage informed the newspapers that the Empress of Austria was staying as their esteemed guest, which was widely reported the next morning. Lucheni happened upon the news and felt his luck turning.

He lay in wait for the empress behind a tree with the file hidden up his sleeve and attacked her as she made her way on the deserted quay. Lucheni's makeshift knife had created such a clean, small aperture in her heart, that she had time to walk to the steamer before her heart's beating slowly faded. Now underway, Countess Sztáray begged the steamer captain to return the boat to shore. She desperately tried to revive Sisi with handkerchiefs dipped in cologne and a combination of sugar and ether, but nothing worked. Once the ship had docked, several people carried the unconscious empress back to the hotel on a makeshift stretcher fashioned from boat oars and deck chairs. They laid her on the bed where the rattling in her throat grew quieter. Finally, around 3 p.m., Elisabeth, Empress of Austria, was pronounced dead.

—m—

At half-past four that day, Franz Joseph's assistant hastily arrived from the Hofburg and marched directly to the Emperor's Schönbrunn study. The blood had drained from Count Paar's face as he presented the emperor with a telegram from Geneva. Franz Joseph rose from his desk, immediately assuming it had to do with his wife's precarious health. He was met with the handwritten words, "Her Majesty the Empress dangerously injured" transcribed across the paper.

But just as quickly as the confusion set in and Franz Joseph begged for his aides to find out more information, a second telegram was placed in the emperor's hand. In a fit of agitation, he tore the paper along with the sealing stamp and scrambled to find the words "Her Majesty the Empress has just passed away," before sinking into his chair.

"So I am to be spared nothing in this world!" the emperor cried. And then, softly to himself, "Nobody knows the love we had for each other."[5]

—⟋⟍—

Lucheni was apprehended almost immediately after fleeing the scene and told the authorities that he had acted alone and had intended to kill.

"I ran toward her and barred her way," he told them. "I bent down and looked under the parasol. I didn't want to catch the wrong one. They were both dressed in black. She wasn't very beautiful. Quite old already. Anybody who says different doesn't know what he is talking about. Or he lies."[6]

Lucheni stood trial in a Geneva court two months after the crime. Time in custody hadn't humbled him; he was as proud of his deed in front of the jury as he had been the day he had committed it. Newspapers reported him laughing throughout the proceedings and yelling, "Long live anarchy!" and "Death to the aristocracy!" When asked if the assassination was premeditated, he readily answered, "I did my utmost to make the stroke fatal." His reasoning, or "doctrine," as he called it, was simple: "No one who does not work should be allowed to live."[7]

It took the jury just twenty minutes to convict Lucheni and sentence him to life. He would have preferred death, but Geneva had no death penalty.

Sisi's assassination was reported worldwide, and the public expressed outrage that the empress had fallen victim to such a brutal crime. Some 16,000 "women and girls of Vienna" signed a scathing letter to Lucheni in jail calling him a "murderer, monster, ravenous wild beast."[8] American writer Mark Twain, who was living in Austria when the news broke, wrote to a friend about his shock at the murder, "which will still be talked of and described and painted a thousand years from now."[9] Scientists struggled to make sense of Lucheni's actions and one even analyzed the anarchist's handwriting to diagnose him as a degenerate with a double personality that was "another of the essential characteristics of hysteria and epilepsy."[10]

Even prominent anarchist Emma Goldman, called "the most dangerous woman in America" for her radical politics, strongly denounced Lucheni's actions in a letter to the *New York World*. She wrote that Lucheni had no justification under the anarchists' code "for slaying a woman who was harmless, unhappy and not unkind." Goldman explained that the philosophy of anarchy went against the useless taking of human life, although she went a step further by condemning Sisi's husband Franz Joseph for destroying his empire and oppressing the Hungarian nationals:

> Had this man chosen Francis Joseph for his victim I would have approved it, because he in his fifty years' reign has succeeded in bringing his empire nearly to dissolution. While yet a young lad, in '48, he was the first one to set an example of cruelty by encircling the captive fighters for freedom and, without giving them a chance to defend themselves by arms or law, ordering them shot down like dogs.[11]

Both friends and foes of the monarchy believed that even though Sisi was spoiled and irresponsible during her lifetime, she did not deserve a barbarous death at the hands of a political dissident. Aside from her role in the Austrian-Hungarian Compromise, which united the two nations instead of tearing them apart, Sisi had played no role in politics during her forty-four years on the imperial throne. She once said that the only honest money she ever earned came to her when performing outside the German beer gardens. Lucheni murdered her in part because she never made her own living and in part because she just happened to be in his path when he was ready to strike.

Like Gerald Blanchard exactly one hundred years later, Lucheni knew nothing of Sisi except what he had read about her in the papers. He didn't hate her because her autocratic husband had repressed the Italian nationalists. In fact, it wasn't clear if he even felt a connection to other Italians and their political causes. He was a radical anarchist, plain and simple, whose goal was to hurt the class of people he felt had wronged the average man. For both criminals, Sisi was nothing more than a wealthy empress who had something each of them wanted to take. Gerald Blanchard would take her famous jewel; Luigi Lucheni would take her privileged life.

XV

"You continue to take pride in your criminal past."

—Parole Board of Canada

On November 8, 2007, thirty-five-year-old Gerald Blanchard was transported some twenty-five miles north of Winnipeg and handed over to authorities at Stony Mountain Federal Penitentiary. He joined more than 500 other medium-security inmates in the white brick fortress that still featured its original guard cupola built in 1877, now flanked by a modern guard tower with its 360-degree observation windows. Gordon Schumacher described it as "an intimidating and depressing place full to capacity with the more serious of offenders."[1] Blanchard's attorney, Danny Gunn, had tried to move his client's incarceration to a facility near Vancouver, the city Blanchard had called home for years, but there hadn't been any room for him in British Columbia. Regardless, Gunn said his client was ready to pay his debt to society and that he was a deeply remorseful man.

"Obviously he went through a lot after the initial arrest," Gunn said. "His entire life came crashing down around him, but ultimately, he's resilient and able to sort of put together the pieces of what was his former life and look forward to something else."[2]

In January 2009, fourteen months into Blanchard's stay at Stony Mountain, he witnessed Manitoba's worst prison riot since the Headingley uprising in 1996. Tensions had been building in the facility since a New Year's Eve crackdown, when prison guards seized more than thirty hand-made shivs. Authorities then ordered a two-day lockdown, confining prisoners to their stifling cells even for meals. The inmates' grumbling turned violent over a week later when rival gangs, the Manitoba Warriors and the Native Syndicate, began battling in the recreation hall. More inmates took advantage of the melee to overtake a kiosk that regulated access to inmate cells in one of the prison's five living units. The prisoners then barricaded themselves inside the unit with mattresses and bed frames, while others wearing masks started fires and threw garbage cans at the prison guards who were trying in vain to regain control. A source inside the prison said officers used copious amounts of pepper spray and displayed their shotguns but were no match for the rioters. Authorities were forced to call in the prison's specially trained emergency response team to quell the violence and transport four seriously injured inmates to Winnipeg's Health Sciences Center. A fifth prisoner was treated and sent back to Stony Mountain. Some six hours after the riot began, all prisoners were back in lockdown while authorities tried to piece together exactly what had transpired. The smell of smoke and pepper spray was said to have remained thick in the air even as the combative mood abated.

A U.S. convict with talents similar to Blanchard's described how harrowing a prison riot can be on weaker inmates. In his book, *The Art of the Heist: Confessions of a Master Thief*, Myles J. Connor, Jr. recounted his stay at the Massachusetts Correctional Institution at Cedar Junction, also known as MCI-Walpole. Connor was from a working-class family and grew up outside of Boston. He developed a taste for fine art early on, and an unwavering contempt for authority even though his father was a decorated police officer. Connor's unique abilities mirrored Blanchards': He was an innate leader who inspired loyalty in his crew members, staged multiple successful bank and museum heists, and had a talent for escaping from police custody. (In one instance in the 1960s, Connor fashioned a pistol from a piece of soap and some shoe polish and used it to break out of a Maine jail.) He also said he deplored violence, although he often carried a gun while perpetrating his crimes and once shot a police officer while making an escape.

In 1975, while facing federal charges of stealing artwork, including paintings by Andrew and N.C. Wyeth from the Woolworth family estate in Monmouth, Maine, Connor decided he would need a "bargaining chip" to keep him from serving a fifteen-year prison sentence. While

169

out on bail, Connor and another man who were both heavily disguised paid their admission fee and strolled into Boston's Museum of Fine Arts, carefully dismounted a million-dollar Rembrandt from the wall (*Portrait of a Girl Wearing a Gold-Trimmed Cloak*), made their getaway, then secreted the masterpiece away under a friend's bed. Connor and his attorney negotiated the return of the Rembrandt with prosecutors in return for a lighter sentence. Just as in Blanchard's case of turning over the Sisi Star in hopes of getting a break from Crown Attorneys, Connor received a reduced prison term of only four years thanks to the stolen Rembrandt.

While Connor was serving time at Walpole for a different convic-tion in 1971, the New York prison riots at Attica sparked disgruntled inmates at Walpole, known as one of the most violent U.S. prisons at the time, to stage their own insurrection. According to Connor, who stood just five-foot-six-inches tall and relied on his wits to survive in prison, "For the weaker inmates, riots are a time of intense fear. Many of these men … spent the duration of the riots barricaded in the prison hospital, terrified for their lives."[3]

Blanchard managed to survive the Stony Mountain riot that involved some one hundred prisoners. Several months later, in a bid to prevent further revolts in what authorities agreed was a vastly over-crowded facility saturated with smuggled narcotics, prison officials decided to completely separate prisoners by gang affiliation. No longer would members of the six crews operating within Stony Mountain inter-mingle while eating, sleeping, exercising, or working in the penitentiary. The president of the Winnipeg Police Association disagreed with the segregation, believing it only strengthened ties within each gang by allowing them to rely solely on one another with no outside influences. But Kevin Grabowsky with the Union of Canadian Correctional Workers said his group had been lobbying to isolate individual gangs for a decade and believed the ruling would drastically reduce violence.

"Rather than try to run a population as big as Stony Mountain's all at one time, especially in the evening, where we have the majority of our problem, they are in smaller more controllable sections, "[4] Grabowsky told *CBC News*.

But Gerald Blanchard wouldn't get to witness whether gang segre-

XV. *"You continue to take pride in your criminal past."*

gation decreased violence at Stony Mountain. The same month that the new rule was enacted, June 2009, he was led through a green mesh, wire-and-steel electronic gate and up a wooden stairwell to the Parole Board of Canada hearing room. Blanchard had applied for day parole six months prior to his date of full parole eligibility, and now he would get to make his case for his earliest possible conditional release. According to Canada's Corrections and Conditional Release Act, "all offenders must be considered for some form of conditional release during their sentence," although parole is never guaranteed.

Blanchard, his attorney, and his appointed parole officer seated themselves in comfortably-cushioned high-backed chairs across a conference table from the parole board members. The parole officer spoke first, addressing the board members and making his case for Blanchard's early release. Next, the members themselves questioned Blanchard on his past criminal behavior, the crimes for which he was serving his time in federal prison, and his conduct for the past two years at Stony Mountain. Blanchard and his attorney were then permitted to address the board about how remorseful he was and how he'd learned his lesson before being escorted out of the room for a few tense moments while the members deliberated and assessed Blanchard's risk to reoffend. When they were called back in, Blanchard received the news he had been hoping for: The parole board was putting its faith in his rehabilitation and releasing him into very closely monitored day parole after serving fewer than two of his original eight-year sentence.

And there was more good news. Blanchard was being assigned to a halfway house in his hometown of Vancouver to serve out the rest of his sentence.

"He's very happy, and he's looking forward to proving the parole board right—that they can trust him and that he can live the life he said that he could," said Attorney Danny Gunn.[5]

But the board had a stern warning for Blanchard. While on parole, he was forbidden from working with certain computers and surveillance equipment, or from contacting known criminals or any members of his former crew. And because it was day parole, he was required to return to the halfway house and check in with staff members each night.

Blanchard complied with the parole board's wishes for a time, but the lure of his previous life continued to pull at him, and authorities grew concerned that the ex-convict was quickly delving back into fraudulent financial activities.

First, police reported him hanging around some former accomplices, then Blanchard tried to volunteer for the 2010 Vancouver Olympics but was denied because of his criminal history. Not to be deterred, Blanchard phoned his old nemesis, Sergeant Mitch McCormick, and tried to get him to pull a few strings for him.

"He'll phone me to touch base and even asked me to call off the Vancouver Police Department from his case, and I told him, no," McCormick said.[6] In fact, far from calling off the Vancouver Police, McCormick and partner Larry Levasseur had given a day-long presentation instructing some 200 officers on Blanchard's devious financial schemes and break-ins.

Levasseur was skeptical that Blanchard would be able to stay on the straight-and-narrow, citing the ex-con's former life of intrigue, fancy homes, and world travel. "He did tell me that he never intends to go back to jail, though," Levasseur said. "He suffered a lot."[7]

Despite any fears he may have had about being locked up again, Blanchard continued to push boundaries. On July 27, 2010, the parole board revoked Blanchard's parole altogether. The Board's decision was based on the grounds that Blanchard had re-entered his "crime cycle" by organizing a shoplifting ring in a large retail store. "(Police) also believe you were engaged in a product return fraud," the report continued, although no charges had been filed.[8] In addition, while performing a room check, the halfway house staff discovered electronics, cell phone SIM cards, computer USB drives, deposit envelopes for two different banks, a pen with audio/video capabilities, and a device called a "spoof card" that disguised a caller's voice and redirected the call through another number. Blanchard was unceremoniously hauled back to prison pending re-evaluation.

—⚹—

Exactly fifteen months later on October 27, 2011, Blanchard was again granted day parole, although the board expressed concerns that he was still "glorifying his crimes." According to the report, "While the board is concerned that you continue to take pride in your criminal past and the board is skeptical about your expressed remorse, there is no reliable and persuasive information to suggest you have returned to your crime cycle or that your risk to reoffend has elevated."[9]

Blanchard stayed under the radar on his second day parole all the way up to his statutory release date of April 23, 2012. At this point, the board had no choice but to discharge him, although with serious strings attached: He was barred from owning more than one cell phone, could not associate with criminals, and was forbidden from owning or using a computer. He also had to reveal his personal financial documents when asked by his parole officer. Despite these limitations, Blanchard told anyone who would listen that he was off to start his own security business. Perhaps he had clung all those years to Judge Oliphant's declaration during his trial that the banking institutions "should hire him and pay him a million dollars a year."[10]

Now finally free, Gerald Blanchard slipped into obscurity to plot his future. He wouldn't be heard from again for nearly a year when his sentence was set to expire.

—〰—

For his crime of murdering the empress, Luigi Lucheni spent the first two years of his life sentence as a relatively well-behaved prisoner. His only malfeasance stemmed from his own grandiosity in which he saw himself as an important political prisoner who resented being housed with Geneva's common criminals. He received countless letters of support from European anarchists calling him a "hero" and congratulating him on his "noble deed,"[11] but the prison guards most likely never delivered them.

As the years wore on, however, Lucheni began to find his neverending incarceration to be unbearable. He started squabbling with the guards and was intermittently thrown into solitary confinement. Finally, on October 16, 1910, Luigi Lucheni decided to carry out the death penalty he had dearly wanted in the first place. When the prison warden checked

173

on Lucheni in his dank, secluded cell around 6 p.m., he found the empress's assassin hanging by his own leather belt.

—⟞⟋⟍—

Although few people took notice when Lucheni died, Sisi's death was lamented on an international scale. But before all of Vienna would be draped in black and ebony horses would bear the caisson through streets lined with throngs of mourners, those who knew Sisi best would first have to prepare the empress for her final voyage home.

While Sisi's body lay on her death bed at the Beau-Rivage, authorities scrambled to determine whether an autopsy would be performed as prescribed by Swiss regulations in cases of murder. A dispatch from Vienna brought Franz Joseph's reply. They were to follow the rule of Swiss law on the Austrian imperial consort, but they would need witnesses from the Austro-Hungarian Empire. Countess Sztáray was horrified to learn that she would be one of them. Ida resolutely stood by Sisi's bedside while three doctors commenced the clinical postmortem. The Empress of Austria and Queen of Hungary was now a specimen to be examined, a fact that struck a sickening blow to the countess's own heart.

The doctors recorded Sisi's height and weight, noted her good teeth and joint swelling due to her self-imposed malnutrition, then focused in on the stab wound that took the form of a small "v," fourteen centimeters below the left collarbone and four centimeters above the nipple of the left breast.[12] When it was time for the doctors to examine the heart itself, Ida must have blanched; she would have to witness them cutting into the woman she had dedicated her life to serving and comforting. Now, she could only watch as Sisi's heart was vulnerably exposed and terribly still.

Once they were able to see inside, the doctors noted that Sisi suffered from an enlarged heart that accounted for her recent weakened state and shortness of breath. The stab wound itself was eight-and-a-half centimeters deep; Lucheni had hit the empress so hard that his file had broken her fourth rib, pierced her lung, and plunged through the left ventricle. But because the file had been so sharp and the heart wound so small, and because Sisi was so tightly corseted, she had been able to rise and walk to the steamer ship while blood trickled ever so slowly into the pericardium. The doctors determined that her heart had stopped pumping little by little during her hundred-yard walk and that her death had been painless. This pronouncement came as a blessed relief to the anguished lady-in-waiting.

Sisi's death mask was most likely cast out of plaster before the embalming process was begun. According to the British Museum, it was important to capture the deceased's visage as soon after death as possible to preserve the true facial contours. Sisi biographer Count Egon Corti wrote that the embalming fluids did, in fact, cause Sisi's face to become swollen and distorted. The doctors assured Countess Sztáray that the effect would not last, and within minutes the once beautiful empress had regained a more natural appearance.

Soon, it was time for the lady-in-waiting and the hairdresser to tend to their empress for the last time. Ida first removed Sisi's jewelry, which included the wedding ring she wore on a plain gold chain around her neck, her simple watch with its frayed leather strap, and two lockets containing a quantity of Rudolf's hair and the ninety-first psalm: "He that dwelleth in the secret place of the most High shall abide under the shadow of the Almighty."[13] When it was time to dress the body, some reports say Ida chose an all-black ensemble while others say Sisi's final dress was pure white. Regardless, Ida undoubtedly dressed the Empress with as much care as if Sisi had been alive to grant her approval.

Fanny Feifalik would have the honor of dressing the empress's hair one last time. Corti wrote that the hairdresser arranged Sisi's hair "as she had usually worn it,"[14] which was most likely in the magnificent crown of braids atop her head. Once the empress was finally ready, she was carefully laid on the white satin lining of a casket fashioned from polished oak. Ida and Fanny undoubtedly fussed over Sisi's clothes and hair to make sure everything was perfect and may have kissed her face for a last time before the lid was closed.

The woman who so hated pomp and ceremony would now be the focus of one of the greatest displays of respect her empire had ever witnessed. Hundreds of thousands of mourners, hats in hand, lined the streets of Vienna as the funeral cortège slowly made its way from the Hofburg to the Church of the Capuchin Friars. Since Sisi had so obviously shunned Vienna during her lifetime, many observers felt the immense turnout was more for the emperor's sake than for Sisi's.

Mark Twain witnessed the procession from a window atop Vienna's newly built Krantz Hotel. He described how carriages full of courtiers first began to arrive, then army and navy officers filled the Neuer Markt square dressed in imperial red, gold, and white. A cardinal, bishops, and archdeacons all filed into the churchyard followed by priests in gold-embroidered robes bearing a crucifix and banners. Bells tolled solemnly throughout the four-hour progress, when at last, the funeral procession itself came into view. Led by the cavalry riding in lines four across, the imperial family's six-horse mourning coaches made their way up to the church. Twain next described how the soldiers presented arms in the midst of a low rumble of drums as the opulent hearse approached pulled by eight ebony horses plumed with matching black ostrich feathers. Finally, the casket was carried to the entrance of the church whose crypt held generations of Habsburg royalty.[15] The controller of the household used his metal-tipped staff to slowly and pur-

Sisi stopped posing for court photographers in her early thirties to preserve her youth and beauty in the minds of her subjects. To approximate what she looked like at the time she was assassinated, photographer Carl Pietzner retouched an original photo taken by Ludwig Angerer around 1869. Pietzner filled out her face, dulled her eyes, and added the high-necked dress and large cross necklace (Library of Congress Prints and Photographs Division, George Grantham Bain Collection).

posefully knock three times on the church doors. What followed was an age-old ceremony meant to humble the Habsburg royal to God's will.

"Who requests entry?" asked the Capuchin monk from inside the church.

"Elisabeth, empress and queen, desires admittance," came the emphatic reply.

"We know her not," answered the monk.

Three more times the controller knocked.

"Who requests entry?" the monk asked again.

The controller's voice lowered. "Elisabeth, a mortal, sinful human being," he said.

Now satisfied, the monk answered, "Come in," and pushed opened the enormous double-doors.

The casket was placed by the church alter where scores of people would file past it to pay their final respects. Next to the coffin was the empress's

This shows the old emperor in uniform. When Sisi died, thousands lined the streets of Vienna to pay their respects, more for their beloved emperor than for his murdered consort. Franz Joseph died on Nov. 21, 1916, in Schönbrunn Palace at the age of eighty-six. His reign had lasted for sixty-eight years, and he was succeeded by his grand-nephew, Karl (Library of Congress Prints and Photographs Division, George Grantham Bain Collection).

coat of arms with the inscription, "Elisabeth, Empress of Austria." The Hungarians present were outraged that she was not also remembered as their beloved queen. Before the day was out the words, "and Queen of Hungary," were added.

Sisi's attendants, Ida Ferenczy and Marie Festetics, stood by comforting one other. The two women talked about how they regretted not being with the empress while she lay dying as Irma Sztáray had. Then,

Ida summed up the reality of having set aside one's own needs to serve the imperial household: "I have lost everything," she sobbed, "husband, children, family, happiness, contentment; for my dear Queen was all these to me."[16]

Sisi's final resting place was the Habsburg Crypt beneath the church, next to her son, Rudolf, and one day, Franz Joseph. But one Habsburg tradition would not be observed: that of burying the heart and viscera separately from the body. Franz Joseph was strongly against this practice that dated back to 1654 when King Ferdinand IV dedicated his heart to the Virgin of Loreto at the Augustinian Church. Subsequent Habsburg rulers followed suit, and there are now fifty-four silver urns containing imperial hearts in the Loreto Chapel's Heart Crypt. Ferdinand's intestines were subsequently buried in the Ducal Crypt at St. Stephen's Cathedral followed by those of dozens of other Habsburgs. The Franciscan custom stemmed from the Bible verse Luke 12:34, "For where your treasure is, there will your heart be also."[17]

Sisi was an exceedingly shy and private person who was thrust into an unrelenting spotlight on a restrictive world stage while still a teenager. She coped the only way she knew how, by fleeing from the intrusion that to her seemed life-threatening. She protected herself each day by donning her armor of tight-laced corsets topped with a perfectly braided crown that became a protective cloak when let loose. Sisi spent a lifetime building a wall around her heart; a silver urn could not have preserved it any better.

Epilogue

"A king among thieves."—*Kronen Zeitung*

In July 2008, the Köchert Diamond Pearl was finally freed from its exhibit locker in Winnipeg's Public Safety Building, where it had been held since being liberated from Blanchard's grandmother's basement a year earlier. A Canadian Crown attorney carried the precious cargo under lock and key for the nine-and-a-half hour nonstop flight from Winnipeg to Vienna. A car met her at the airport and drove a half hour to Schönbrunn Palace where officials waited anxiously to take possession of the star that had been adrift for exactly a decade. The star's original owner had been adrift, too, in 1898, and her homecoming had been mournful. Now a piece of Sisi's past had finally found its way home, and the mood was decidedly uplifted. Planning would begin immediately to decide how and where to display the star again. Security had improved vastly in the past decade, and this time, all angles would be properly covered to fend off the likes of another Gerald Blanchard.

Remarkably, news of the Köchert Diamond Pearl's homecoming did not generate the front-page headlines the theft had in 1998. Perhaps it had been eclipsed by the recovery of another priceless treasure the same week in Vienna: A Stradivarius violin created in 1680 and worth nearly four million dollars had been stolen by a Georgian gang two weeks earlier. It was safely returned to an acclaimed Viennese musician around the same time the Sisi Star arrived back at Schönbrunn Palace.

"Art Thief's Grandmother Hid Sisi's Star," is how *Kronen Zeitung* erroneously reported the story, buried on page sixteen. Though it had been hidden in his grandmother's basement, only Gerald Blanchard ever knew the star's whereabouts. For his audacious theft, the paper dubbed Blanchard, "a king among thieves."

In the same article, an official from Austria's Federal Criminal Police Office commented that the investigation into the star's theft was still open. "The group of criminals was mainly involved in ATM thefts," Rupert Sprinzl told the paper. "We are still investigating whether the individuals are responsible for other cases in Austria."[1]

On Valentine's Day, 2013, a story ran in *The Province*, a Vancouver daily newspaper, about a cable company employee named Rick White who was petitioning officials in British Columbia to allow exotic serval cats to be kept as pets. Eight months earlier, White had been ticketed by a Vancouver city animal control officer for walking his serval in the city's Portside Park. Even though servals weren't specifically named in the city's animal control bylaw as cheetahs and jaguars were, the ticket still cited White under "Prohibition against keeping certain exotic or wild animals," which carried a hefty fine of $2,000. White told the paper he would fight to have the bylaw clarified so that servals could be kept in Vancouver without fear of prosecution.

The Province story featured a photo of White in a safari outfit with the pet in question, his one-year-old serval cat, Ramsey, sporting a jeweled collar. Servals like Ramsey are bred in captivity and can sell for up to $8,000.

"I love this cat," said the forty-one-year-old White. "He is super adorable. I walk him on a leash. He's like a dog."[2] White added that Ramsey was his second serval; he told *The Province* that he was also co-owner of Ramsey's father, Stewie.

Servals are cheetah-like African wildcats that are closely related to the African golden cat and the desert lynx. Animal organizations like the Society for the Prevention of Cruelty to Animals and the Vancouver Humane Society fear that these natural predators, weighing up to thirty pounds, could act upon their instincts and seriously injure people and other pets.

Gerald Blanchard with his serval cat, Ramsey. Following his incarceration for bank robbery, fraud, and possessing the Köchert Diamond Pearl, Blanchard turned up in the Vancouver newspaper as exotic cat activist "Rick White" (photograph by Jason Payne/*The Province*).

According to a Humane Society official, "Even if they're bred in captivity, they retain the same bahavioural and biological needs as their wild counterparts. We don't think they make good pets because they're basically being deprived of the ability to engage in their natural behaviour."[3]

As soon as the serval story ran, *Province* reporter Frank Luba received several phone calls not about the exotic cat issue but about the cat's owner. The tipsters said that Rick White wasn't exactly who he seemed and encouraged Luba to look into his background. After doing some digging, Luba learned that his interviewee's real name was Gerald Daniel Blanchard and that he had a notorious past within the Canadian legal system. Luba contacted "White" for comment and was surprised when the ex-con came clean. "That's me," Blanchard admitted to Luba. "I changed my life around."

When asked whether it was prudent for a high-profile criminal mastermind to court the media spotlight, Blanchard said it was all part of his plan to rebuild his life.

"It's positive for me," Blanchard said. "Now I'm just basically a regular cable guy with a normal job and volunteering at animal shelters and working with these cats."[4]

Blanchard admitted to *The Province* that it was difficult going from having millions of illicit dollars to living paycheck to paycheck working for the cable company. He never mentioned anything, however, about starting his own security consulting business, his dream since his confinement to Stony Mountain Penitentiary in 2007. But if Blanchard is to be believed, his career goals have taken a back seat to an ardent desire to repair his personal relationships.

"Being the criminal that I used to be," Blanchard said, "I never realized that there was such negative impacts on your family and your friends. I was basically selfish and just thought about how much money I could make and kept that life super secretive.

"You realize after you've been incarcerated, what matters in life is your family and friends."[5]

Blanchard's work with serval cats did, in fact, seem to be introducing him to a whole new world of law-abiding citizens. A prominent photo on his group's web site, the Domestic Serval Society of B.C., features Blanchard affectionately rubbing foreheads with one of the pet felines. He can also be seen posing with his new found friends and their cats outside of a British Columbian municipal office building where they were appealing for Green Party support. Blanchard blends in seamlessly with the group, wearing his safari outfit in one shot and a dark windbreaker and jeans in another. He is smiling and gives the impression that he truly values being an important part of the group that has a common purpose of good will. There is no hint of Blanchard's nefarious past.

The web site features a video montage of servals fetching toys and splashing in baby pools stocked with wriggling goldfish. It's set to a Canadian rock band's power ballad with earnest lyrics about pushing on even when life leaves you feeling hopeless and abandoned: "Stop thinking about the easy way out ... there's no need to go and blow the candle out. Because you're not done, you're far too young, and the best is yet to come...."[6]

The lyrics could easily pertain to Blanchard's own life, and it is possible that with his penchant for videotaping his past escapades, Blanchard is the one behind the camera, capturing some of the animal friends he now says he treasures more than money and editing the piece to an emotional soundtrack.

On Blanchard's Facebook page named after one of his servals, he has posted dozens of photographs of cats posing with children, attending animal expos, and cozying up to patients in their hospital beds. There are also shots of the cats at lavish events, posing with flashy cars like a Lamborghini and Rolls Royce and with the likes of Miss World Canada 2013. Blanchard sports a media pass around his neck in one shot, and in another, he posted a photo of the animal control citation he received as "Rick White." Next to the ticket is an ATM transaction receipt for a checking account showing $299,847.95 with the words:

Called Lawyer $$$$
Money in Bank $$$$
Fight for the Animals (priceless)

An earlier photo posted March 13, 2013, shows a serval cat next to an ATM slip displaying a balance of close to $200,000 with a smiley-face doodle and the words "Smile Ramsey" penned in blue marker. One friend commented, "Ramsey is one rich cat!!"

It was not clear whether the ATM slips were for a personal account or one maintained by the B.C. serval group.

One of the most extraordinary photos was posted on the same day Blanchard added an old shot, taken during his crime spree days of his pet black-and-white spaniel stretched out on a bed of $100 Canadian bills. The new photograph featured a serval cat wearing a jewel-studded collar and luxuriating on a pile of cash all his own, only this time the bills were twenties instead of hundreds. For a man who maintained he was moving on with a legitimate life and had even tried changing his name, the reenactment of a photo from his criminal past seemed like an ill-advised move. But perhaps it was just Blanchard's curious attempt at humor.

Blanchard's Facebook page also revealed that his love of surveillance gadgets remains in tact; he posted several videos of high-flying adventures taken with multirotor drones.

—⟋⟋⟍—

The Winnipeg Police officers who headed up Project Kite, one of the largest probes in the city's history, received national accolades for their investigative skills and tenacity. Inspector Tom Legge, commander of the Criminal Investigations Bureau; Sergeant Larry Levasseur of the Commercial Crime Unit; and Sergeant Mitch McCormick of the Major Crimes Unit received the prestigious 2007 Canadian Banks' Law Enforcement Award for solving the string of bank robberies perpetuated by the Gerald Blanchard Criminal Organization between 2000 and 2006. Levasseur and McCormick have also parlayed their invaluable experience into a business of their own; since retiring from the Winnipeg Police Service, the two have been in demand as lecturers, sharing what they've gleaned from the Blanchard case with investigators around the world.

Superintendent Gordon Schumacher received Manitoba's 2006 Excellence in Law Enforcement Award and in 2008 was inducted by the lieutenant governor of Canada as an officer into the Canadian Order of Merit, Canada's highest and most prestigious award for serving police officers. After thirty years of service, Schumacher retired in 2009 and went on to continue the fight against organized crime as an attorney within the Manitoba Justice Department.

The arrest of Gerald Blanchard and the copious amounts of admissible bank robbery and fraud evidence that the Project Kite team gathered against him inevitably led Blanchard to give up the Sisi Star. Without the officers' diligent detective work, Blanchard might not have felt as pressured, and the Köchert Diamond Pearl might still be tucked away in his grandmother's basement. To what end, only Blanchard would have known.

Epilogue

"You know, it had its ups and downs," Schumacher said of Project Kite. "It had some nonbelievers in the early stages and even as we were going through [it], some people were just like, 'this isn't the investigation you guys are holding it out to be.' Once the [Sisi Star] showed up, that was a great culmination to the entire investigation."[7]

Following Blanchard's trial, the warehouse full of tens of thousands of pieces of evidence was dismantled. Some of the more important items were placed into police storage while personal effects were returned to Blanchard. As for the surveillance systems, electronics, and computers that Blanchard methodically employed for his most brazen crimes, that equipment was reconfigured and is now being used by analysts in the Winnipeg Police Criminal Intelligence Unit to continue the crackdown on organized crime.

Sisi's myth of eternal beauty and the reality of her obsessions and lifelong unhappiness have been preserved for posterity in the Hofburg's Sisi Museum. The museum celebrated its tenth anniversary in 2014 with more than six million visitors desiring to learn more about the elegant and mysterious Empress. Of the three hundred exhibits dedicated to Sisi, the one considered most valuable is the Winterhalter portrait of the young Empress in her star-spangled ball gown with the diamond Köchert Stars affixed to her masterfully braided hair. The portrait, measuring eleven feet by seven feet, was painstakingly restored in 2012 to mark Sisi's 175th birthday. It is certainly the single image by which Sisi aspired to be remembered, and the restoration ensures her wish will continue to be fulfilled.

Another desire realized concerns Sisi's poetry and the Hungarian people she loved enough to repress her pathological shyness in order to take a political stand. Around 1890, Sisi deposited six hundred pages of verse in an iron box fixed with her personal seal featuring a seagull. Her attendant, Ida Ferenczy, was instructed to turn over the container to the empress's brother, Duke Karl Theodor, after Sisi's death. He, in turn, delivered it to the Austrian Academy of Sciences with Sisi's express instructions that the poetry belonged to "the souls of the future" and should not be published for sixty years.

In 1951, according to Sisi's will, the academy delivered the package to the Swiss Federal Council, requesting that the poems it contained finally be published. Sisi's work was ultimately printed in German under the title "*Kaiserin Elisabeth: Das Poetische Tagebuch*" and later in English. In 2010, the United Nations High Commissioner for Refugees announced it would donate sales from Sisi's poetic diary to a Hungarian school that supports children from immigrant families. An excerpt from *Words To Souls Of The Future* advises the misunderstood to take heart:

> I wander lonely before me on this planet earth
> All yearning long since gone, and life;
> To share my innermost is no companion.
> There never was a soul who understood.
>
> I flee this world, its pleasures too,
> And its people are distant to me now;
> Their joys are foreign and their distress;
> I wander lonely as if upon a star.
>
> And my soul, heavy to burst,
> Mute sensuality is not enough.
> What it needs is found in song
> And this I am burying in my book.
>
> This will keep you faithfully into age
> From souls who understand you not in this life;
> Till one day, following lengthy years of change,
> These songs, blooming, do revive.[8]

As for the Köchert Diamond Pearl, no one was ever charged with actually stealing it. The piece was acquired by the Hofburg's Sisi Museum from the private collector who owned it when it was stolen from Schönbrunn in 1998. Perhaps the jewel became too expensive to insure or the owner simply felt it should belong to the people of the former empire whose sovereign made it famous. Whatever the reason, the last remaining Sisi Star available for public viewing is now resting permanently on a rotating lilac-hued velvet pillow, forever a glittering symbol of a woman who continues to be considered one of the most beautiful—and intriguing—the world has ever known.

Chapter Notes

Preface

1. Gerald Blanchard, phone interview with author, January 14, 2014.

Prologue

1. Doug Struck, "An Empress's Jeweled Hairpin Buffs a Canadian Crook's Rep," *The Washington Post*, June 19, 2007.
2. Alan Palmer, *Twilight of the Habsburgs: The Life and Times of Emperor Francis Joseph* (New York: Grove Press, 1994), 234.

Chapter I

1. Brigitte Hamann, *The Reluctant Empress: A Biography of Empress Elisabeth of Austria* (New York: Alfred A. Knopf, 1986), 16.
2. Joan Haslip, *The Lonely Empress* (London: Sterling Publishing, 1965), 59.
3. Andrew Sinclair, *Death By Fame: A Life Of Elisabeth Empress of Austria* (New York: St. Martin's Press, 1998), 4.
4. Sinclair, 123.
5. Palmer, 69.
6. Andrew Wheatcroft, *The Habsburgs: Embodying Empire* (New York: Penguin Putnam Inc., 1996), 272–273.
7. Sinclair, 13.
8. Hamann, *The Reluctant Empress*, 16.
9. George R. Marek, *The Eagles Die: Franz Joseph, Elisabeth and Their Austria* (New York: Harper & Row, 1974), 102.
10. Hamann, *The Reluctant Empress*, 53.
11. Brigitte Hamann, *Sisi: Elisabeth, Empress of Austria* (London: Taschen, 1997), 15.
12. Anthony Phelan, *Reading Heinrich Heine* (Cambridge: Cambridge University Press, 2010), x.
13. Louis Untermeyer, ed. "Lyrical Intermezzo, 57," In *Poems of Heinrich Heine: Three Hundred and Twenty-five Poems* (New York: Henry Holt and Company, 1917), 73.
14. Renate Hotbauer, *Empress Elisabeth of Austria: The Fate of a Woman under the Yoke of the Imperial Court* (Vienna: Lindenau Productions GmbH, 1998), 30.
15. Sinclair, 26.
16. Hamann, *The Reluctant Empress*, 78.
17. Wheatcroft, 274.
18. "Foreign Intelligence, Austria and Hungary," *The Irish Times*, November 21, 1860.
19. *The Irish Times*, November 27, 1860.
20. Hamann, *The Reluctant Empress*, 111.
21. Gemma Blackshaw, ed., *Journeys Into Madness: Mapping Mental Illness in the Austro-Hungarian Empire* (New York: Berghahn Books, 2012), 98.
22. Hamann, *The Reluctant Empress*, 109.
23. Hamann, *The Reluctant Empress*, 105.
24. Sinclair, 37.
25. *Dublin Evening Mail*, September 29, 1862, 3.
26. Katrin Unterreiner, *Sisi: Myth and Truth* (Vienna: Verlag Christian Brandstatter, 2005), 51.
27. "A Royal Pupil," *The Irish Times*, May 8, 1863.
28. Count Egon Corti, *Elizabeth, Empress of Austria* (New Haven: Yale University Press, 1936), 186.
29. Corti, 452.

30. Palmer, 119.
31. Corti, 446.
32. Unterreiner, 59–60.
33. Corti, 443–444.

Chapter II

1. "Super Thief Eyes Career as Security Consultant," *Daily Motion*, video, 12:46. January 11, 2010. http://www.dailymotion.com/video/xfrt5q_super-thief-eyes-career-as-security-consultant_news.
2. *Daily Motion.*
3. Joshuah Bearman, "Art of the Steal: On the Trail of the World's Most Ingenious Thief," *Wired Magazine*, March 22, 2010.
4. "High-tech Crook Gets 8 years from String of Thefts, Frauds," *CBC News*, Nov. 7, 2007, http://www.cbc.ca/news/canada/manitoba/high-tech-crook-gets-8-years-for-string-of-thefts-frauds-1.640262.
5. Bearman.
6. *CBC News*, Nov. 7, 2007.
7. *CBC News*, Nov. 7, 2007.
8. Bearman.
9. Struck.
10. Struck.
11. Joe Friesen, "Jet-set Thief Had Designs on Gems, Police Say," *The Globe and Mail*, June 2, 2007.
12. *Daily Motion.*
13. Bearman.
14. Ibid.
15. Ibid.
16. Mary De Zutter, "Deportation Ordered for Man Who Eluded Police in Two Cities," *Omaha World Herald*, June 10, 1993.
17. "He's a Man of Mystery Even to His Family," *Winnipeg Free Press*, May 30, 2007.

Chapter III

1. Gerald Blanchard, phone interview with author, January 14, 2014.
2. Palmer, 47.
3. *Nottinghamshire Guardian*, April 8, 1887, 12.
4. "Talks With the Empress of Austria," *The San Francisco Call* 85, no. 67, February 5, 1899.
5. Sinclair, 155.
6. *The San Francisco Call.*

7. Haslip, 278.
8. Hamann, *The Reluctant Empress*, 136.
9. Haslip, 175.
10. Baroness Staffe, *The Lady's Dressing Room* (London: Cassell & Company, 1892), 107.
11. Hamann, *The Reluctant Empress*. 137.
12. The Sisi Museum, "Imperial Apartments: Lavatory and Bathroom," http://www.hofburg-wien.at/en/things-to-know/imperial-apartments/tour-of-the-imperial-apartments/lavatory-and-bathroom.html.
13. Unterreiner, 68–69.
14. Marek, 108.

Chapter IV

1. Bearman.
2. *Morgenpost*, April 27, 1863.
3. Sinclair, 171.
4. Olivia Gruber Florek, "I Am a Slave to My Hair: Empress Elisabeth of Austria, Fetishism, and Nineteenth-Century Austrian Sexuality," *Modern Austrian Literature* 42, no. 2, (2009), 8.
5. Constantin Christomanos, Elisabeth von Österreich. *Tagebuchblätter von Constantin Christomanos*, (Vienna, 1899), 84.
6. *Newcastle Courant*, December 9, 1881, 3.
7. Unterreiner, 43.
8. Countess Marie Larisch, *Secrets of a Royal House* (London: J. Long, Limited,1936), 17.
9. *The San Francisco Call.*
10. Hamann, *The Reluctant Empress*, 136.
11. Christomanos, 84.
12. "Wigs of Empress Elisabeth in the Sisi Museum," http://www.hofburg-wien.at/en/things-to-know/sisi-museum/wigs-of-empress-elisabeth-in-the-sisi-museum.html.

Chapter V

1. Bearman.
2. Gerald Blanchard, phone interview with author, January 2014.
3. Blanchard.

Chapter VI

1. Hamann, *The Reluctant Empress*, 131.
2. *Bath Chronicle and Weekly Gazette*, October 13, 1864, 7.
3. Helen Rappaport, "Winterhalter, Franz Xaver (1805–1873)" In *Queen Victoria: A Biographical Companion* (Denver: ABC-CLIO, 2003), 422–423.
4. Rappaport, 425.
5. Rappaport, 422.
6. Frank Anderson Trapp, "The Universal Exhibition of 1855," *The Burlington Magazine* 107, no. 747, June 1965, 302.
7. Haslip, 179.
8. Hotbauer, 68.
9. "The Cholera," *The Wrexham Advertiser*, Clwyd, Wales, July 28, 1866
10. Corti, 253.
11. Hamann, *The Reluctant Empress*, 131.
12. Unterreiner, 83.
13. "A Novel Fashion," *The Irish Times*, February 8, 1866.
14. Kate Culkin, *Harriet Hosmer: A Cultural Biography* (Amherst: University of Massachusetts Press, 2010), 113.
15. Hamann, *The Reluctant Empress*, 129.
16. Ulla Fischer-Westhauser, "Court Photographers—Photographers for the Court?" *Photography Research in Austria: Vienna, the Door to the European East*, Symposium 2001 Vienna, European Society for the History of Photography, (Vienna: Dietmar Klinger, 2002), 74–75.
17. Unterreiner, 43.
18. Unterreiner, 42.
19. Palmer, 244.
20. Sinclair, 160.
21. Hamann, *The Reluctant Empress*, 128.
22. Haslip, 175.
23. Sinclair, 123.
24. Corti, 347.
25. Blackshaw, 99.
26. Sinclair, 106.
27. Sinclair, 129.
28. Marek, 259.
29. Sinclair, 134.
30. Crown Prince Rudolf, "Final Letter," Mayerling Museum, Austria, January, 1889, http://commons.wikimedia.org/wiki/File:Mayerling.final_letter.jpg.
31. Palmer, 264–265

32. Sinclair, 143.
33. Haman, 342.
34. Corti, 402.
35. The Hofburg Sisi Museum, "The Sisi Museum Celebrates its 10th Anniversary: A Temporary Exhibition Allows a Fascinating Glimpse Behind the Doors of Elisabeth's Wardrobe," http://www.hofburg-wien.at/en/nc/services/news/news-detail-start/artikel/zehn-jahre-sisi-museum-sonderschau-gewaehrt-einblick-in-elisabeths-garderobenschrank-1.html, June 21, 2014.
36. "A Royal Wedding," *The Queenslander*, March 22, 1902, 648.

Chapter VII

1. *Kronen Zeitung*, July 21, 1998.
2. Ibid.
3. Franz Sattlecker, email interview with author, March 4, 2014.
4. *Daily Motion*.
5. Bearman.
6. *Daily Motion*.
7. "Boss of Global Theft Ring Pleads Guilty to Theft Crimes Stretching Across Country," *Winnipeg Free Press*, November 7, 2007.
8. Bearman.
9. Ibid.
10. Schumacher.
11. *Daily Motion*.
12. Schumacher.
13. Ibid.

Chapter VIII

1. Haslip, 197.
2. Haslip, 179.
3. Unterreiner, 47.
4. Hamann, *The Reluctant Empress*, 131.
5. Fischer-Westhauser, 75.
6. Diana de Marly, *The History of Haute Couture 1850–1950* (New York: Holmes & Meier Publishers, Inc., 1980), 22.
7. de Marly, 19.
8. Regina Schulte, ed., *The Body of the Queen: Gender and Rule in the Courtly World, 1500–2000* (New York: Berghahn Books, 2006), 223.
9. Hotbauer, 74.

10. Corti, 341.
11. Palmer, 177–178.
12. *Sheffield Daily Telegraph*, August 20, 1874, 2.
13. *Edinburgh Evening News*, March 6, 1876, 4.
14. Haslip, 411.
15. Unterreiner, 58.
16. Corti, 247.

Chapter IX

1. Hotbauer, 100.
2. Unterreiner, 46.
3. G.K. Fortescue, ed., *Memoirs of Madame Campan on Marie-Antoinette and Her Court* (Boston: J.B. Millet Company, 1909), 89.
4. Palmer, 324.
5. Ian Traynor, "Pope to Beatify 'Buffoon' Who Was Austria's Last Emperor," *The Guardian*, January 18, 2004.
6. Justin O. Vovk, *Imperial Requiem: Four Royal Women and the Fall of the Age of Empires* (Bloomington, iUniverse, 2012), 220–221.
7. Vovk, 480.

Chapter X

1. Struck.
2. Corti, 36.
3. Palmer, 193.
4. Marek, 165.
5. *Western Daily Press*, Bristol, England, February 16, 1882, 7.
6. Hotbauer, 87.
7. *Western Daily Press*, Bristol, England, February 16, 1882, 7.
8. *The Irish Times*, August 31, 1878.
9. Corti, 272.
10. Unterreiner, 64–65.
11. Hamann, *The Reluctant Empress*, 234.
12. Hamann, *The Reluctant Empress*, 217–218.
13. Marek, 192.
14. Hamann, *The Reluctant Empress*, 55.
15. *The Irish Times*, August, 26, 1874.
16. *The Wrexham Advertiser*.
17. Sinclair, 100–101.
18. Hamann, *The Reluctant Empress*, 94.
19. Unterreiner, 88.

20. Corti, 425.
21. Carmen Sylva, *Golden Thoughts of Carmen Sylva, Queen of Rumania* (New York: John Lane Company, 1910), 62.
22. Corti, 357.
23. Ibid.
24. Unterreiner, 100.
25. Hamann, *The Reluctant Empress*, 338.
26. Unterreiner, 97.
27. Corti, 429.
28. Corti, 438.
29. Hans Koning, *The Almost World* (Hong Kong: Longriver, Hk Books, 1995), 183.

Chapter XI

1. Gordon Schumacher, phone interview with author, August 12, 2014.
2. Schumacher.
3. Bearman.
4. Schumacher.
5. Ibid.
6. *Daily Motion*.
7. *Daily Motion*.
8. Schumacher.
9. Bearman.
10. Gordon Schumacher, email interview with author, August 18, 2014.
11. Bearman.
12. *Daily Motion*.
13. Ibid.
14. Judge Jeffrey Oliphant, email interview with author, July 15, 2014.
15. Bearman.
16. Schumacher.
17. Dean Pritchard, "Accused Criminal Mastermind's Lair Raided," *Sun Media*, July 12, 2007.
18. Mike McIntyre, "Police Raids, Arrests Targeted Hells Angels," *Winnipeg Free Press*, March 16, 2012.
19. Struck.
20. "Con Man Repentant for Crimes," *Winnipeg Free Press*, November 8, 2007.
21. Bearman.
22. Schumacher.
23. Bearman.

Chapter XII

1. Unterreiner, 101.
2. Unterreiner, 39.

3. William and Robert Chambers, "Royal Pleasure Ships," *Chamber's Journal of Popular Literature, Science and Art, Fifth Edition,* June 7, 1890.
4. Corti, 328–329.
5. Unterreiner, 98–99.
6. Corti, 443.
7. Unterreiner, 100–101.
8. Hamann, *The Reluctant Empress,* 353.
9. Corti, 422.
10. Corti, 400.
11. Corti, 231–232.
12. Hamann, *The Reluctant Empress,* 285.
13. Clifton Fadiman and Andre Bernard, Eds., *Bartlett's Book of Anecdotes Revised,* (New York: Little, Brown and Company, 2000), 8–9.
14. Sinclair, 157–158.
15. Corti, 448.
16. Hamann, *The Reluctant Empress,* 360.
17. *Western Daily Press,* Bristol, England, September 5, 1890, 7.
18. Sinclair, 175.
19. Corti, 415.

Chapter XIII

1. Bearman.
2. *Daily Motion.*
3. Gerald Blanchard, phone interview with author, January 14, 2014.
4. Gordon Schumacher, phone interview with author, August 12, 2014.
5. "Criminal Mastermind's Thefts Funded Muslim Extremists, Court Hears," *Winnipeg Free Press,* November 7, 2007.
6. "Palace Ecstatic Queen's Gem Recovered," *Winnipeg Free Press,* June 3, 2007.
7. Schumacher.
8. "Scams Funded Terror in Iraq," *The Truth Seeker,* November 11, 2007, http://www.thetruthseeker.co.uk/?p=7585.
9. Judge Jeffrey Oliphant, email interview with author, July 15, 2014.
10. *CBC News,* Nov. 7, 2007
11. "Boss of Global Theft Ring Pleads Guilty to Theft Crimes Stretching Across Country," *Winnipeg Free Press,* November 7, 2007.
12. Gordon Schumacher, email interview with author, August 18, 2014.

13. Mike McIntyre, "Scams Funded Terror in Iraq," *Winnipeg Free Press,* November 7, 2007.
14. *Winnipeg Free Press,* November 7, 2007.
15. Blanchard.
16. *CBC News,* Nov. 7, 2007.
17. "Alert Wal-Mart Employee Sparked Investigation," *Winnipeg Free Press,* November 8, 2007.
18. "Boss of Global Theft Ring Pleads Guilty to Theft Crimes Stretching Across Country," *Winnipeg Free Press,* November 7, 2007.
19. Bearman.
20. *Daily Motion.*
21. Schumacher.
22. Canadian Bankers Association, "Debit Card Fraud," http://www.cba.ca/en/consumer-information/42-safeguarding-your-money/59-debit-card-fraud.
23. Schumacher.
24. "Criminal Mastermind's Cousin Pleads Guilty, Gets Break from Judge," *Winnipeg Free Press,* July 2, 2008.
25. Bearman.
26. "Judge Punishes Minor Players in Global Scam," *Winnipeg Free Press,* April 8, 2008.
27. "Crime Boss's Ex-girlfriend Gets One-year Conditional Sentence," *The Vancouver Province,* September 25, 2008.
28. Dean Pritchard, "Man Sentenced for Aiding Ringleader," *Sun Media,* April 9, 2009.
29. Schumacher.
30. Judge Jeffrey Oliphant, email interview with author, July 15, 2014.
31. Nancy Koreen, email interview with author, July 17, 2014.
32. Nancy Koreen, phone interview with author, July 16, 2014.
33. Oliphant.

Chapter XIV

1. Unterreiner, 102.
2. Corti, 475.
3. Hamann, *The Reluctant Empress,* 368.
4. "For Killing The Empress, The Fate of Luigi Luccheni," *The New York Times,* November 11, 1898.

5. Palmer, 285.
6. Sinclair, 176.
7. *The New York Times.*
8. Corti, 486.
9. Charles Neider, ed., "The Memorable Assassination," In *The Complete Essays of Mark Twain* (Cambridge: Da Capo Press, 2000), 536.
10. Cesare Lombroso, "A Study of Luigi Luccheni (Assassin of the Empress of Austria), *Popular Science Monthly*55, June 1899.
11. Candace Falk, ed., *Emma Goldman: A Documentary History of the American Years, Vol. 1: Made for America 1890–1901* (Champaign: University of Illinois Press, 2003), 346–347.

Suspect Again, *Winnipeg Sun*, September 13, 2010.
9. "Serial Thief Out Since Last Fall," *Winnipeg Sun*, May 2, 2012.
10. Bearman.
11. Corti, 486.
12. Corti, 487.
13. *The King James Version Bible*, Psalm 91:1, (New York: Thomas Nelson, Inc., 1990).
14. Corti, 488.
15. Neider, 543.
16. Corti, 489.
17. *The King James Version Bible*, Luke 12:34, (New York: Thomas Nelson, Inc., 1990).

Chapter XV

1. Gordon Schumacher, email interview with author, August 13, 2014.
2. *CBC News*, Nov. 7, 2007.
3. Myles J. Connor, Jr. and Jenny Siler, *The Art of the Heist: Confessions of a Master Art Thief, Rock-and-Roller, and Prodigal Son*, (New York: Collins, 2009), 93.
4. "Gang Members Separated to Curb Violence in Stony Mountain Prison," *CBC News*, June 9, 2009.
5. Arielle Godbout, "Mastermind of ATM Heist Granted Day Parole," *Winnipeg Free Press*, June 19, 2009.
6. Suzanne Fournier, "Police Put Thief on Olympic Radar," *The Province*, January 13, 2010.
7. Fournier.
8. Paul Turenne, "Master Criminal a

Epilogue

1. Michael Pommer, *Kronen Zeitung*, June 2007, 16.
2. Frank Luba, "Cat Fight Brewing over African Serval Pets," *The Province*, February 14, 2013.
3. Ibid.
4. Frank Luba, "Cat Owner Admits Criminal Past," *The Province*, February 15, 2013.
5. Chad Kroeger, "Lullaby," *Here and Now*, Roadrunner/Universal Music Canada, 2012.
6. Luba, "Cat Owner Admits Criminal Past."
7. Gordon Schumacher, phone interview with author, August 12, 2014.
8. Hotbauer, 91.

Bibliography

Appleton, D. & Company. *Appleton's Annual Cyclopædia and Register of Important Events*. Foreign Obituaries, Volume 1898.

The Art Loss Register. www.artloss.org.

Association of Certified Forensic Investigators of Canada. "ACFI 15th Annual Fraud Conference Speaker Bios: Larry Levasseur and Mitch McCormick." https://secure.acfi.ca/Conf2013Bios.htm.

Bath Chronicle and Weekly Gazette. October 13, 1864.

BBC News. "Austria finds stolen Stradivarius." June 6, 2007.

BBC News. "Body Art Goes on Show." March 22, 2002.

Bearman, Joshuah. "Art of the Steal: On the Trail of the World's Most Ingenious Thief." *Wired Magazine*, March 22, 2010.

Beevor, Antony. *The Second World War*. Columbus: Phoenix, 2013.

Blackshaw, Gemma, ed. *Journeys into Madness: Mapping Mental Illness in the Austro-Hungarian Empire*. New York: Berghahn, 2012.

Blanchard, Gerald, phone interview with author, January 14, 2014.

The British Museum. "Death Mask of George Bernard Shaw." http://www.cba.ca/en/consumer-information/42-safeguarding-your-money/59-debit-card-fraud.

Brooks, Derek. "Empress Sisi's Wardrobe Goes on Display in Vienna." *Reuters*, April 24, 2014.

Brown, David. "Criminal Mastermind Ends Jewel Mystery." *The Australian*, November 27, 2007.

Brumberg, Joan Jacobs. *Fasting Girls: The History of Anorexia Nervosa*. New York: Vintage, 2000.

Canadian Bankers Association. "Debit Card Fraud." http://www.cba.ca/en/consumer-information/42-safeguarding-your-money/59-debit-card-fraud.

Canadian Police College. http://www. cpc. gc. ca/en.

CBC News. "Gang Members Separated to Curb Violence in Stony Mountain Prison." June 9, 2009.

CBC News. "High-tech Crook Gets 8 Years from String of Thefts, Frauds." Nov. 7, 2007.

CBC News. "7 Arrested in Western Canadian Bank-theft Ring." January 26, 2007.

CBC News. "Alleged Fraud Ring Leader Facing New Charges." May 29, 2007.

CBC News. "Super-thief Blanchard has parole revoked." September 13, 2010.

CBC News. "Three Guilty in Headingley Jail Riot." July 3, 1999.

Centers for Disease Control and Prevention. "Gonorrhea." http://www.cdc.gov/std/gonorrhea/STDFact-Gonorrhea.htm.

Centers for Disease Control and Prevention. "Syphilis." http://www.cdc.gov/std/syphilis/stdfact-syphilis.htm.

Chambers, William, and Robert Chambers. "Royal Pleasure Ships." *Chamber's Journal of Popular Literature, Science and Art* 5 (June 7, 1890).

Chan, Marcus. "The Art of the Steal: Lessons from a Hired Scammer." *Bloomburg.com*, March 6, 2012.

Chrisp, Peter. *A History of Fashion and Costume: The Victorian Age*. Hove, East Sussex: Bailey, 2005.

Christomanos, Constantin. *Elisabeth von Österreich. Tagebuchblätter von ConstantinChristomanos*. Vienna, 1899.

Cone, Polly, ed. *The Imperial Style: Fashions*

Bibliography

of the Hapsburg Era. New York: The Metropolitan Museum of Art, 1980.

Congressional Serial Set, Currency of Austria-Hungary. U.S. Government Printing Office, 1896.

Connor, Myles J., Jr., and Jenny Siler. *The Art of the Heist: Confessions of a Master Art Thief, Rock-and-Roller, and Prodigal Son*. New York: Collins, 2009.

Corti, Count Egon. *Elizabeth, Empress of Austria*. New Haven: Yale University Press, 1936.

CTV News. "Suspect in Austrian Jewel Theft Faces New Charges." June 12, 2007.

Culkin, Kate. *Harriet Hosmer: A Cultural Biography*. Amherst: University of Massachusetts Press, 2010.

Daily Motion. "Super Thief Eyes Career as Security Consultant," January 11, 2010. http://www. dailymotion. com/video/xfrt5q_super-thief-eyes-career-as-security-consultant_news.

De Burgh, Edward Morgan Alborough. *Elizabeth, Empress of Austria: A Memoir*. J. B. Lippencott, 1899.

De Marly, Diana. *The History of Haute Couture, 1850–1950*. New York: Holmes & Meier, 1980.

De Marly, Diana. *Worth: Father of Haute Couture*. New York: Holmes & Meier, 1990.

De Zutter, Mary. "Deportation Ordered for Man Who Eluded Police in Two Cities." *Omaha World Herald*, June 10, 1993.

The Domestic Serval Society of B.C. Accessed July 30, 2014. http://www.domesticatedservals.com. *Dublin Evening Mail*. September 29, 1862.

Edinburgh Evening News. March 6, 1876.

Fadima, Clifton, and Andre Bernard, eds. *Bartlett's Book of Anecdotes, Revised Edition*. New York: Little, Brown & Co., 2000.

Falk, Candace, ed. *Emma Goldman: A Documentary History of the American Years, Vol. 1: Made for America 1890–1901*. Champaign: University of Illinois Press, 2003.

Falk, Ophir, and Henry Morgenstern, eds. *Suicide Terror: Understanding and Confronting the Threat*. Hoboken: John Wiley & Sons, Inc., 2009.

Florek, Olivia Gruber, "'I Am a Slave to My Hair': Empress Elisabeth of Austria, Fetishism, and Nineteenth-Century Austrian Sexuality." *Modern Austrian Literature* 42, no. 2 (2009).

Fortescue, G. K., ed. *Memoirs of Madame Campan on Marie-Antoinette and Her Court*. Boston: J. B. Millet, 1909. http://archive.org/stream/memoirsofmadamec02campuoft/memoirsofmadamec02campuoft_djvu. txt.

Fournier, Suzanne. "Police Put Thief on Olympic Radar." *The Province*, January 13, 2010.

Friesen, Joe. "Jet-set Thief Had Designs on Gems, Police Say." *The Globe and Mail*, June 2, 2007.

Godbout, Arielle. "Mastermind of ATM Heist Granted Day Parole." *Winnipeg Free Press*, June 19, 2009.

Habsburger.net. "Habsburgs in Exile—the Dynasty after 1918." http://www.habsburger.net/en/printpdf/stories/habsburgs-exile-dynasty-after-1918?language=en.

Hamann, Brigitte. *The Reluctant Empress: A Biography of Empress Elisabeth of Austria*. New York: Alfred A. Knopf, 1986.

Hamann, Brigitte. *Sissi: Elisabeth, Empress of Austria*. London: Taschen, 1997.

Haslinger, Ingrid and Katrin Unterreiner. *The Residence of Empress Elisabeth*. Vienna: The Vienna Hofburg, 2000.

Haslip, Joan. *The Lonely Empress*. London: Sterling, 1965.

Hofburg Sisi Museum. "The Sisi Museum Celebrates its 10th Aanniversary: A Temporary Exhibition Allows a Fascinating Glimpse Behind the Doors of Elisabeth's Wardrobe." http://www.hofburg-wien.at/en/nc/services/news/news-detail-start/artikel/zehn-jahre-sisi-museum-sonderschau-gewaehrt-einblick-in-elisabeths-garderobenschrank-1.html.

Hofburg Sisi Museum. "Star Jewelry of Empress Elisabeth." http://www.hofburg-wien.at/en/nc/services/news/news-detail-start/artikel/sternenschmuck-der-kaiserin-elisabeth.html.

Hofburg Sisi Museum. "Wigs of Empress Elisabeth in the Sisi Museum." http://www.hofburg-wien.at/en/things-to-know/sisi-museum/wigs-of-empress-elisabeth-in-the-sisi-museum.html.

Hotbauer, Renate. *Empress Elisabeth of Austria: The Fate of a Woman under the*

Yoke of the Imperial Court. Vienna: Lindenau Productions GmbH, 1998.

The Institute of Internal Auditors, Winnipeg Chapter. "2014 Fraud Summit: Larry Levasseur, Speaker." https://chapters.theiia.org/winnipeg/Events/Pages/2014-Fraud-Summit.aspx.

The Irish Times. August, 26, 1874

The Irish Times. August, 31, 1878.

The Irish Times. November 27, 1860.

The Irish Times. "Foreign Intelligence, Austria and Hungary," November 21, 1860.

The Irish Times. "A Novel Fashion," February 8, 1866

The Irish Times. "A Royal Pupil," May 8, 1863.

Kent, Jacqueline C. *Business Builders in Fashion.* Minneapolis: Oliver Press, 2003.

Kives, Bart and Lindsey Wiebe. "Gangs Staged Bloody Battle at Stony Mountain Penitentiary." *Winnipeg Free Press,* January 12, 2009.

Köchert, A. E. "history." http://www.koechert.com/geschichte/1.

Koning, Hans. *The Almost World.* Hong Kong: Longriver Hk, 1995.

Kronen Zeitung, July 21, 1998.

Koreen, Nancy, Director of Sport Promotion, United States Parachute Association, phone interview with author, July 16, 2014; email interview with author, July 17, 2014.

Larisch, Countess Marie. *Secrets of a Royal House.* London: J. Long, Ltd., 1936.

Laurent, Lea. *Our Lady of Belgium.* London: The Iris, 1916.

Lewiston Daily Sun. "Some Stolen Wyeth Paintings Recovered." July 19, 1974.

The Library of Congress. Prints & Photographs Online Catalog, www.loc.gov.

Lobell, Steven E. and Philip Mauceri, eds. *Ethnic Conflict and International Politics: Explaining Diffusion and Escallation.* New York: Palgrave Macmillan, 2004.

Lombroso, Cesare. "A Study of Luigi Luccheni (Assassin of the Empress of Austria)." *Popular Science Monthly.* June 1899.

Los Angeles Times. "The Empress and Old Vienna." Sept. 13, 1998.

Luba, Frank. "Cat Fight Brewing Over African Serval Pets." *The Province,* February 14,2013.

Luba, Frank. "Cat Owner Admits Criminal Past." *The Province,* February 15, 2013.

Malkin, Bonnie. "'The Boss' Who Organised Crimes to Fund Kurdish Terrorists." *The Daily Telegraph,* November 26, 2007.

Manitoba News Release. "2002 Attorney General Safer Communities and Excellence in Law Enforcement Awards." November 27, 2002. http://news.gov.mb.ca/news/?item=26222&posted=2002-11-27.

Marek, George R. *The Eagles Die: Franz Joseph, Elisabeth and Their Austria.* New York: Harper & Row, 1974.

McIntosh, Christopher. *The Swan King: Ludwig II of Bavaria.* New York: I. B. Tauris, 2012.

McIntyre, Mike. "Inmates Riot at Stony Mountain Penitentiary." *Winnipeg Free Press,* January 10, 2009.

McIntyre, Mike. "Last Link in Racket Admits to Crime." *Winnipeg Free Press,* April 9, 2009.

McIntyre, Mike. "Police Raids, Arrests Targeted Hells Angels." *Winnipeg Free Press,* March 16, 2012.

McIntyre, Mike. "Scams Funded terror in Iraq." *Winnipeg Free Press,* November 7, 2007.

Melnychuk, Phil. "African Cats May Still Be Allowed in Maple Ridge." *Maple Ridge News,* November 30, 2012.

Morgenpost. April 27, 1863.

Murad, Anatol. *Franz Joseph I of Austria and His Empire.* New York: Twayne, 1968.

Murphy, Shelley. "A Prodigal Art Thief Still Rocks 'n' Rolls." *The Boston Globe,* June 5, 2009.

Neider, Charles, ed. "The Memorable Assassination." *The Complete Essays of Mark Twain.* Cambridge: Da Capo Press, 2000.

New York Times. "For Killing the Empress, the Fate of Luigi Luccheni." November 11, 1898.

Newcastle Courant. December 9, 1881.

Nottinghamshire Guardian. April 8, 1887.

Oliphant, Jeffrey, email interview with author, July 15, 2014.

ONPA Architets. "Headingley Correctional Institution." http://www.onpa.ca/portfolio/portfolio-project/72.

Owen, Bruce and Wency Leung. "Fraud Ring Got Away with Millions." *CanWest News Service* and *Vancouver Sun,* January 27, 2007.

Bibliography

Owens, Karen. *Franz Joseph and Elisabeth.* Jefferson, NC: McFarland, 2014.

Palmer, Alan. *Twilight of the Habsburgs: The Life and Times of Emperor Francis Joseph.* New York: Grove Press, 1994.

Panek, Carl J. "321 Inmates Surrender After Rampage." *Chicago Tribune,* April 28, 1996.

Parole Board of Canada. http://pbc-clcc.gc. ca/.

Perlez, Jane. "WHAT'S DOING IN; Vienna." *New York Times,* August 2, 1998.

Phelan, Anthony. *Reading Heinrich Heine.* Cambridge University Press, 2010.

Pirnie, Bruce. *Counterinsurgency in Iraq (2003–2006).* Pittsburgh: The RAND Corporation, 2008.

Polan, Brenda and Roger Tredre. *The Great Fashion Designers.* Oxford: Berg, 2009.

Pritchard, Dean. "Accused Criminal Mastermind's Lair Raided." *Sun Media,* July 12, 2007. Pritchard, Dean. "Crime Spree Mastermind Gets Day Parole." *Sun Media,* June 19, 2009.

Pritchard, Dean. "Man Sentenced for Aiding Ringleader." *Sun Media,* April 9, 2009.

The Queenslander. "A Royal Wedding." March 22, 1902.

Rappaport, Helen. "Winterhalter, Franz Xaver (1805–1873)." *Queen Victoria: A Biographical Companion.* Denver: ABC-CLIO, 2003.

Rau Antiques, M. S., New Orleans. "The Empress of Austria's Jewel Case." http://www.rauantiques. com/about-us/press/the-empress-of-austria-s-jewel-case-1170.html.The Royal Jewlry Box. http://thero yaljewelrybox.blogspot.com/2013/03/the-empress-of-austrias-jewel-case.html.

Rudolf, Crown Prince. *Final Letter.* Mayerling Museum, Austria, January, 1889. http://commons.wikimedia. org/wiki/Fil e:Mayerling.finalletter.jpg.

Ruth, John A. *Decorum: Treatise on Etiquette and Dress.* Chicago: J. A. Ruth, 1877.

The San Francisco Call. "Talks with the Empress of Austria." Volume 85, Number 67,February 5, 1899.

Sattlecker, Franz, email interview with author, March 4, 2014.

Schulte, Regina, ed. *The Body of the Queen: Gender and Rule in the Courtly World, 1500–2000.* New York: Berghahn, 2006.

Schumacher, Gordon, phone interview with author, August 12, 2014; email interviews with author, August 13 and 18, 2014.

Sheffield Daily Telegraph. August 20, 1874.

Sinclair, Andrew. *Death by Fame: A Life of Elizabeth Empress of Austria.* London: Constable, 1998.

SMS Engineering. "Projects: Headingley Correctional Centre Medium and Maximum Security Wings." http://www.smseng.com/sms-engineering-projects/correctional-headingley-correctional-centre.cfm.

Staffe, Baroness. *The Lady's Dressing Room.* London: Victorian London Publications, 1893.

Steele, Philip. *A History of Fashion and Costumes: Volume 7, The Nineteenth Century.* Hove, East Sussex: Bailey, 2005.

Struck, Doug. "An Empress's Jeweled Hairpin Buffs a Canadian Crook's Rep." *The Washington Post,* June 19, 2007.

Sylva, Carmen. *Golden Thoughts of Carmen Sylva, Queen of Rumania.* New York: John Lane Co., 1910.

Taylor, Andrew. *Random Acts of Politeness: Eccentric, Quirky and Occasionally Suicidal Examples of Selflessness and Courtesy.* Gloucestershire: The History Press, 2011.

Trapp, Frank Anderson. "The Universal Exhibition of 1855." *The Burlington Magazine,* June 1965.

Traynor, Ian. "Pope to Beatify 'Buffoon' Who Was Austria's Last Emperor." *The Guardian,* January 18, 2004.

Tschudi, Clara. *Elizabeth, Empress of Austria and Queen of Hungary.* New York: E. P. Dutton, 1901.

Tschudi, Clara. *Maria Sophia, Queen of Naples.* New York: E. P. Dutton, 1905.

Turenne, Mike. "Master Criminal a Suspect Again." *Winnipeg Sun,* September 13, 2010.

Tuveri, Matteo. "Elizabeth of Austria: A Beauvoirian Perspective." *Simone de Beauvoir Studies: Celebrating a Centenary,* Vol. 24, 2007–2008.

Ulla Fischer-Westhauser. "Court Photographers—Photographers for the Court?" *Photography Research in Austria: Vienna, the Door to the European East.* Symposium 2001, Vienna, European Society for

Bibliography

the History of Photography. Vienna: Dietmar Klinger, 2002.

Untermeyer, Louis, ed. "Lyrical Intermezzo, 57." *Poems of Heinrich Heine: Three Hundred and Twenty-five Poems.* New York: Henry Holt and Co., 1917.

Unterreiner, Katrin. *Sisi: Myth and Truth.* Vienna: Verlag Christian Brandstatter, 2005.

The Vancouver Province. "Cat Owner Admits Criminal Past." February 15, 2013.

The Vancouver Province. "Crime Boss's Ex-girlfriend Gets One-year Conditional Sentence." September 25, 2008.

The Vancouver Province. "Exotic Cat Snared by Bylaw; Owner Asks Vancouver City Hall to Change Rules for Cheetah-like Creatures." February 14, 2013

Vovk, Justin O. *Imperial Requiem: Four Royal Women and the Fall of the Age of Empires.* Bloomington: iUniverse, 2012.

Weiss-Krejci, Estella. "Heart Burial in Medieval and Early Post-medieval Central Europe." *Body Parts and Bodies Whole.* Oxford: Oxbow, 2010, 119–134.

Western Daily Press, Bristol, England. February 16, 1882. Western Daily Press, Bristol, England. September 5, 1890.

Wheatcroft, Andrew. *The Habsburgs: Embodying Empire.* New York: Penguin Putnam Inc., 1996.

Winnipeg Free Press. "Alert Wal-Mart Employee Sparked Investigation." November 8, 2007.

Winnipeg Free Press. "Boss of Global Theft Ring Pleads Guilty to Theft Crimes Stretching across Country." November 7, 2007.

Winnipeg Free Press. "City Police Get Patted on the Back for Bust." August 24, 2007.

Winnipeg Free Press. "Con Man Repentant for Crimes." November 8, 2007.

Winnipeg Free Press. "Criminal Mastermind's Cousin Pleads Guilty, Gets Break From Judge." July 2, 2008.

Winnipeg Free Press. "Criminal Mastermind's Thefts Funded Muslim Extremists, Court Hears." November 7, 2007.

Winnipeg Free Press. "Judge Punishes Minor Players in Global Scam." April 8, 2008.

Winnipeg Free Press. "Model Admits to Aiding Bank Robber's Schemes." September 25, 2008.

Winnipeg Free Press. "Notorious Fraud Artist's Parole Revoked Following New Concerns." September 14, 2010.

Winnipeg Free Press. "Palace Ecstatic Queen's Gem Recovered." June 3, 2007.

Winnipeg Free Press. "Police Raids, Arrests Targeted Hells Angels." March 16, 2012.

Winnipeg Free Press. "Winnipeg Police Recover Rare Austrian Gem as Part of Crime Ring Investigation." June 1, 2007.

Winnipeg Police Service. "Media Release: Project Kite Arrests." June 1, 2007. http://www.winnipeg.ca/police/press/2007/06june/2007_06_01.stm.

Winnipeg Police Service. "Project Kite Draws International Attention." In AnnualReport 2007. http://www.winnipeg.ca/police/annualreports/2007/2007_wps_annual_report_english.pdf.

Winnipeg Police Service. "Project Kite Yields National Award." August 22,2007. http://www.winnipeg.ca/police/press/2007/08aug/2007_08_22.stm.

The Winnipeg Sun. "Serial Thief Out Since Last Fall." May 2, 2012.

Wong, Edward. "Saddam Charged with Genocide of Kurds." *New York Times,* April 5, 2006.

The Wrexham Advertiser, Clwyd, Wales. July 28, 1866.

Index

Numbers in **_bold italics_** indicate pages with photographs.

Index

Christomanos, Konstantine (E.'s Greek tutor) 44–46, 57–58, 123, 142
Church of the Capuchin Friars 84, 123, 176
Clary-Aldringen, Prince Alfons 146
Collett, John 46 (E.'s acquaintance) 46
Combined Forces Special Enforcement Unit of British Columbia 128
Connor, Myles J., Jr. 169–170
Corfu, Greece 25, 27, 86, 121, 123, 125
Corti, Count Egon 105, 175
The Court of Queen's Bench, Manitoba 153
Crimean War 19, 143
Criminal Investigation Bureau, Canada 92, 129, 184

Decorum: Treatise on Etiquette and Dress 47
de Crenneville, Count Franz Folliot 118
demoiselles de magasin 98
de Sondheimer, Alphonse 111
de Vera d'Aragona, Prince Raniero 163–164
diadem 8
Dickens, Charles 97
Domestic Serval Society of British Columbia 182
Drummond, Victor 78
Dublin, Ireland 24
Duke Maximilian 12

Elisabeth ("Erzsi," E.'s granddaughter) 81, 84, **86**, 87
Elisabeth, Empress of Austria (Sisi): on the Achilleion 121, 123–124; album of beauties 73; arrival in Vienna 15; assassination 162–165; autopsy 174–175; battles with mother-in-law 22; beauty recipes 30, 47, 49, 114; binges 30–31; child birth 21, 23, 101; death 165; on death 123, 147, 162; depression 14, 22–23, 147; on disliking her mother-in-law 19; early personality 13–14; exercise 30; on family life 26; family lineage 12; fashion 44, 73, 97, 116; feelings toward Stephanie (Rudolf's wife) 85; flees court 24, 140; funeral 175–176; hair 13, 25, 27, 29, 32, 44–48, 50, 51–52, 54–55, **56**, 57–58, **68–69**, 108, 116, 175; horseback riding 14, 116; hunting excursions 116–117; illness 19–20, 24, 25–26, 31, 45–46, 145–146; incompatibility with Franz Joseph 19; jewelry 86–87, 107,

114, 175; languages 28–29, 46, 82; liberalism 119–121; love of Hungary 28, 94–96; marriage to Franz Joseph **14**; *Morgengabe* ("morning gift") 19; obsessions 29, 49, 122; physical beauty 15, 27, 29–30, 65, **69**, 70, 72–73, 94, 145–146, 147, **176**; poetry 20, 54–55, 72, 75, 76, 95–96, 140, 141, 185–186; pre-marriage title 12; Queen of Hungary **96**, 97, 108, 177; reaction to Ludwig II's death 79; reaction to Madame Tussauds Wax Museum 71–72; reaction to mother-in-law taking her children 21; reaction to Rudolf's death 82–84; refusal to eat 25, 29–32; relationship with Andrássy 95–96, 101; relationship with Bay Middleton 117–118; relationship with Franz Joseph 18–19; relationship with Marie Valerie 102; on religion 147–148; self-confidence 22, 27; shyness 16, 72–73; silver wedding anniversary 106–107; sketchbook 21; tattoo 122; talents 14; traveling incognito 102–103, 164; wedding 16; on Winterhalter **69**; yellow domino affair 105
Empress Elisabeth in a Star-spangled Dress **69**
Empress Elisabeth with Flowing Hair **68**
The Empress Eugénie Surrounded by Her Ladies in Waiting 67
endogamy 14
Esterházy-Liechtenstein, Countess (E.'s mistress of the household) 16, 17, 28
Eugénie, French Empress 65, 67, 70, 72, 73, 98, 98–99

fasting girls 31
Fedoruk, Dale 158
Feifalik, Fanny (née Angerer) 53–55, **56**, 57–59, 142, 175
Feifalik, Hugo 53
Ferdinand I, Emperor of Austria (Franz Joseph's uncle) 18, 42–44, 98, 115
Ferdinand d'Orléans, Duke of Alençon 144
Ferdinand Maximilian, Archduke (Franz Joseph's brother) 74; Emperor of Mexico 80; execution 100; marriage 23
Ferenczy, Ida (E.'s Hungarian tutor) 29, 82, 95, 103, 105, 141, 177, 185
Festetics, Countess Marie (E.'s lady-in-waiting) 54, 57, 79, 118, 119, 142–143, 177
Fischer, Dr. 25
Florinda 67
Francis II, Emperor of Austria 42–43

Index

Index

Index

Index